BEGINNING

LANGUAGE ARTS

INSTRUCTION

WITH CHILDREN

HAROLD G. SHANE

Professor of Elementary Education and Dean
The School of Education, Indiana University

MARY E. REDDIN

Assistant Professor of Education
Pre-School Primary Division and Elementary Division
Teachers College, University of Hawaii

MARGARET C. GILLESPIE

Supervisor of Pre-School Primary Education
Instructor in the Language Arts
Teachers College, University of Hawaii

CHARLES E. MERRILL BOOKS, INC., Columbus, Ohio

BEGINNING
LANGUAGE ARTS
INSTRUCTION
WITH CHILDREN

To the children with whom we have worked, and from whom we three have learned so much—with affection and respect.

H.G.S.

M.E.R.

M.C.G.

Illustrations by G. A. Wellmes

Library of Congress Catalog Card Number: 61-7060

Printed in the United States of America

PREFACE

One of the great tasks that relentlessly has confronted mankind in the twentieth century is that of improving human understanding—both among individuals and among the many culture-groups of which they are a part. And with each passing year it has become more obvious that one of the most important impediments to the quest for better understanding is the cluster of problems created by faulty communications.

It is easy to comprehend why communication has become of vastly increased significance. The earth's peoples—speaking a myriad of languages and dialects—have been thrown together as never before in history. They encounter one another on hundreds of new frontiers that are no longer merely geographical but also scientific, economic, social, political, and cultural. If our encounters with others, both at home and overseas, are to strengthen rather than to impair human understanding, we must learn to become more skilled in our efforts to refine and interpret the "meaning of meaning." The measure of our success will be the extent to which we can create a climate of mutual trust and respect in which the world's billions can not only exist but also move toward the self-realization and self-respect which are prerequisites to enduring peace and the humane civilization which men have thus far sought in vain for more years than history has preserved remembrance.

Beginning Language Arts Instruction with Children was designed in an effort to make a small contribution to the enormous job of improving receptive and expressive communications in our schools. It represents an attempt to help both inexperienced and seasoned teachers to infuse even

v

more effective language arts experiences into the lives of boys and girls as they progress through the years of early and middle childhood. The book concentrates on both theory *(what* makes a good language arts program *good)* and methods *(how* to teach more effectively). While the remorseless alchemy of time ultimately will determine whether our ideas be gold or dross, on the eve of its publication we cannot but hope that there will be those who say, "Here is something I can do to make my teaching better tomorrow than it was today!" as they explore our chapters.

The writers wish to acknowledge with appreciation the opportunities they have had to work with able classroom teachers from whom, over the years, they have accumulated the ideas and suggestions incorporated in *Beginning Language Arts Instruction with Children.* We also are grateful for the helpful criticisms of many professional colleagues, particularly E. T. McSwain, Dora V. Smith, and Paul A. Witty who read the manuscript or helped in screening the lists of references and materials in the concluding chapter.

HAROLD G. SHANE
MARY E. REDDIN
MARGARET C. GILLESPIE

Bloomington, Indiana
and
Honolulu, Hawaii
January, 1961

CONTENTS

vii

PART II   GUIDING LANGUAGE LEARNINGS DURING CHILDREN'S EARLY YEARS IN SCHOOL

Reading Activities That Help to Build Language Usage Power in Children

Activities That Pave the Way for Skill in Written Expression   219

14

PART ONE

Developing An Effective Program

In The Language Arts

A resumé of principles governing the effective use of methods and materials in the kindergarten-primary years.

CHAPTER 1

Language and Learning

The New Importance of Communication

Our Symbol-Saturated World
The Phantom Curriculum
Human Relations and Language Skills
Linking the Past and the Present
Language Skill and Academic Success

The Four Components of Communication

What Are the Language Arts?

Why This Book Was Written

Language and Human Development

The Living Nature of Language Development
The Language Growth Continuum

Language and Learning

The children with whom we work in school live in a world that surrounds them with wonders that are ever new. It is a world of light and color, a world of imagination and beauty. Wherever a boy or girl may live, there are fascinating things to learn in the flash of color in a bird's wings, in the luminous haze of a summer sunset, in slowly ripening fruit, or in the thunder of a great machine.

Children during the primary years stand on the threshold of a world of new meanings. Perhaps at no other age levels is it such fun to work with the young as when they are in the delightful fives, the lively sixes, and the steady sevens of kindergarten and the first two grades. Much of what these children are to become has yet to be determined. What they will do in and for the world—what life will do to them and for them—remains undecided.

But of one thing the primary teacher can be certain. She has much to do with the meanings and interpretations which children will carry with them in the years that stretch ahead in their lifetimes. She has much to do with their sense of beauty and power of expression, their feeling for words and their meanings, their ability to recognize the sublime and to laugh—albeit kindly—at the ridiculous.

These primary years more than any others in school are the language-centered years. Here it is that the powers to grasp the meanings of life and living ripen most quickly. It is here too that satisfactions found in effective, creative expression stir within the child. In *Beginning Language Arts Instruction with Children* we seek to help teachers lend even greater meaning to the experiences they plan with and for boys and girls to help them over the threshold of meanings and toward rich and more complete understandings of the things they read, hear, and see, and of which they speak and write. First, however, a word on the growing importance of a command of language.

THE NEW IMPORTANCE OF COMMUNICATION

The task of helping children become successful in their use and understanding of language has for generations uncounted been one on which the efforts of the elementary teacher have focused. Now, in the later decades of the twentieth century, language skills have become even more vital. It is one of the ironies of modern life that as the technical means of communication have improved and increased, the coherence and clarity of communication as reflected in radio, TV, and published material have, at least in some ways, failed to realize their promise as constructive educational forces. Let us examine some of the reasons why effective language teaching is becoming of even greater importance than when the parents of today were themselves children.

Our Symbol-Saturated World. Children today live in a world that teems with verbal and visual language symbols. There are several reasons —both positive and negative—why the increase in the quantity of words which surround us requires effort from primary teachers to develop the language power of children even more effectively than in past decades.

In the first place, the close contact that children have with TV and radio from the earliest years of their lives creates opportunities for learning that can greatly extend the child's understanding of his world if they are wisely developed. Indeed, primary age children now spend about as much time viewing TV as they spend in school—well over twenty hours per week. With proper teacher guidance in the development of language-listening skills, the educational value of TV has tremendous potential merit.

The Phantom Curriculum. Children's books (including comic books), radio, and especially television, are creating a "phantom curriculum" for children and youth. This phantom curriculum, one steeped in language, is bringing to children a wealth of information which spans the centuries. It hurries the child from a re-creation of King Arthur's court to dramatic on-the-spot news that is literally seen as it happens. The mixture of times and of places —the transition from dinosaurs to space travel with a flip of a TV channel selector or a comic book page—may be confusing but it is educational, too. What a challenge and opportunity it is for the kindergarten-primary teacher to help make this new out-of-school curriculum meaningful to children as quickly as possible through developmental language experiences. It is wonderful, too, to contemplate the way in which the phantom curriculum helps the school by providing children with experiences which, while disorganized, can be "sorted out" in the school situation so as to extend greatly the knowledge assimilated during the kindergarten-primary years.

Human Relations and Language Skill. Because the technical means of communication have been so improved, and because of a transportation system which has brought any place on the earth within a day's journey, there is an even greater need for language skill at the present time than when the parents of today were themselves children. Americans are visiting and residing everywhere in the habitable world. People are meeting daily who would never even have seen one another in 1900. As a result of the ease and speed with which people of different cultures can now meet and communicate, there has never been a greater need for better human relations than there is today.

And what has this to do with language skills? Perhaps one of the greatest problems in human relations is faulty communication: the use of words which alienate others; the failure of the written or the spoken word to convey the intended meaning; the deliberate misuse of language to create ill-will. We must exist successfully with peoples of many different cultures in a world made small by man's ingenuity. The primary teacher must therefore see her-

self as a part of the team of workers in education who are laying the
foundation for the use of language in ways that will create and strengthen
a feeling of outreaching friendliness in others.

Linking the Past and the Present. There is so much to learn today,
and knowledge is increasing so rapidly, that children and young people
are under an increasing burden as they try to understand the past, deal
with the present, and attempt to do a better job of shaping the future
than past generations have done. Here, too, there is a new need for communication skills. Language binds the past to the present and it is only
through language power—the ability to read, comprehend, and interpret
accurately—that the child can claim the inheritance of knowledge to
be gleaned from mankind's eventful history.

Scholars who have studied words, their origins, meanings, and effects
on human behavior, are quick to point out that language is man's greatest
invention. They point to what is called the "time-binding" power of the
written and spoken word, the ability of language to preserve knowledge,
meanings, and values over the centuries. As noted above, with all the
accumulating information of the present era, how important it has become for us to put forth our best effort to help the child of today and
adult of tomorrow to cope with language so that he can make the best
of mankind's past a part of his growing self. This goal calls for the
fullest possible development of the ability to observe, to interpret, to
listen, to read, and to express himself.

Here again, the work of the primary teacher assumes enlarged importance in her efforts to increase each child's grasp of "the meaning
of meaning" in language, to foster his ability to link past knowledge to
the challenging task of improving the future.

Language Skill and Academic Success. Although the points already made more than justify the teacher's best efforts in sharing language learnings with boys and girls, one more cogent reason must be included in our inventory of reasons why communication skills are the most important dimension of the kindergarten-primary teacher's work. Research has repeatedly demonstrated that ability in language arts, including reading, is an excellent index to general achievement in the elementary school— for example, in arithmetic and in the social studies.

It seems an inescapable conclusion that an important reason for emphasizing language skills at the kindergarten-primary level is that language power serves to undergird the future academic progress of children more than does any other single asset that a boy or girl can develop. Teachers will also wish to remember that fluency in language—that is, highly developed word power—is the one measurable quality which seems to be shared by leaders in adult life, whether they are industrialists, soldiers, statesmen, or professional men. Success in school and in becoming a contributive adult is undoubtedly related to linguistic ability.

In summary, helping children learn to communicate is a vital responsibility of teachers (1) because of the increasingly verbal environment in America today, (2) because of the "phantom curriculum" which surrounds children with knowledge that they can gain fully only through developing language skill, and (3) because of the need for children to use language in ways which improve human relations. (4) Language also helps the child to link the past and present and (5) to enhance his chances for future success in school and as an adult.

THE FOUR COMPONENTS OF COMMUNICATION

There are two types of communication skills which concern the teacher in the early years of elementary school. These are *receptive* and *expressive* language skills. In broad terms, receptive communication includes *listening*

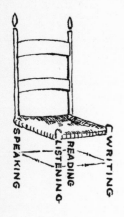

and *reading* ability, and expressive skills involve *speaking* and *writing*.

All four of these components of communication are of equal importance. Each is like the leg of a chair. All four are needed to support a balanced language program. Even at the kindergarten level, for instance, reading readiness experiences are an important harbinger of the more structured work in reading which begins at the six-year-old level. Hence, such kindergarten activities may be considered as preliminary learnings in the receptive communication skills, although reading, as such, is postponed until grade one.

WHAT ARE THE LANGUAGE ARTS?

The four components of communication are taught in the elementary school as the language arts. The term *language arts* is used to designate the fusion of many language skills into one broad field in which the related phases of expressive and receptive communication are taught *in relationship*. As a general rule, the language arts include reading, creative writing and creative expression (such as choral speech), handwriting skill, children's literature, spelling, grammar and usage, listening, vocabulary building, and, in some schools, instruction in a second language.

WHY THIS BOOK WAS WRITTEN

It is the purpose of this book to review with the classroom teacher of young children her understanding of the nature and purpose of effective language instruction in the areas listed above. But we do not expect to limit ourselves to a mere exploration of theory. We hope to devote the bulk of our pages to a down-to-earth group of suggestions on *how* language learnings can be made rich in meaning and *how* the communications experiences of fives, sixes, and sevens can be tailored to the uniquely personal qualities which make each boy and girl an individual challenge to the classroom teacher.

In the several brief chapters that follow, *Beginning Language Arts Instruction with Children* will sketch or review current trends and research findings which illuminate and support good practices. In the latter—and larger—portion of the volume, techniques, procedures, and resources will be listed for the improvement of oral language, the strengthening of listening and observing, and the building of language power and skill in written expression. Lists of professional references, children's materials, and teaching aids are included.

Before attention is directed toward recent trends in the language arts, however, it is in order to say a few words about the nature of language and children.

LANGUAGE AND HUMAN DEVELOPMENT

One of the most important truths for the teacher of kindergarten-primary age children to bear in mind is that language development is a living or *organic* aspect of children's experiences in school.

The Living Nature of Language Development. Effective language development is not sterile and academic. As Mario Pei, the widely known semanticist, points out,[1] new developments in the spoken and written word are constantly being minted. Yesterday's slang becomes accepted as respectable, old words acquire new meanings, and new words are created to fit new concepts or to describe new social and technical developments. Again, as peoples of the world meet and mingle, one language influences the vocabulary and structure of another.

In our work with children in the language arts we need constantly to be alert to *two* aspects of the vital nature of language: (1) that *language*

---

[1] In his delightful and informative book, *The Story of Language* (see bibliography for teachers).

Interpretation: Children vary in age, intelligence, the rate at which they mature, and in many other ways. While all of them—within the wide range we call "normal" progress—move toward mature skill in communication, their rates of progress may differ dramatically. Often there is almost as much difference in communication powers within a single group of children as there is between two or even three different grade levels.

One of the great challenges to the teacher, both in beginning and sustaining good language instruction, is that of recognizing that children are spread over a language growth continuum and that there is need to adjust and to individualize the learning experiences of boys and girls accordingly. Note the wide range of language power that may be encountered at any given grade level.

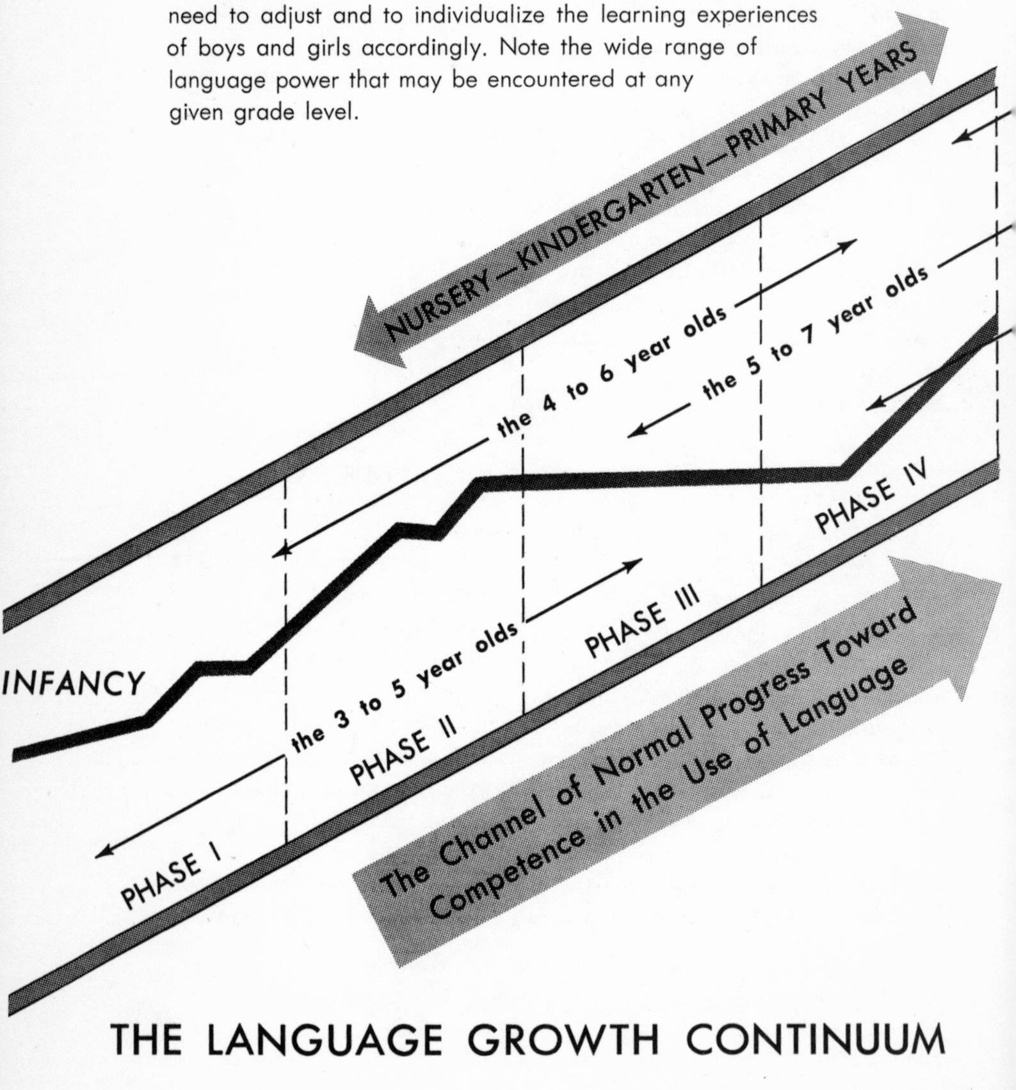

NURSERY—KINDERGARTEN—PRIMARY YEARS

the 4 to 6 year olds

the 5 to 7 year olds

INFANCY

the 3 to 5 year olds

PHASE II

PHASE III

PHASE IV

PHASE I

The Channel of Normal Progress Toward Competence in the Use of Language

THE LANGUAGE GROWTH CONTINUUM

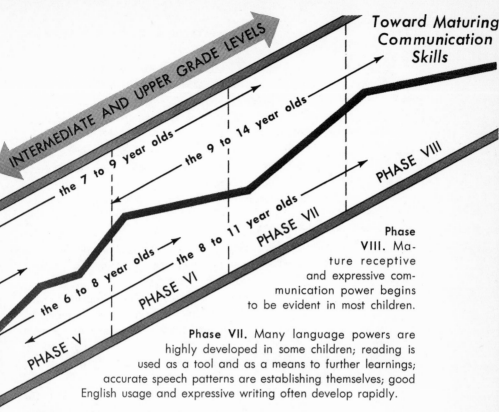

Toward Maturing Communication Skills

INTERMEDIATE AND UPPER GRADE LEVELS

the 7 to 9 year olds

the 9 to 14 year olds

the 6 to 8 year olds

the 8 to 11 year olds

PHASE VIII

PHASE VII

PHASE VI

PHASE V

Phase VIII. Mature receptive and expressive communication power begins to be evident in most children.

Phase VII. Many language powers are highly developed in some children; reading is used as a tool and as a means to further learnings; accurate speech patterns are establishing themselves; good English usage and expressive writing often develop rapidly.

Phase VI. Rapid growth of many language skills which some children are well on the way to mastering, especially in effective oral expression and independence in reading.

Phase V. Upward extension and consolidation of communications powers; increased recognition of language as a tool and as a means of controlling one's environment.

Phase IV. Reading experiences begin to become a source of pleasure and of satisfaction; simple creative oral expression begins to flower.

Phase III. Functional use of language increases; the child begins to sense more fully the meaning and use of verbal and visual symbols. There is a continued need for readiness experiences.

Phase II. Effective communication begins; guided experiences promote readiness for using expressive language and for interpreting receptive communication.

Phase I. Early language understandings begin; first words are used in simple combinations; language begins to be recognized as a means of indicating and satisfying wants and needs and for gaining satisfactions.

itself is a flexible, changing thing, and (2) that the *children* in our groups are motivated by their purposes and understandings; hence language experiences must have meaning in their active, young lives if learning is to occur in an efficient and effective manner.

Like any other living thing, language cannot be pulled to pieces and doled out in small bits but must be seen as a whole. In other words, any teaching *in* English is the teaching *of* English. As they *listen*, children are also learning speech habits, laying a foundation for vocabulary development and for reading. As children *read*, they are also improving their power to listen, extending their oral vocabularies, and acquiring the raw material of words with which to express themselves creatively.

Likewise, children's literature, work in spelling, even the study of a second language, are parts of the total pattern of emerging language power. As teachers we must never forget the basic unity or one-ness of any teaching we do in any realm of language. True, for purposes of instruction we may single out some elements of the totality of language, but even as we stress a reading skill, for example, we need to remember that all phases of language are in some degree a part of language experiences as a whole.

The Language Growth Continuum. Because children grow continually, like flowers or plants, their language power, too, grows continually. Dr. James L. Hymes, the nationally known expert and author in early childhood education, has used an interesting analogy in describing the teacher's task in guiding total child development, including communication skills.

The teacher, says Dr. Hymes, needs to develop a professional "green thumb" like a good gardener. She needs to know when youngsters (in the manner of flowers) need the "sunshine" of stimulation, the "shade" of relaxation, the "fertilizer" of rich experience. We cannot effectively teach live children dead, dull language learnings. Rather we need to have the "green thumb" skill of the professional classroom worker who knows how to guide continually the progress her group is making toward linguistic competence.

It is helpful to think of achievements in language skill as spread over a continuum of growth gradients in not only the kindergarten-primary years but throughout the elementary school. As shown by the zig-zag line in the diagram on pages 12 and 13, each child follows a continuum of language growth. The drawing suggests the "average" or "typical" upward progress which an individual or a group of children might make toward mature interpretation and usage of language. Yet note that a four- or five- or six-year-old may vary with respect to his ability in language arts. There may be, even in grade one, a two-, three-, or even four-year range with respect to the ability of a slow maturing child on the one hand and a rapidly maturing child on the other to comprehend and to use English.

These individual differences in language powers usually tend to increase rather than to decrease as children move into the intermediate grades. As any seasoned fourth or fifth grade teacher will verify, a four- to eight-year range in language skills (e.g., in reading ability) is the rule rather than the exception in most classrooms. It is because of this striking individuality reflected in children's ability that it is so important for the primary teacher to think of language skills not in terms of norms or minimum essentials but in terms of the widening range or spread in accomplishment which is characteristic of even the most "normal" of groups.

We suggest the idea of the continuum at the outset of this book to make the point that good beginning language instruction is not made up of a few fixed teaching methods. Instead, language instruction is made up of many and varied practices which are associated not so much with an exact grade level as with the stage of development of individual children—that is, with their language maturity—at a particular time.

Good language teaching, it will be made clear, is most readily achieved when it is a vigorous approach to living, active sharing of communication skills which mirrors the teacher's understanding of the subtle fact that no two children in her kindergarten or primary group are likely to be at exactly the same stage of linguistic competence.

CHAPTER 2

Making Language Meaningful

Language and "Classroom Climate"

The Physical Setting for Learning
The Psychological Climate

Establishing Readiness for the Effective Use of Language

Language Learnings Wither in an Intellectual Vacuum
Creating a Concrete Foundation of Meaningful Experiences
What Influences the Child's Readiness for Developing
Communications Skills?

Some Basic Concepts Related to Communication Skills

Language Development Is Personal and Creative
The Development of Communication Skills Is a Social Process
Sound Language Development Is an Integrating Process for the Child
Significant Communication Experiences Build Self-Direction
and Self-Control and Lead to Still Further Increases in
Language Powers

Making Language Meaningful

A State Department supervisor of elementary education in a middle-western state was visiting schools in early autumn. One afternoon he stopped at a small rural building where he spent some time in a first grade classroom.

The teacher was an imperturbable person—the sort who has had one year of experience many times. As the supervisor entered, she motioned him toward a chair at the back of the room and went on reading some Mother Goose rhymes to the six-year-olds. Among them were "Hickety-Pickety, My Black Hen," "Little Miss Moffett," and "Diddle-Diddle-Dumpling, My Son John."

When she had finished the rhymes, the teacher said with somewhat exaggerated enthusiasm, "Now, boys and girls, I'm going to pass the manila paper. Take out your crayons and draw the pictures that you thought of while I was reading from *Mother Goose.*"

In a few moments the children had settled down to work and the State Department visitor strolled up the aisle to see what kinds of pictures the nursery rhymes had prompted. He paused and peered over the shoulder of a lad who had just finished a recognizable picture of a bed—like this:

As the supervisor watched, the picture grew like this:

until at last it looked like this:

    The supervisor pointed at the coverlet on the bed and said, "That's a nice design you've put on the quilt, my boy."

    The lad looked up with a puzzled expression, and the supervisor decided that the child did not know the meaning of the word *design*. He tried again. Pointing to the marks on the quilt, he said, "I mean that's a nice pattern you've drawn on the bedclothes."

The expression of the six-year-old brightened. "Oh, that's no pattern, Mister," he said. "Those are the mice!"

"Mice?" the supervisor repeated in astonishment.

"Sure," said the boy. "Didn't you hear that nursery rhyme I'm drawin'? It's 'Diddle-Diddle-Dumplin', Mice on John.' Those are the *mice on John*, Mister!"

How little we know of what children really make of what they hear. How often we are unaware of the under-the-skin interpretation they may make of a word or phrase they hear. How seldom we fully recognize that the content, or meaning, of language is self-created by the young learner. Does the five-year-old who hears you speak know that "cocker" or "German shepherd" refers to a dog in the story you are telling him? Making sure that he does know—and that he builds up a good fund of visual and aural-oral understandings—is one of the most important aspects of the kindergarten-primary teacher's job. But how does one go about making written and verbal symbols come alive with meanings?

LANGUAGE AND "CLASSROOM CLIMATE"

One of the factors that helps to make language meaningful is the "climate" or atmosphere of the classroom. If children are to acquire a rapidly growing and functional store of language meanings, they need a rich diet of experience rather than the thin gruel of rote learning. There are two main elements in a classroom milieu that help communication skills to mature with reasonable speed. These are the visible physical setting and the invisible psychological environment for language learnings.

The Physical Setting for Learning. A good visible environment for youngsters in the five- to eight-year-old age range has several general qualities. It has a touch of the familiar for security and homelikeness. It has unfamiliar elements to stretch the imagination and to open new channels of language understandings. And it has "freshness"—a frequently changing array of new things to see and to manipulate.

The familiar in the kindergarten-primary language field includes, for example, such things as well-loved books to examine or to re-read, phonograph records to instruct or to delight the children, some toys to play with (especially at the five- and early six-year-old level), or twice-told tales that the teacher, seemingly, can share with them almost endlessly.

The unfamiliar in the classroom may encompass new books, records, and appropriate playthings. A pet animal, come to stay for a few days

and to be cared for, a compass, something from a faraway land such as a doll in native costume, a dozen polliwogs or a turtle in faintly brown-tinted water scooped from the pond, these—and many more similar objects—represent the unfamiliar on the way to becoming familiar because they are talked about, read about, or are the focal point of teacher- or pupil-told stories.

And what of the quality of "freshness" in the classroom that has a physical setting conducive to language development? Freshness is the quality descriptive of the carefully tempered flow of new things and new ideas into the world of the school. Freshness is attained when the unfamiliar becomes the familiar, is artfully replaced by new things which promote questions and conversation and, with older boys and girls, the desire to read as well as to look, listen, and inquire.

The purpose of a good physical setting, of course, is not merely to entertain or to please the child but to encourage language power. Experiences that are varied and fraught with meaning are the raw material from which word comprehension grows. Before he can comprehend the written or spoken word, the beginner must have experience with the concept which a word represents. That is why a stimulating classroom is so necessary. Children, figuratively speaking, see and hear with their experiences, as well as with their eyes and ears.

The Psychological Climate. Even more significant than the physical surroundings provided by the school is a psychological climate conducive to language development. This climate may be thought of as related to the spirit or the quality of teacher-pupil relationships. The good climate provided by the teacher and reflected by her attitudes is one in which, for example:

An inquiring mind is encouraged.

Children are treated with respect.

Mistakes are met with sympathy rather than derision.

Children are accepted for what they *are* rather than for what they can *do* at a given time in their development.

It is recognized that there are no "problem children" although some children may come from problem situations.

The teacher is firm (rather than harsh) with respect to reasonable standards of behavior and achievement.

The teacher is warm and friendly rather than sentimental or too familiar in relationships with children.

Premature pressure for *unreasonable* achievement is not placed on children because the teacher takes a shallow satisfaction in having the class "above grade" in language arts skills.

The children, are continually learning from the teacher through her example as well as through her precepts—by what she *does* as well as by what she *says*.

As the nine examples above imply, the psychological climate is intangible but nonetheless real and potent. Its importance must not be belittled simply because of its intangibility. A humorist once said that "A hole in the ground is 'a lot of nothing' but you can break your neck if you trip in it!" Likewise, a program of beginning language experiences can be shattered by the teacher's lack of sensitivity to the contribution of the vital intangibles of a classroom atmosphere that makes children *want* to learn by *freeing* all children to learn to whatever degree their human endowment permits.

ESTABLISHING READINESS FOR THE EFFECTIVE USE OF LANGUAGE

Entire books have been written on the subject of readiness for learning and it is not our purpose to provide—nor does space permit—a review of the points pertaining to readiness which have already been made by astute and sensitive writers such as Gertrude Hildreth or James Hymes.[1] At the same time, it is pertinent to mention a few things especially related to readiness in the language arts fields.

Language Learnings Wither·in an Intellectual Vacuum. The ancient Romans had a saying that "Out of nothing, nothing comes." This is an important maxim to remember when guiding pupil progress in language. If children are to speak effectively, they must have something to talk about—something which they *want* to talk about. If children are to write creatively, they require a diet of experiences that illuminate and motivate creative expression. Good writing cannot germinate in a vacuum or in an atmosphere of arid, sterile assignments.

---

[1]The interested reader is referred to Dr. Hildreth's scholarly *Readiness for School Beginners,* and to Dr. Hymes's helpful *Before the Child Reads.*(See teacher's bibliography in Chapter 15.)

Creating a Concrete Foundation of Meaningful Experience.
As children mature, they find themselves, more and more, living in a
world of abstractions—in an environment of words both heard and seen
—which they need to interpret accurately if they are to make any sense
of the bewildering surroundings in which they find themselves at birth.

There are those persons who argue that, since children are going to
live in a world of abstractions, we might as well confront them with and
drill them in abstract language learning as quickly as possible. Actually,
an opposite approach is better. The kindergarten-primary classroom
teacher seeking to build readiness for learning needs to create a concrete
rather than an abstract foundation for the abstractions encountered in
life.

Concrete, firsthand learnings are more rich in *real* meaning to young
children than abstract symbols which merely *represent* meanings. The
foundation for interpreting the abstract, verbal ideas in adult life found
in magazine, book, or newspaper and heard or seen over such mass media
as radio and TV is therefore a substantial amount of direct experience
which most fully conveys meaning and understanding.

Building readiness for learning through experience takes time, but
any enduring structure must have a firm foundation. Hence, whatever
time is required to help the kindergartener or first or second grader
develop a good stock of accurate meanings is not only time well spent;
it is time that *must* be invested in order to ensure the long-range success
of children in mastering language skills and in dealing with problems
in human communications.

The simplified diagram below suggests how the elementary school
language program should emphasize a concrete or "firsthand experience"

approach to learning, with an increase in abstract learnings (as through the verbal symbols on a printed page) being reserved for the upper grades.

Note that the elementary program, as illustrated, never *does* become completely abstract. The extent of direct experience decreases somewhat each year, but even in seventh and eighth grade there remains a need for contact with learnings at firsthand through such means as field trips or direct contact with resource persons.

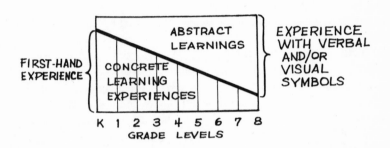

The importance of concrete experience in establishing meaning is aptly illustrated by a conversation transcribed in a second grade. The children listened to the familiar Pledge of Allegiance and then were asked, a phrase at a time, to tell the meaning of the Pledge which they had just learned by heart. Here are their interesting interpretations:

"I pledge allegiance to the flag of the United States of America . . ."

LINDA: It shows respect for the flag.

ROBBIE: That's when you put your hand over your heart.

BRUCE: *Allegiance* is an organization that gets together.

PAM: (When asked to indicate the United States on the map also pointed to South America and asked if she should include that, too.)

"And to the Republic for which it stands . . ."

BOBBIE: Like a public school—it belongs to the country.

BECKY: It's the states—all the states.

HUGH: You're supposed to be republic to the flag.

"One nation under God indivisible . . ."

LINDA: One person in this world is invisible. It could be God who you can't see.

"With liberty . . ."

PAUL: No fighting or anything—be free.

BOBBIE: Be free to do anything you like. In some countries you can't do what you want, like vote.

JEFF: Free to be good and not too bad.

VICKY: I know another kind of liberty: The Statue of Liberty. *"And justice for all."*

BOBBIE: Certain rules—you can't go out and wreck everything like in a nice hotel, or kill people and all that stuff.

MARION: Be careful when the patrol boy tells you not to do something like run out in the street.

BRUCE: When we all have peace. You shouldn't go out and fight someone.

VICKY: That's when you just can't bear to hurt your country.

JEFF: You shouldn't bomb buildings unless someone starts it.

The dialogue recorded above was provided by youngsters who came from excellent homes, youngsters with many cultural advantages. Even so, note the inaccuracy, confusion, and lack of understanding shown in most instances. We must recognize clearly that children do not necessarily *understand* that which they can repeat or the words they sometimes attempt to use, unless experience has provided the *means* of comprehension. The seven-year-olds who had memorized the familiar Pledge simply were not yet ready fully to grasp the verbal symbols upon which its concepts depended. There was as yet no firm foundation of meaning.

What Influences the Child's Readiness for Developing Language Skills? What, specifically, can be done in the school to cultivate readiness and a grasp of meanings? Essentially, language readiness can be promoted by many diversified yet simple means.

1. Use words in the classroom which will expand each child's stock of meanings and concepts. Say the same or similar things in different ways. Insofar as possible, associate these words with objects and situations which are concrete.

2. Read stories frequently. Take time to explain and to talk about words used by the author which may need interpretation.

3. Bring in, and encourage children to bring to the classroom, objects of interest that stimulate conversation and build vocabularies.

4. As conditions permit, plan simple trips. With very young children, even an "excursion" within the building in early autumn may introduce words like *custodian* or *janitor, corridor, lavatory, principal,* or *library.*

5. Frequently replenish the supply of books and similar reading materials kept on hand as in a library corner.

6. Play word games and guessing games that "stretch" children's ability to use words, both the names of objects and descriptive words like *buzz, slipping,* or *crawl.*

7. Make good educational use of bulletin board and chalkboard space and of signs or labels. Especially at the five- and six-year-old level, the not-yet-reading child can learn from labels, including picture labels.

8. Recognize the "readiness-building value" of such teaching aids as phonograph records, tape recorders, and filmstrips, which can serve so pleasantly to extend the "meaning of meaning" for boys and girls.

You will think of many similar means of building language readiness to suit a particular group of children in a particular situation. Also, explicit ideas are presented in the second portion of this book.

SOME BASIC IDEAS RELATED TO COMMUNICATION SKILLS

In addition to the principles defined in the preceding discussion, there are several basic ideas which should govern the development of meaningful language learnings in the kindergarten-primary years. It would be helpful to summarize these ideas before we turn to such aspects of the language arts as reading, spelling, or language usage.

Language Development Is Personal and Creative. Each child must build *his own personalized meanings.* In one sense, the teacher does not "teach" so much as she frees children to develop their concepts through guided experience. (Or, perhaps, in the best sense of the word, this *is* teaching.)

The Development of Communication Skills Is a Social Process. Communication skills are *social* skills. It must be recognized that, by the very nature of language, the growth of language power is a social process. This point is of twofold importance. First, effective use of language in its many forms depends on wholesome social relationships so that learning is unimpeded by the psychological problems which are bred by poor human relations. Second, good social situations are a requisite for the effective use or application of expressive communication (speaking, writing) and a basis for the motivation pupils must have for optimum receptive communication experiences (reading, listening).

Sound Language Development Is an Integrating Process for the Child. Integrating experiences—which good education constantly seeks—may be thought of as those experiences which "knit together" the personalities of children. As we seek to make language meaningful in the classroom, one of the criteria for gauging our effectiveness should be the way in which boys and girls become more effective and contributive human beings through the growth of their receptive and communicative abilities.

Significant Communication Experiences Build Self-Direction and Self-Control and Lead to Self-Maintained Increases in Language Powers. This fourth and final principle may seem a bit wordy, but the idea involved is not easily stated in a simple phrase or sentence. In a nutshell, successful language experiences, beginning in the kindergarten and nurtured through the primary years, are in themselves one of the best means to *continued* success in the language arts realms.

If we can make language meaningful with ever-increasing success for each group of youngsters, each child—self-motivated and self-propelled by his initial success and satisfaction—will do a great deal to ensure his progress toward linguistic maturity by and for himself.

In her contacts with parents, persons who have an immeasurable but great influence on their child's progress toward mature language ability, the teacher encounters additional significant challenges and responsibilities. These reside in the task of "sizing up" or appraising parents and then helping them to grasp more fully the four points made above. Particular skill needs to be displayed by the teacher—plus tact—in sensitizing mothers and fathers to ways in which they can create a meaningful language climate in the home, through family travel, and by means of the books, records, and other learning materials they provide. Since parents vary a great deal in age, socio-economic background, education, and insight, each child's home environment presents unique opportunities for the teacher, through her parent relationships, to find ways of helping parents to reinforce the work of the school.

CHAPTER 3

Language Development
through Reading

The Reading Growth Continuum

Reading and the Total Language Program during Children's
Early Years in School

Strengthening General Language Usage through Reading

Language Development
through Reading

This is the first of seven chapters in which many aspects of the child's progress toward mature competencies in the use of language are reviewed. These chapters contain illustrations of the nature of language growth, references to practices supported by research, interpretations of current trends, and critical examinations of obsolete or dubious practices.

Because it permeates other aspects of the language arts, and because it constitutes such a major part of the curriculum in the kindergarten-primary years, let us concentrate first on reading in the total language program.

THE READING GROWTH CONTINUUM

One of the most important concepts for the teacher of young children to bear in mind is that of the language growth continuum which has already been introduced in Chapter 1. (See pp. 12-15.) When applied in greater detail to the teaching of reading, the continuum illustrates clearly the challenge of teaching reading to a group of

children, each of whom is unique, each of whom has a different native endowment, a varied background of experience, and a personalized or under-the-skin interpretation of the world in which he finds himself.

What Is the Reading Growth Continuum? At one time the teaching of reading was closely linked to grade levels. That is, our elementary schools used graded readers and also attempted the grade placement of various supplementary or leisure reading materials. One is reminded of the story of the six-year-old who brought a butterfly to the first grade and asked whether he could show it to the other children. "No, I'm afraid not," replied the teacher. "You've brought a third grade bug into the first grade room."

In somewhat the same fashion, a few decades ago certain books were allocated to each grade and both teachers and children were confined to the use of those readers or supplementary volumes which some curriculum "experts" and reading "specialists" had preordained that youngsters should read at a given time. This was all very "scientific." Studies had been made to suggest what a seven-year-old could read—an "average" seven-year-old, that is—and all sevens were expected to conform.

Fortunately, it was eventually recognized that the "average" reader was a myth. Every boy and girl, it was seen, was at some time or another either above or below "normal." As a result, we began to think of reading *levels.*

some children being at a higher level of reading ability than others in a particular group. But even this more flexible interpretation was not a completely adequate one. As able teachers had previously sensed, reading skill is a personal or individualized ability. In other words, the reading ability of children in a given group is spread over a spectrum of reading power, each individual being somewhere on a gradient of skill ranging from the very slow or retarded reader to the over-achiever and the fast reader.[1] This brings us to the new concept of the reading continuum or reading gradient.

As illustrated by the accompanying diagram of the reading continuum (see p. 36), children *do* progress through certain levels of reading ability. But the performance of children in a given group or grade is characterized more by *diversity* than by *uniformity* in reading power.

Consider the first of the eight phases included in the diagram, a phase involving such experiences as the sharing of books to be enjoyed, listening to musical and story records, listening to jingles and poems for pleasure, recognizing similarities and differences in pictures, signs, or labels, and so forth. This pre-reading phase, one which creates readiness for meaningful interpretation of the printed page, is not restricted to the fives in kindergarten or to the sixes in the early months of grade one. A few rapidly maturing children are already on the threshold of—or moving into—the second phase of the continuum when they enter kindergarten. Conversely, the slow maturing boy or girl may linger in phase one in the high first grade and even when in grade two. These are the kinds of dramatic differences that exist among youngsters in the wide range of *normal* developmental patterns.

One of our great challenges as kindergarten-primary teachers beginning language instruction is that of grasping the implications of the continuum concept and interpreting it in terms of gradients of the maturity and ability possessed by the children whose progress we guide.

Interpreting and Applying the Reading Continuum Concept. Because the human element in each teaching-learning situation is in certain ways unique, the teacher cannot and should not be *told* explicitly how to adapt instruction in reading and in other language skills to her pupils' needs, purposes, and manifest socio-cultural lacks. This task is one which calls for the application of professional study and judgment, and

---

[1]The so-called slow or retarded reader (as distinct from the mentally handicapped reader) is one of average or high mental ability who is nonetheless encountering difficulty in learning to read. The "over-achiever" displays ability in excess of his apparent native endowment.

The Concept of the Language Growth Continuum
Applied to Reading and Illustrating Eight Gradients
Or Phases of Child Progress Toward Mature Reading Power

THE READING GROWTH CONTINUUM

GRADES 4-6 and above

GRADES 3-5

GRADES 1-3 or 1-4

NURSERY — KINDERGARTEN

Phase or gradient:

VIII. Mature and creative use of reading skills for personally desirable and socially worthy purposes.

VII. Reading as a mastered process with respect to comprehension, fluency, and steadily increasing insight into word meanings and relationships. Reading also a well-honed tool for research, information-seeking, problem-solving actitivies and for the gradual enhancement of cultural understandings.

VI. While verging on Phase VII, reading is also characterized by individual and group instruction in such skills as advanced structural and phonetic analysis, contextual clues, interpretation of graphic, diagrammatic, and similar visual elements. Oral work encompasses nuances of meaning, inflection, double meanings, etc. Dictionary skills are refined.

V. Consolidation and extension of reading skills introduced and developed in phases I-IV of the continuum.

IV. The power of visual discrimination increases with respect to initial consonants and phonograms (symbols representing a word, sound, or syllable), and so forth. Phonetic and structural analysis become meaningful; children sense that some words are not phonetically consistent. Individualized reading stressed.

III. Broadening of the sight vocabulary occurs. Children begin to use context clues. Auditory and visual discrimination grow.

II. The picture story phase begins and a few words are introduced. Pre-primer material is introduced. Readiness is increased by experiences in listening, speaking, story hour, etc. First organized reading experiences are begun with reading charts, primers, and simple collateral books as suggested by the teacher's professional judgment and organismic analysis of children.

I. Enjoyment of stories, interpretation of pictures, signs, and labels; poetry-for-fun; listening to phonograph records, etc. Foundations of reading readiness are strengthened.

creative planning and teaching in response to a particular classroom situation. Various *general* reading activities that help to build language usage power in children are, however, suggested in Chapter 13. These have been selected so as to provide resource-suggestions consistent with pupil growth gradients in the kindergarten-primary years.

READING AND THE TOTAL LANGUAGE PROGRAM DURING CHILDREN'S EARLY YEARS IN SCHOOL

Throughout their years in school—and of course in their later adult life, too—children's ability to read well is of the utmost importance in enhancing their chances for success in *all* aspects of the language arts. Also, research has shown that able readers are the youngsters most likely to fare very well academically in such fields as the social studies and even in arithmetic. (A bit of reflection, for instance, quickly makes apparent the importance of reading in the interpretation of word problems involving arithmetical computation.)

The relationship between reading and generalized success in communication is, of course, more subtle than the simple "equation":

(1) Success in reading ⟶ (2) success in other language skills ⟶ (3) success in other academic areas.

In individual cases slow readers may do very well in certain other aspects of their work. Also, an able pupil in reading may do ordinary work in spelling or grammar in the upper grades and stumble rather badly in arithmetic. Yet the fact remains that good work in reading tends to presage academic success even as excellent vocabularies and "word power" usually characterize men who are (at least by material standards) prominent and successful in managerial, executive, political, and professional leadership. Hence, research inquiries *have* shown reading to be an especially vital skill in the total language program.

Selected Research Findings Which Have a Bearing on Reading Programs. Since well-designed reading experiences in the total language arts program should, whenever possible, be based on research findings rather than on mere intuition or "hunches," it seems fitting to review here a few research highlights which support viewpoints and practices in reading and in pre-reading activities. Here is a list of points, many of them familiar ones, for the kindergarten-primary teacher to keep in mind when planning reading experiences and in evaluating pupil progress.

1. Reading readiness can be determined with considerable accuracy, but no *single* index of readiness should determine the teacher's appraisal of the *individual* child's status.

2. The cultural setting or home environment of the child may appreciably influence his level of readiness even as it permeates his score on an I.Q. test.

3. The "right" time for initiating organized instruction in reading varies appreciably from one child to another.

4. There is evidence to suggest that a mental age of at least 6.2 years, and preferably 6.6, is appropriate for beginning organized work in reading instruction.

5. Reading rate, recall, vocabulary, and comprehension can be improved by systematic instruction, but *stress* on meaningful practice or drill *for which children see a reason* should be postponed until at least the second grade for most children.

6. Functional word analysis is a helpful practice, but emphasis on phonetics should usually be postponed until the child has attained an M.A. (or mental age) of at least 7.0 years.

7. The reading program, for optimum success, must be modified in recognition of the individual child's status on the reading ability continuum. (Individualized approaches to reading are receiving great emphasis at present.)

8. Reading disabilities of individual children nearly always stem from more than one problem, often being produced by two or more of the following: physical illness or deprivation, unwholesome or culturally barren environment, limited intelligence, psychological or faulty social adjustment.

9. An appraisal of the individual child's progress in reading should reflect the axiom that professional judgments cannot be made without preliminary study of the many factors that influence good achievement or the multiple causes of the problems encountered by the under-achieving pupil.

The Teacher's Insight into the Reading Process. The fact that a teacher is a competent person does not automatically ensure that every child in her class will learn to read in a manner consistent with his potential for learning and his environmental opportunities—but teacher competence certainly helps! And the uninterested, poorly informed, or misinformed school worker invariably slows the progress of her group.

Here is a list of professional understandings which characterize the insightful teacher who has a grasp of reading in the over-all elementary program.

1. Reading is a complex process of translating printed or written language symbols into psychologically meaningful ideas or thought units.

2. Reading requires that the child undertake a complex process, that of grasping the ideas of others through abstract printed symbols. Since he must face this difficult developmental task at an early age, he merits our best understanding and sympathetic help in avoiding the social disapproval and pressures that result when he achieves slowly.

3. When the materials and purpose of a reading experience are identified with the interests and needs of the child, reading becomes a more meaningful "thought-getting" process and the rate of achievement is accelerated in most instances.

4. In the last analysis, each child determines the rate and the mental processes he employs in reading. The professional teacher makes every effort to recognize and utilize clues to the "under-the-skin processes" that the child uses in making his interpretations of the printed page and strives to improve them.

5. Because success is a powerful motivating force, each child should be helped to experience continuous progress in organizing and improving his reading abilities and his skills in *all* class activities that lend themselves to reading-to-learn activities.

6. Since reading ability involves translating, interpreting, and evaluating information and concepts, it is strengthened through all experiences, both in and out of school, which lend meaning to language symbols. In a manner of speaking, all language learning directly or indirectly increases the child's potential for reading achievement.

7. Since reading is an inner, psychological process, each child literally teaches himself to read. *Ergo*, the teacher really helps boys and girls to help themselves to read.

If some of the major understandings presented above do not seem clear to the beginning kindergarten-primary teacher, or to the seasoned teacher newly assigned to work with younger children, the suggested professional readings (see pp. 246 to 253) should prove extremely helpful.

STRENGTHENING GENERAL LANGUAGE
USAGE THROUGH READING

The teaching of reading, especially when adequately individualized, is also the teaching of general language skills. Properly developed in the kindergarten-primary range, ability to read undergirds later experiences involving, for instance, spelling, English usage, and vocabulary development, or enjoyment through a sense of literary appreciation.

How Reading Helps to Enrich Other Language Learnings. Several specific procedures can be used to enhance the contribution reading can make to other aspects of receptive and expressive communication. While many of these procedures are spelled out in the second half of our book, which describes promising methods, a few broad points merit special mention here..

In the first place, a basal reading program in the primary grades is not, in itself, adequate. Various kinds of enrichment materials—trade books, co-basals, varied teaching aids such as records and films, and so forth—are minimum additions or supplements to a basal program. In short, there needs to be balance and variety in reading experiences which are personalized and which fertilize over-all language gains.

In the second place, reading experience which "carries over" strongly to reinforce general language power should reach beyond the familiar "3-group" or "Fairies, Elves, and Brownies" approach to grouping in order to recognize and provide for human differences. Many approaches to individualized reading, artfully described by Leland B. Jacobs and others,[2] need to be explored and applied.

"Individualized reading" is a practice which good teachers have used for years, but only of late has it received the scrutiny and stress that it deserves. By its inherent nature, individualized reading cannot be formalized in a precise definition. It is a point of view through which professional know-how and value judgments are applied to the guidance of reading/language growth in a child development context.

Perhaps the simplest way to characterize the individualized reading concept is to say that it:

Helps each child experience success.

Enables the individual to move at his own pace.

Encourages a child to sense how to choose reading material linked to his interests and with which he can cope.

---

[2]In Leland B. Jacobs *et al., Individualizing Reading Practices* (New York: Bureau of Publications, Teachers College, Columbia University, 1958).

Motivates children to seek help as needed.

Provides for sharing one's pleasure in what he has read.

Facilitates flexible reading groups.

Encourages increased power in the self-selection of materials.

Stimulates discussions.

Leaps beyond the confines of word lists established so far back as to be obsolescent now.

Encourages and facilitates diversified approaches to the appraisal of an individual child's success in reading.

Given such qualities as the ten listed above, reading will almost inevitably foster rapid progress in total language power in the slow and fast achiever alike.

The Challenge of Language in Childhood. Some years ago a young teacher was working with American Indian children in a southwestern state. Many were nimble-minded youngsters, but untutored in the cultural conventions and concepts identified with a reading program designed for the "average" U.S. classroom.

To start a reading lesson, the teacher wrote *boy* on the chalkboard and explained its meaning. Then, somewhat prematurely for her unsophisticated six-year-olds, she wrote BOY on the board to illustrate the difference between upper and lower case letters.

"Tell me," she said, "if boy spells *boy*, what does BOY spell?"

There was a pause. Then a Navajo lad ventured, "It must spell *man*. It's bigger than *boy*."

Good thinking, that! An unschooled mind, yes, but not an unintelligent one. And how well the little tale illustrates the challenge of childhood found in the quick minds of children. How richly they deserve our best individualized attention in the task of "making sense" out of the language symbols that complicate the inner world of childhood.

CHAPTER 4

Developing Creativeness and Competence in Writing

Creative Expression and Handwriting Skill

Kindling the Creative Spark

Developing Handwriting Skills

Developing Creativeness and
Competence in Writing

Young children have a flair for interesting, creative oral expression. The very fact that their vocabularies are somewhat limited often encourages them to use the words they *do* possess in fresh and original ways. Also, their eagerness to communicate and to learn powerfully motivates versatile expression.

Because they speak long before they write, the task of *writing* something which one can so much more easily *say* can be most frustrating. This fact puts the primary teacher on her mettle to preserve the spontaneity and color of children's oral expression until their ability in written expression ripens to a point where they can begin to capture what they wish to say on paper.

One of the teacher's chief tasks in the cultivation of creative written expression is to protect creativeness from the self-consciousness which some youngsters begin to develop with respect to "neat" and well-spaced handwriting. Boys and girls may become so preoccupied—especially in grade two and above—with the proper physical appearance of their papers that a lively, spirited approach to expressive and vivid writing evaporates.

It is helpful to think of written work in the elementary school language arts program in two dimensions. These are (1) creative written expression and (2) the technical skill of handwriting. In the post-primary years, of course, these dimensions are further complicated by the amenities of form in writing letters, paragraphing, tense, agreement, modifiers, and similar considerations. But such matters are not appreciably involved in the age groups with which we are presently concerned.

CREATIVE EXPRESSION AND HANDWRITING SKILL

Creative expression and skill in manuscript and cursive writing are, in a material sense, intimately related. Obviously, a child who cannot yet write can express himself only orally and through gestures. At the same time, creative expression and handwriting should not become so closely identified that so-called creative writing becomes a thinly veiled pretext for lessons in penmanship. To emphasize the point that mere writing exercises should not be confused with self-expressive experiences, let us consider creative power and technical skill separately.

The kindergarten-primary teacher can do a great deal to build the power of creative self-expression. But such ability is "caught rather than taught." That is, the teacher can work to create a classroom climate that is conducive to creativity. However, this is done by freeing children, by maintaining the glowing spark of human individuality, rather than by any specific routines or methods.

KINDLING THE CREATIVE SPARK

Since every child has a unique background of experiences which have helped to make him what he is, every child has a unique *potential* for creative expression. This potential is most likely to be nourished and harvested when the kindergarten-primary program mirrors the qualities of an effective environment for language development as presented and described in earlier chapters. However, let us now become more explicit with regard to the child's development of the power to write creatively.

Creative ability in *writing* cannot be assayed and encouraged in isolation. It is but one phase of general creativity. The child must engage in all kinds of creative activities and experiences if his written expression is gradually to sprout in the upper primary grades and eventually to bud and flower. If the school climate is a good one, it will automatically stimulate the maturing powers and skills which should characterize middle and later childhood.

The viewpoint that creative written expression is a product of rich, *total* creative living in school enhances the importance of the kindergarten-primary teachers who guide the experiences of early and middle childhood, a period in which children either have not yet begun to express themselves in writing or are taking their first steps—sometimes shy and faltering steps—in the direction of skillful expression.

The kindling of the creative spark, teachers must recognize, begins long before the child is ready to take pencil in hand to express his thoughts, describe his actions, or express his feelings on paper.

Teachers who encourage imaginative and vital work in art—with chalk, clay, and brush—are building readiness and strengthening personal qualities that will emerge subsequently in written work. Freedom to talk, to discuss, and to tell stories at the pre-writing stage also helps to provide an oral foundation for later expression of feeling with pencil and paper.

Again, hearing stories and perhaps dramatizing them, listening to records, and examining well-chosen books before actual reading begins subtly promote the child's uneven progress through the writing readiness stage. And, above all, if they are to write with freedom and with fluency, boys and girls must have a quality of experience that gives them something about which to write and about which they *want* to write.

To sum up, creative written expression does not appear abruptly when a child's first few halting words are preserved on a page. It does not appear merely because a group is assigned to write what is sometimes euphemistically called a "creative" composition. The creative spark is first fanned to a glow and then to a blaze by a design for school living in which the child is respected and his life enriched.

Can we "create creative power" in boys and girls? Of course we can if we teach creatively and free ourselves from narrow conceptions of free expression. Techniques and procedures which pave the way to skill in creative writing and which should be of interest and practical value to the classroom teacher are shared with the reader in the "how-to-do-it" portion of this book. (See pp. 223 to 227 in Chapter 14.)

DEVELOPING HANDWRITING SKILLS

One of the long-standing debates familiar to primary-level teachers revolves around the relative merits of manuscript and cursive writing. Even when manuscript writing is accepted at the primary level, dis-cussion waxes hot as to when a transition should be made from manu-script to cursive letter forms. Let us look at some questions pertaining to handwriting skills for which research and practice support or suggest desirable policies.

Is Manuscript Superior to Cursive Writing for Use at the Primary Level? Research, teachers' attitudes, and current practice combine to support the use of manuscript letter forms during the early years children spend in school. The consensus among language arts authorities is that manuscript writing is preferable to cursive at the primary level because it more nearly resembles the printed letter forms in children's books. Also, since each separate manuscript letter "stands alone" as in the word toy , the task of writing places fewer demands on muscle coordination than does the linked cursive letters of the word *toy*. Research surveys also suggest that teachers prefer manuscript forms in the early grades, finding the work easier for children to master and easier to present. Apparently speed does not suffer and clarity of handwriting is increased when youngsters use the manuscript form.

Insofar as practice is concerned, probably well over 90 per cent of U.S. schools now begin children's writing through the use of the manu-script alphabet.

Readiness for Writing. Since "readiness" is a quality or condition that permeates the child, there is readiness for writing—both in creative form and as penmanship—just as there is readiness for reading, spelling, or listening. Among the factors that affect ability to write are mental maturity and perceptual maturity. Also, linguistic maturity, social and emotional adjustment, and one's background of experience are important. Physical condition and development, too, help to govern the success with which writing, along with other school activities, is approached.

It is important to reiterate with reference to any type of writing, whether to develop expressive power or technical skill in the primary years, that *ideas* to be communicated rather than mere *form* should be stressed. Readiness for expression can be delayed or impeded by making children overly self-conscious about packing letters properly and spacing words neatly.

The Change-Over from Manuscript to Cursive Writing. Although surveys have shown that many teachers *think* that there are problems and difficulties in shifting from manuscript to cursive letters, research actually indicates that change-over is less troublesome than is generally believed. In one study it was learned that a group of children who had first learned manuscript subsequently wrote more easily in cursive script than a comparable group which had been instructed only in cursive writing. In addition, the "manuscript children" wrote longer compositions than did the cursive group.[1]

At the present time, in a majority of schools, it is the practice to begin cursive writing in the third grade, about two-thirds of our schools making the change-over in grade three. The range of practice is great, however, since a few schools do not introduce manuscript writing at all, and some never require children to switch to cursive writing.

There are two suggestions which teachers may wish to weigh carefully concerning the arguments which continue to smoulder with respect to manuscript and cursive writing: (1) all children should not be expected to switch from one form to the other at the same time, and (2) all boys and girls should be encouraged to keep alive their ability to write in manuscript after cursive writing is introduced. Several common-sense points support each of these proposals.

Why is a *gradual* shift to the use of cursive writing recommended when it appears easier, at first glance, for the teacher to introduce linked letters to an entire group? The answer resides in the marked developmental differences that exist among children in the same age or grade group. Some are eager and ready to write much sooner than others. Therefore, it seems reasonable to begin a change-over to cursive script with fast-maturing children in the high second grade and to delay the switch for others who are less ready until as late as the fourth grade. Only this gradual approach seems consistent with the idea of the growth continuum originally illustrated on page 12. Since children differ, why not encourage them to write in a manner consistent with their inner patterns of growth?

The need to sustain skill in *both* manuscript and cursive writing seems self-evident. For all of us there are times when one type of letter form is more useful than another. For example, many people use manuscript

---

[1]Prudence Cutright, "Script-Print and Beginning Reading and Spelling," *Elementary English Review*, 13:139-40, 160; April, 1936.

writing for lettering a graph or a drawing, for addressing packages or when note-taking in a lecture course. Yet they may prefer a cursive script for writing personal letters. Surely there is reason to encourage children to "do what comes naturally" in selecting the form that seems more appropriate in a particular writing situation.

Pencil Size and Handwriting Achievement. Some teachers favor the oversize "beginner's pencil" in the first two grades, while others contend with vehemence that boys and girls might as well begin at once to use the standard-sized writing tool that they will use in the years of later childhood.

Available research suggests a happy solution to the question of pencil size. Apparently it makes no difference whether the large or standard pencil is used. Handwriting achievement and the physical reactions of pupils are not affected by the teacher's preferences or requirements with respect to pencils. Would that all language arts controversies could be resolved so conveniently!

"Troublesome" Letter Forms and Legibility. Some professional workers, who undoubtedly deserve a medal for patience and an "A+" for perseverance, examined 1,344,905 letters of the alphabet which were used in the writings of several thousand persons of all ages. They found that four letters—a, e, r, and t—were the most "troublesome." That is, these four were most often illegibly written.

Primary teachers will be pleased and perhaps a bit amused by another conclusion reached in the same study. Illegibilities tend to increase with age. Adults wrote three and a half times as many indecipherable letter forms as did children.

Boys—and girls—may not write a hand that is "pretty," but the writing we help them to achieve in the early years has the virtue of being more easily translated than may be the case twenty years later.

Handedness and Human Individuality. At present there is less concern about left-handed children (or *sinistrals,* as they are sometimes called) than was the case twenty or thirty years ago. There seems to be little reason to arrange for primary children who are left-handed to undergo vigorous right-hand training in any case. Both right- and left-handed youngsters make about the same number of letter reversal errors, and the sinistral may write just as legibly and rapidly as the *dextral*, or right-handed child.

The fact that parents and teachers no longer seem to strive so vigorously to make children use their right hands when writing may help to explain the increase in left-handedness noted in recent years.[2] Between 8 per cent and 10 per cent of the children now in school write with their left hands, while in the 1930's an estimated 5 per cent were sinistrals. Freed of parental pressure and less often urged to use the right hand in school, boys and girls now seem to follow their natural inclination to use whichever hand is dominant.

It may be of passing interest to note *why* some children are left-handed. A number of things seem to create or to influence handedness. These include instructional policies of the school, environment or example, convenience, previous habits, hand strength, the nature or familiarity of the task to be performed, and, at least to some degree, genetic factors. When handedness is governed by so many complex elements, often in combination, it is easy to see why attempts to convert children to right-handedness have waned since 1930.

---

[2]Cf. George C. Carrothers, "Left-Handedness Among School Pupils," *American School Board Journal*, May, 1947, pp. 17-19, and Luella Cole, *The Elementary School Subjects* (New York: Rinehart & Co., 1946), p. 209.

CHAPTER 5

Sharing Books, Poems, and
Stories with Children

Children's Literature and Twice-Told Tales as Sources of
   Language Power

How Shall We Select Poems and Stories for Sharing?

   What Kinds of Tales Do Children Like?
   Be Sure the Librarian Is a Friend of Yours!
   Clues from Children's Reading Interests
   Poetry Preferences
   Story Selection and Sex Differences

Reviving the Art of Good Story-Telling

Five Types of Story-Telling

   Personal Experience Story-Telling
   Paraphrased Stories
   Creative Story Reading
   Memorized Story-Telling
   The Conjured Tale
   Tailor Your Tale!

Sharing Books, Poems, and Stories with Children

Much has been written elsewhere about the "realms of gold" that are reached through children's stories and poetry. Even the use of literature to help children improve in their attitudes toward others and better to cope with personal problems has been discussed rather widely. But one important aspect of sharing books and stories with youngsters is sometimes slighted. This is the contribution of such sharing to the child's *general* competence in language.

CHILDREN'S LITERATURE AND TWICE-TOLD TALES AS SOURCES OF LANGUAGE POWER

Sharing literature with children is one of the more important means to strengthening their total communications skill. By "sharing literature" is meant not only reading prose and poetry to children, but also story-telling and providing a classroom environment that invites the child to read.

The link between sharing literature and *reading* instruc-

tion is obvious. Good poems and tales, thoroughly enjoyed, are for the child a source of powerful motivation for unlocking the wonders of the printed page for himself. Yet also in *vocabulary* building (which in turn influences spelling ability) literature plays its important part. Why do youngsters often surprise us with the words they use? Partly it is because of books in which the words appeared (although TV has become a tremendous word-power builder, too).[1]

And what of the neglected language art of *listening*. Few if any means to increased ability to recognize, interpret, and comprehend spoken language are superior to the rapt attention children give to a rousing good story. *Grammar and usage*, likewise, tend to be improved through the child's continued exposure to good English in stories from which good language habits seep into his skin.

Outside the language arts field, geography, history, and science are content areas likely to be strengthened through tales which draw upon the social sciences and science to make people and places, times past, and the fascination of technology and invention very real in the child's mind.

Because many children in the kindergarten-primary years have not yet begun to read, or can read only the more simple books, well-chosen readings and artfully told stories are of an importance unequaled in later childhood. Let us make the most of them during this so-important era in childhood.

---

[1]Edgar Dale, specialist in the field of teaching aids has, for decades, studied the vocabulary development of children in the Winnetka, Illinois, public elementary schools. For the first time, since the 1920's, at the close of the 1950's, he found that a significant increase had occurred in the vocabularies of children. Television helped to create this change, Dr. Dale concluded.

HOW SHALL WE SELECT POEMS AND STORIES FOR SHARING?

What Kinds of Tales Do Children Like? There are many varieties of children's book lists. Some are *comprehensive* lists in which a book appears merely because it has been published. Others are *selected* lists containing books that an association or organization has hand-picked as of special value or interest to children. Then there are *specialized* lists in which books are categorized on one basis or another—perhaps because they deal with a phase of science, a particular country or topic, or have been deemed useful for children who are in need of absorbing stories which are nonetheless not too difficult for them to read. In short, book lists are most helpful, but they do not always supply an answer to the primary teacher's question, "What story can I find that the children will like and that is 'just right' for them?"

Professional judgment and teaching experience help the teacher develop an invaluable knack for story selection, and nothing we can suggest is more valuable than this talent. There are, however, several suggestions with respect to story selection that are worth passing along.

Be Sure the Librarian Is a Friend of Yours! Librarians are a wonderful breed of people who delight in helping others in a most selfless fashion—especially children's librarians. Since teachers cannot keep up with every new book that comes along, and since they cannot remember all of the "children's classics" that they loved in childhood, they should count on the librarian as a mainstay in making initial selections from among the flood of new titles that appear each year and in choosing forgotten favorites.

The good children's librarian—one who thinks of books as treasures to be *used* rather than merely guarded—has another tremendous asset. She knows what children are reading and relishing. Book withdrawals tell that story. Be sure to enlist her help.

Clues from Children's Reading Interests. A number of investigations have been made of children's voluntary reading interests and these provide some assistance to the teacher as she makes preliminary selections from among the inviting shelves. At the primary level many boys and girls like stories in which children are the main characters. Animal stories and fairy tales are top favorites, too. Research also suggests that with young children elements of surprise and a fast-moving plot are important attention-holders. Adventure stories and tales that are slowed down by description are best deferred until grade three or above.

The reading interests of *individual* children, it must be noted, do not conform to any set pattern. You may have a fast-achieving or gifted seven-year-old who dotes on stories designed for much older children or who loses himself in the encyclopedia or even the dictionary.

The "packaging" or format of children's books often attracts adult buyers, but with youngsters "the story's the thing." A tale that brings something of the world's meanings, its delights and sorrows, to children will be liked regardless of whether it has glowing four-color illustrations or a drab brown jacket. Ironically, books acclaimed by critics and given awards are not always successful with the youthful clientele for whom they were intended. Never force a book on children because an expert, or a purported expert, has decreed that a book is "a delight to the eye and a feast for the mind." Children are the jurors. Their judgment is surprisingly good—and as seasoned children's editors have learned, the juvenile jury takes precedence over the book reviewer in determining the titles that will long survive.

Poetry Preferences. Research tells us very little about children's poetry preferences or, for that matter, about the teaching of poetry. In general, if a poem is enjoyed by children, it is likely to be popular over a wide age range. However, children at the kindergarten level seem slightly to prefer unrhymed, cadenced verses, while in grades one and two rhymed material becomes more popular.

Story Selection and Sex Differences. Children at the kindergarten and six-year-old level are likely to enjoy similar tales, but in the upper primary and intermediate grades sex preferences begin to appear. These become most pronounced after children are nine years of age. Boys seem to like animal yarns even more than girls do in the primary grades, while girls favor tales in which a youngster of about their age is the central character.

Toward the upper end of the kindergarten-primary range, it is wise to choose stories to be read aloud to children because they are liked by the boys. Girls will listen to boys' favorite tales, but the boys often will not listen to books designed for girls.

REVIVING THE ART OF GOOD STORY-TELLING

Prior to the era of mass media story-telling was an acknowledged art and an important part of community and family life. Listeners old and young hung on the words of the teller-of-tales in historical times and the professional *raconteur* was a welcome and respected guest in village and manor house in Western Europe. The East, too, had its story-tellers who preserved and interpreted the culture for the illiterate and beguiled Caliph, khan, and nabob. Wherever there is life, there is story-telling. It is through this vehicle that man has captured the essence of living and preserved the sum of human emotions and experience.

Even though mass media bring the artistry of talented or gifted persons to millions, there remains a vital role for story-telling in preserving meaning, charm, beauty, drama, and similar elements that are woven into the tapestry of life in any day or era.

It seems important for a number of reasons to give more time and heed to twice-told tales, than many teachers do. This is true not only at the primary level, but throughout the elementary school. For one thing, children love to listen to stories. When encouraged a bit, they often become expert story-tellers themselves and grow accordingly in language power. Stories told orally also build a bond of shared pleasure between teacher and group. As we will shortly see, tales also can be adapted creatively to the needs and backgrounds of children by utilizing the several forms of story-telling described below.

There are good reasons, psychologically speaking, for story-telling both *to* and *by* children. Their education and insights can be furthered on the one hand by adeptly retold or original yarns, and there are deep satisfactions for the child who receives recognition for his budding ability to fabricate or to re-present stories he knows in an audience situation.

FIVE TYPES OF STORY-TELLING[2]

Although the kindergarten-primary teacher does not need to know

---

[2]We are indebted to Dr. William Martin, Jr., nationally known story-teller and principal of the Crow Island School, Winnetka, Illinois, for suggesting the interesting classifications presented here.

the five kinds of story-telling in order to tell a story well, it is important to be aware of the several ways in which stories can be shared. Variety is important to sharing tales with youngsters and the points below may help you to increase your versatility.

Personal Experience Story-Telling. A first type of story-telling probably stems from our strong desire to be the hero of our own tale. This is the personal-experience type of story-telling.

The personal story is likely to develop unrehearsed when a child asks, "What did you do when you went to school?" or when some incident or turn of conversation in a gathering prompts one of the group to say, "Oh, that reminds me of the time when I was . . . ." The bluff and hearty or extroverted type of person is likely to embroider his story so as to enhance the importance of his role in the personal experience tale. Introverts, whether they are five years old or fifty, are likely to minimize their part in the events described. Indeed, listening to the story a young child tells is a good means of helping a teacher to understand his under-the-skin personality.

No special training or preparation is needed for recounting personalized stories. However, they usually are most interesting when the narrator's vocabulary, "sentence sense," personality, memory, and depth of experience combine to lend strength and flavor to a tale. Some forethought, or previous tellings, may improve this type of story-telling, but (as in most communication) enthusiasm and self-involvement—the remembrance of past joys or sorrows —are the life-giving substances blended in personal experience stories.

Paraphrased Stories. The paraphrased type of story is widely used in speaking and writing when one attempts to communicate to others a vicarious experience which he has absorbed either by listening or reading. The child who retells a tale heard during the library story hour or the mother who shares with her four-year-old *Peter Rabbit* without resorting to Beatrix Potter's book is *paraphrasing* the stories.

As in the personal experience type of story-telling, the

effectiveness of the paraphrased yarn is influenced by the teller's personality. The intensity and recency of his vicarious experience with the story also may influence its effectiveness.

Creative Story Reading. The reading of stories is probably the most widespread method of story-telling now used in the elementary school. Reading is, of course, an extremely important way of sharing literature and experiences. *Creative* story interpretation occurs, however, only when the reader has assimilated the story experience from the printed word-symbols on a page and endows them with a living spirit through nuances of inflection, characterizing figures in the story, varying the pace of the reading, and so on.

Memorized Story-Telling. Memorized story-telling is the most highly specialized and the least important of the five types. While it verges on the theatrical because of the memory-work involved, stories repeated "by heart" are a natural method of tale-telling for those kindergarten-primary teachers who have a flair for memorizing easily plus a knack for repeating exact phrasing in a natural manner.

There are certain stories that, in order to be told effectively, must be memorized. This is obviously true of stories told in lines of verse: nursery rhymes, for instance, or gems such as "To Think That It Happened on Mulberry Street." Also, the prose of tales like Kipling's *The Just-So Stories* is best when memorized—or read expressively. Descriptive phrases, such as "the great, gray, green, greasy Limpopo River," should not be debased by whittling away their impact in a paraphrase.

Just as most of us can sing a song from memory, so most of us can—within reasonable limits—learn some of the grand tales and poems that merit the work that goes into making them a part of ourselves. Also, young children respect and appreciate the efforts and skill of the teacher who holds them enrapt by memorized literature in both poetry and prose. The eagerness radiated by the eyes and ears of boys and girls is the reward of the artist teacher who recreates well loved writing word for word from within herself.

The Conjured Tale. A fifth and imaginative-creative type of story-telling is the conjured tale. Unfortunately, many adults lose the power to create a spontaneous, original yarn as adeptly as the young can during their unself-conscious years of childhood. Lucky is the child who can experience the great original story-spinner, for such stories usually are preserved only in the mind of the teller and in the memory of the listener.

Conjured story-telling owes its charm and appeal to its great flexibility and to the child-adult rapport which it builds and upon which it thrives. The teller of such tales often creates his narrative from day to day with the help of his audience. The enthusiasm of the listener when all goes well is in itself a help—and if the story-teller is "stumped" in the search for a new episode, she need never be at a loss for long. She need only ask in a soft but impressive voice, ". . . and, boys and girls, what do *you* think happened next?" A dozen ideas will appear to make the plot soar on and on.

You'll never know how good *you* are at conjuring or "making up" stories for the fives, sixes, or sevens until you try. So—why don't you?

Tailor Your Tale. No one of the five types of story-telling is the best of the five. It depends on the story, and on the group of children —and on the talents and background of the teller.

The primary-level story-spinner need observe but one axiom: "Tailor your story to the time, the place, and the company—and share more than one type of story with the group."

A lady who must be a wonderful grandmother, indeed, summed up so much of what we have tried to say—and did it so spiritedly—that we would like to share with you her letter on story-telling.[3]

PALO ALTO, CALIFORNIA

DEAR EDITORS:

Have you told and retold the story of the three bears so often that you want to pull up the covers of the baby's bed and smother Goldilocks once and for all? Something like that started me on my own story-telling.

My husband and I had taken our three-year-old granddaughter and a ten-year-old niece to spend the summer with us at our cabin. I had *A Child's Garden of Verses,* thinking to read a verse or two to the children at night. But after three weeks of reading the book (and telling all the children's stories I could recall) over and over, I was decidedly bored. If I wanted to continue the storytime and keep my own sanity, I'd have to make up my own tales.

I had no delusions about my ability as a story-teller. All day I wondered what I could talk about. My only hope lay in finding a character to put through a series of adventures. But what character? What would interest both a three-year-old and a ten-year-old?

That evening I took a deep breath. I began a tale about a little boy named Jack who wandered off into the redwood forest to hunt squirrels. When Jack and I got tired, I let him lie down and drop off to sleep. And then, wonder of wonders, a door in the trunk of a huge tree opened, and out swarmed a zillion little men. That ended the night's chapter.

---

[3]The letter was written by Mrs. Clare Bowman and appeared in the *Ladies Home Journal,* 74:7-8, August, 1957. Reproduced with the permission of the *Journal.*

The next night, the children bombarded me with questions. "Tell us what happened to Jack," they begged. That was my first lesson in storytelling for children. You may think those characters are only figments of your imagination, but to the children they are real.

Not all my stories were serials or adventure stories. I soon learned that even the ten-year-old preferred simple, familiar settings. One favorite was about three ants walking up to a chrysanthemum bush. It was simple. It had no plot. It taught no lesson. I don't think it was even a story. But the three ants were garbed in colorful attire, right down to the handkerchiefs in their hip pockets.

The three-year-old demanded this story again and again until I was ready to call for the ant powder. And when I wasn't telling it to her, she was telling it to herself. All day long she went around muttering, "Three ants were walking up a chrysantenan bush." And therein lay the secret of success. "Chrysanthemum" was a mouthful, and she loved it.

Later I told about the animals in the woods around us. To bring the children into it, I had the animals peering into our lighted windows, wondering what manner of animals we were. Then followed a story about the sea, a little girl named Alice and a sea turtle named Mehitable.

Sometimes I wondered whether I or the children told the stories. Their pertinent questions, excited exclamations, even their attitudes cued me on how to continue. One time I started telling how mamma rabbit took her twin babies to get food. "And did the baby rabbits push the grocery-store cart?" my little one interrupted. I hadn't exactly planned on taking the rabbits to a supermarket, but apparently that was how she saw it. The two girls, on familiar ground, finished the story to suit themselves.

When the summer was over and we had returned home, I began to read a book to my cherubs, bedded down for the night. "We don't want to hear that," they chorused. "You tell us a story." That for me who once thought I couldn't even hold my listeners' attention!

Maybe it's just because children are more polite than their elders. But I think it's because your children like to hear *you* tell of things *you* know or imagine. And if they can play a part in the tales, so much the better. I'll start you by giving you the opening sentence that never failed to leave my little listener squirming with anticipation: "Once there was a little girl and, you know, she looked almost like you."

Sincerely,
CLARE BOWMAN

As long as there are people like Mrs. Bowman, and the many kindergarten-primary teachers who are certain to agree with her as to the delights of story-telling, the future of this wonderful and important language art seems secure.

CHAPTER **6**

Making a Good Start in Spelling

Problems of Spelling in English

When Spelling Begins . . . .

Readiness for Spelling
Making Spelling Functional

Spelling Word-Lists

Vocabulary Studies

Helping Children Learn to Spell

General Reasons for Spelling Difficulties
Specific Sources of Individual Problems
Qualities of a Good Program in Spelling

Making a Good Start in Spelling

Spelling in English is difficult for children because of many apparent inconsistencies. Indeed, spelling is difficult for adults, too. Time and again words used in everyday speech send us hustling to the dictionary when we use them in written form. Words like *accommodate, parallel, apparel,* and *opportunity* are examples of familiar terms sometimes misspelled, even in graduate school term papers. Less familiar words like *concomitant* and *desiccated* cause even more grief.

PROBLEMS OF SPELLING IN ENGLISH

One of the explanations of the peculiarities of our spelling is the fact that American English has evolved from so many sources: Latin, Greek, Anglo-Saxon, German, Spanish, French, Arabic, to name but a few. Often in a simple sentence one can find words derived from three or more languages. For example, "The gymnasium was open to the public during the basketball season" contains root words from Greek *(gymnasium)*, Latin *(public)*, Old French and Latin *(during)*, Middle English *(basket* and *ball)*, and French *(season)*.

The mixed ancestry of our language helps to explain why so many words that rhyme are spelled so differently. Consider these confusing rhyming words and how they *might* look if spelled in the same way:

colonel—*colonel*	yacht—*yacht*
journal—*jolonel*	not—*nächt*
infernal—*infolonel*	spot—*spacht*

choir—*choir*
higher—*hoir*
spire—*spoir*

Some verses attributed to a visiting European college student are further illustrations of the amusing result of attempting to spell homonyms in a fashion consistent with their sounds.

The wind was *rough*
And cold and *blough:*
She kept her hands inside her *mough.*

It chilled her *through*
Her nose turned *blough,*
And still the squall the faster *flough.*

And yet *although*
There was no *snough,*
The weather was a cruel *fough.*

It made her *cough*
(Please do not scough) ;
She coughed until her hat *flough ough.*

Sometimes when we stress phonetic analysis with children the results with respect to spelling may be weird. The story is told of an editor who found a sheet of ruled paper on his young son's desk. It bore the letters *e-g-a-k-s-h-i-o-n.* "And what is that supposed to spell?" he asked the boy.

"Oh," replied the lad with an air of great confidence, "I was just spelling *education.*"

Clearly, skill in spelling is a challenge to all from the primary years to adult maturity. But now let us turn to some common-sense ways of beginning spelling experiences during children's early years in school.

WHEN SPELLING BEGINS ....

Some confusion prevails as to just when spelling experiences should begin in the kindergarten-primary span. The developmental approach to language arts instruction makes this an exceedingly difficult question to answer specifically because:

The readiness and level of maturity of children vary.

The experiences and cultural environments of children may be quite different.

Research suggests that children learn to spell in different ways and that "timing" and procedures in spelling may be successful even though they are different.

Readiness for Spelling. In rather general terms it may be said that a number of children acquire *readiness* for spelling in the latter months of grade one. However, this research-conclusion should not be construed as supporting formal instruction in the high first grade. Also, many slow maturing or culturally deprived youngsters may not be ready to spell until considerably later.

As we have already attempted to make clear, readiness for spelling is a part of total language arts readiness and language development. Therefore, spelling readiness tests are unnecessary because reading readiness data for a child also indicate his probable readiness for spelling.

Making Spelling Functional. A foundation for spelling, as well as other language skills, is laid in kindergarten by the teacher who makes language meaningful and a source of satisfaction and pleasure for her group.

The so-called functional approach to spelling is best conceived as one aspect of totally meaningful language experiences in school and out. The four- or five-year-old who writes a "scribble letter" to be enclosed with his mother's note to grandma, or the six who slowly manuscripts a few lines to dad who is away on business for a week, is having a functional experience. He is *spelling for a reason.* At this period of his growth it matters little that the six-year-old's note is copied from an example "spelled out" by his mother. *He* is writing a letter and finding it rewarding to do so.

At the first grade level, in the absence of a formal program in spelling, the sixes are nevertheless growing toward the ability to spell. In these early years, reading instruction and later familiarity with simple phonetic analysis are in a very real sense the beginnings of work in spelling. By the time boys and girls are moving through grade two, an awareness of parts of words, their similarities and differences, and recognition of "word families" have undoubtedly fostered initial success in spelling.

Suggestions are made in the second portion of this book (see p. 236) as to how both readiness for and initial accomplishment in spelling can be fostered in the kindergarten-primary age range.

SPELLING WORD-LISTS

Spelling word-lists become of greatest importance and value at an age level with which this book is not directly concerned. At the same time, there is information pertaining to such lists with which teachers of young children should be acquainted for professional reasons.

VOCABULARY STUDIES

Much patient work has gone into the preparation of lists of words which are valuable resources for instruction in spelling. Recommendations which research workers have made with respect to basic spelling lists begin to become important as more direct attention is given to spelling in grade two.

The words that children and adults employ most often in writing have been used as a basis for compiling the vocabulary lists which have ultimately been boiled down to wieldy size for classroom use. One research team, for instance, has isolated 44 words which make up about 28 per cent of those which appear in all the basic writing of children.[1]

Some interesting data related to word lists include the following:

As many as 6,000,000 words have been checked in a single research project to determine those most often used in writing.

[1]Esther J. Swenson and Charles J. Caldwell, "Spelling in Children's Letters," *Elementary School Journal*, 49:224-235, December, 1948.

Nine hundred and seventy words, with repetitions, comprise about 85 per cent of the words written by elementary school pupils.

Some 95 per cent of elementary school written work involves but 2,650 words.

By the end of elementary school, a child normally has learned to spell about 3500 words.

Rather few words (one investigator identified 222) may cause about 65 per cent of the spelling errors in grades two through six.

must
full
been
rode
at
began
d?

Words frequently missed in the first six grades often are apparently "easy" ones: *pretty, getting, when, their, right,* etc. (The fact that they are often *used,* of course, helps to account for the fact that they are often misspelled.)

Despite the excellent and helpful data at our disposal, it is unwise to be guided by research without applying common sense in the process. Because 222 words seem to cause most spelling errors it does not necessarily follow that we should try to teach these words as soon as possible. Rather we must develop a sensitivity to the sources and nature of such difficulties as may be characteristic of each unique child in our group. Let us look more closely at the question of why children do (or don't) spell well.

HELPING CHILDREN LEARN TO SPELL

There are a number of general reasons and some specific reasons why children encounter difficulty in spelling.

General Reasons for Spelling Difficulties. Among the broad or general causes of poor spelling may be a faulty approach to the teaching of spelling. That is, a child may not have been helped to develop for himself an efficient means of learning to spell a word. Again, it may be that a group of children have been presented with words they do not need and, in consequence, that there is little interest in spelling. Finally, a group's spelling record may be mediocre because time has been wasted in teaching words that they already knew or words that were either too easy or unrelated to their experience. Since spelling is related to other language skills, a sterile "classroom climate" or a poorly conceived program in reading may have an adverse effect on spelling.

Specific Sources of Individual Problems. Individual children may experience difficulties in spelling because of visual defects, although this is not necessarily a source of trouble, and even when it is, may be corrected through the help of an ophthalmologist, the medical specialist who is concerned with the functions and diseases of the eye. Vocabulary deficiencies may, to some extent, impede progress in spelling. Other factors that have at least a minor effect on success in spelling are intelligence, of course, and skill in pronunciation and articulation. Children from bilingual homes and those who frequently have moved from one school to another may encounter difficulties in spelling as well as in other language skills.

Research indicates that there is a close relationship between success in spelling and (1) good visual discrimination, (2) phonetic ability, and to a lesser extent (3) mental age. Good spellers have fewer and briefer eye fixations than do the poor spellers. Reading ability and success in spelling improve together, by the way. Children who are slow in their growth patterns, and hence may read belatedly, can be expected to forge ahead in spelling as they succeed in reading.

Qualities of a Good Program in Spelling. Although Chapter 14 in particular offers "how-to-do-it" suggestions with respect to readiness and to the initiation of spelling, a few points regarding an effective program may be presented here with profit.

1. Since individual children vary in the ways in which they learn to spell, no single method of teaching should be used to the exclusion of others.

2. Although spelling experiences should be functional (i.e., related to

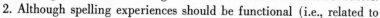

children's purposes and their need to use words), some type of foundation word list should be selected from among the excellent ones available
to avoid gaps in a group's background of spelling experience. This recommendation becomes especially important in grade three and above.

3. There is some disagreement as to whether the "test-study" or the
"study-test" approach to spelling is superior. In grade two it seems wise
to use the "study-test" approach; that is, to study new words *before* testing. This recommendation is made with due regard for the fact that
some research studies show that the "test-and-then-study" procedure is
productive of good results. At the primary level, children sometimes
feel insecure if confronted with certain words which they are expected
to spell without the preliminary experience needed to make them
meaningful.

In the later years of elementary school, the pretest or test-study method
seems to be more feasible and fruitful. Many children may already know
most of the words given on the pretest, hence should not be obliged to
spend spelling periods for an entire week on a list that they already know.

4. Children should be expected to learn only those words for which
clear-cut meaning has been developed. Experiences in the *use* and in
the *pronunciation* of terms are important. Next, each child should be
helped (a) to "see" or visualize new words in his mind's eye, (b) to
"hear" them, and (c) to "feel" them through his muscle sense (the
kinesthetic approach). *Recalling* and *writing* spelling words are the subsequent steps toward mastery.

5. The teacher should supplement any spelling materials used by add-
ing or replacing words in the spelling list. But this needs to be done
with professional judgment. It is unwise to include items that boys and
girls are unlikely to use in the immediate future or words that they see
no reason for spelling.

6. Even at the second grade level, some use can be made of individual
word lists or "personal dictionaries" in which children write correctly
the words they use and which serve as an adjunct to words learned by
the group as a whole. Individualized spelling of this sort not only helps
to meet the needs of children of varied ability; it also allows for the fact
that television and other mass media are changing and enriching the
vocabulary growth of children and gradually making even the best of
word lists obsolescent.

The reader again is referred to Chapter 14 for additional specific hints
related to the good spelling program conceived as an aspect of the total
improvement of power in written expression.

CHAPTER 7

Grammar and Functional
English Usage

Clarifying the Meaning of Good English Education in the
Elementary School

    What Do We Mean Today When We Speak of Grammar and Usage?
    What Is "Functional Development" of Language Power?

The Challenge of Good English Usage during Children's Early
Years in School

    The Problem of Motivation
    Semantics in the Classroom
    How "Pure" Should We Expect Children's Usage to Be?

Some Simple Criteria for Appraising Kindergarten-Primary
English Usage Experiences

Grammar and Functional
English Usage

One of the interesting issues in elementary education is that of how grammar and correct usage of English should be taught. No one denies the need for pupil growth in accepted forms of speech, word usage, or the conventions of written form, but there is confusion and disagreement as to the placement of such learning, the rigidity or flexibility of the standards to be sought, and the amount of information the schools should seek to impart.

The "meaning of meaning" is also a problem for elementary school workers. What is "grammar" in the elementary school? What is "usage"? What is "formal" and what is "functional" experience in grammar? Perhaps one of the most important first steps in attempting to clarify the meaning of a good program which builds power and clarity in the use of English is that of reaching agreement on the terminology and concepts with which we are dealing.

CLARIFYING THE MEANING OF GOOD ENGLISH EDUCATION IN THE ELEMENTARY SCHOOL

Technically speaking, grammar is a science which treats the classes of words, their syntactical relations and functions, and their inflections.

77

The concepts suggested by the term *grammar* are very old ones and were greatly influenced by Aelius Donatus, a Roman grammarian who lived in the fourth century A.D. For over 1,000 years the dictates of Donatus with respect to parts of speech, figures of speech, and so forth, governed the teaching of Latin and greatly influenced instruction in formal English grammar well into the nineteenth century.

The "Donatus approach" to grammar and usage was based on a grasp of complex rules. It lacked meaning and functional value even for our grandparents or great-grandparents when they were called upon to parse[1] sentences in the schools of yesteryear. It was this arid grammatical analysis, in the tradition of Donatus, that led many specialists in English education to revolt, in recent decades, against meaningless exercises in grammar which failed to carry over into actual use of language in clear, concise spoken or written form.

Some "rebels" against formalism have been so vehemently opposed to ritualized grammar that they may have inadvertently created the impression that little if any attention should be given to good English usage. Actually, the issue is not that of the teaching of grammar versus no teaching of grammar in the elementary school.

It is patently absurd to say that children need not learn proper grammar and good usage. The child begins to learn grammar when he combines words in early childhood to form simple sentences. Hence, the real problem is that of determining how we can best help boys and girls to attain the level of skill in communication which is of such major importance for successful living in a world saturated with verbal symbols. Indeed

---

[1]*Parsing* involves *"dissecting"* a sentence so as to identify parts of speech and their interrelationships.

the school which minimizes the importance of accurate, persuasive, and interpretative language power is in effect tacitly condoning faulty communication at a time when more lucid language is one of our great social needs.

What Do We Mean Today When We Speak of Grammar and Usage? Rather than continue to expand the pointless debate on formal grammar versus no grammar, let us examine a middle-of-the-road position, namely that there are ways of helping children use language effectively without basing instruction on rote memory work and sterile drill.

In popular elementary school usage, the term *grammar* is often used to describe two different concepts: (1) the classical concept of grammar as the formal study of the *structure* of the English language, and (2) the appropriate use of capitalization, punctuation, plurals, and so forth.

In order to avoid the semantic snarl of meanings, let us hereafter in these pages not think of *grammar* as the organized study of structure. Rather, let us identify grammar with correct spoken and written English *usage*. There is no place for the formal or rote study of *grammar* (identified as the memorizing of rules pertaining to structure) in the kindergarten-primary years. There is, however, a place for helping children improve their *usage* of correct spoken and written language. There is also a place for instruction in the *amenities* in English which govern practices and forms of oral and written language. Here again, there are simple ways in which teachers of young children can help them to acquire a feeling for, and to make use of, such amenities or conventional practices as generally govern telephoning, simple note-writing, and comparable language experiences that are a part of life.

What Is "Functional Development" of Language Power? Simply stated, the "functional approach" to grammar (interpreted to mean clear and appropriate *usage* of language and the amenities of language) is a process— begun in kindergarten—of guiding the language development of children in ways that will help them to understand, accept, and use English as a means of precise expressive and receptive communication. Many means serve to improve the young child's skill in good English usage. In this broad sense even the teacher of four-or five-year-olds "teaches grammar."

Usage of English is potentially strengthened and improved when the very young child hears the teacher speak correctly or listens to stories, radio, or records. When reading begins and reading ability matures, growth in usage is subtly improved by the printed page. The purpose of capitalization and punctuation, for instance, are often sensed long before they are discussed with a child because he has "just naturally" come to understand and to accept them through his reading. Chapters 11 and 13 in particular suggest some of the rich classroom experiences that pave the way to good English usage.

THE CHALLENGE OF GOOD ENGLISH USAGE DURING CHILDREN'S EARLY YEARS IN SCHOOL

The task of helping boys and girls mature in their ability to write and to speak is an especially challenging one for a simple reason. When they first come to school normal children already have learned more or less successfully the art of communicating basic ideas through speech and gesture. For practical purposes the child who says "he don't" or "I'll lay down here" is understood as well by his listeners as is the child whose usage is more correct.

The Problem of Motivation. In the social studies, mathematics, reading, or science the child is confronted by information, by tasks, by the need to obtain new information. Often he is stimulated and motivated by new experiences involving number concepts or simple principles of science which require that he apply himself in order to satisfy interests or curiosity—or simply to conform to social pressures which demand that certain developmental tasks (e.g., learning to read or to add) be accomplished. The situation is decidedly different with respect to faulty habits of usage in language. Indeed, a number of children feel little if any concern about improving their use of

English because they have been expressing themselves understandably, at least to their own satisfaction, for years past.

There is no easy or specific answer to how children can be helped in the primary grades to *want* to improve English usage. Nagging children for the use of "ain't" or for saying "they have went home" is more than likely to be a useless tactic. Continued exposure to good English in an atmosphere that stimulates free and fluent use of language in kindergarten through grade two seems to be the best way of providing a good foundation for both proper usage and for increased ability in, and desire to observe, the amenities in communication.

Semantics in the Classroom. Another subtle challenge to the teacher of young children is that of making them aware of both the meaning of meaning and the power of English usage as a means of influencing human behavior. How this awareness can best be built depends on circumstances and on the teacher's creative power.

Whenever possible the teacher should seek to help children avoid stereotyping in their speech—e.g., "Dutch children all wear wooden shoes," or "All Italians love opera." She should also quietly point out how epithets like *stinker* can hurt the person to whom they are directed. Properly speaking, such semantic learnings may not be associated with the conventional concept of "usage." Nevertheless they should be, and it is not too early, even at the five-year-old level, to begin to help the young have experiences which deliberately introduce them to nuances and power of language meanings.

How "Pure" Should We Expect Children's Usage to Be? In recent years there has been a division of opinion as to how "pure" we should expect the language usage of children to be. For one thing, usage should be sufficiently crisp and clear so as to leave no doubt as to meaning. Distinctions between words such as *who* and *whom* or *among* and *between* need to be preserved and understood for purposes of sound communication of ideas.

But teachers need not be so over-refined in their standards of oral and written English as to reduce expression to colorless mediocrity. A story attributed to Winston Churchill illustrates the absurdity of effete linguistic rules. When informed that a young member of Parliament had criticized him for ending a sentence with a preposition, the doughty Churchill with a twinkle in his eye growled, "That is the kind of impudence up with which I will not put!"

Clearly, we do not want our usage to be so pure as to be stilted or absurd. We should seek a balance between lax usage on the one hand

and making language a strait jacket for expression on the other.

SOME SIMPLE CRITERIA FOR USE IN APPRAISING KINDERGARTEN-PRIMARY USAGE EXPERIENCES

Although stress has been placed on meaningful and functional English usage experiences for children, such experiences should not be left to chance or handled in an incidental fashion. Here are some suggestions for improving children's expression which make it clear that grammar, interpreted as good usage, deliberately can be woven into the kindergarten-primary years.

The effective language usage program in the early grades is one in which:

1. The teacher is aware of her speech patterns and consciously provides a good example of correct English usage.

2. There are numerous opportunities for functional use of the amenities or conventions used in English. These include introductions, as when the children present a simple program and have guests come to their school room. "Telephone manners" practiced with a toy telephone in kindergarten afford another example.

3. The teacher strives to substitute good examples of usage rather than merely nagging children for using faulty speech.

4. The commonplace and simple errors in usage receive attention rather than the more obscure ones. Use of *brung*, substitution of *yourn* for *your*, or *I drunk* are more appropriate items to be corrected with a six-year-old, for instance, than the use of *lay* for *lie* or his confusion over the use of *teach* and *learn*.

5. *Readiness* for *usage* is consistently developed. For example, kindergarten or first grade children can dictate a letter of invitation inviting parents to a program which creates readiness long before they actually write notes and letters for themselves.

6. Children initially learn good usage by meaningful examples rather than by rules. Learning good speech habits is an outgrowth of experiences in usage which have utility in their lives.

7. Children's literature, reading, show-and-tell time and similar language experiences are recognized as resources for improving language usage skills. All forms of language growth, including, of course, creative expression, are used to improve communication skill.

8. As older primary level children begin to write, the teacher helps children to understand simple and familiar items first. For example, the

pronoun *I* is probably the most frequently used by children. Therefore, when the teacher introduces the concept of capitalization, *I* is a good item to use for an illustration.

9. It is recognized that creative expression can be smothered by premature emphasis on form when a child begins to write.

10. Care is exercised lest children be made to feel self-conscious or even guilty with respect to their English usage. Guidance of speech habits is subtle and kindly. Sarcasm is completely avoided when a child errs in his use of language.

11. The teacher is aware of the fact that each child has a unique background. Some have enjoyed a much better language environment in the home than have their age-mates. Therefore, the teacher's standards of usage vary from one child to another. *Rate* of growth rather than *level* of ability in the use of language is recognized as the more significant evidence in evaluating pupil progress.

CHAPTER 8

Listening and Observing

We "Listen and Observe with Our Experiences"

What Is Listening? What Is Observing?
The Importance of Listening and Observing during the
  Kindergarten-Primary Years

The Listening-Observing Spectrum

The Range of Listening-Observing Power in Children
How Much and How Well Do Children Listen?
How Long Can We Expect Children to Listen or Observe
  at One Time?

Creating a Good Environment for Listening and Observing

Listening, Observing, and Retaining Ideas and Concepts
Mass Media and the Child's Interpretations of His World

Listening and Observing

For many years able and creative kindergarten-primary teachers have recognized that children do not listen merely because they have the ability to hear nor do they necessarily observe merely because they can see. Many factors influence the ability of boys and girls to *interpret* what they see and hear, so let us examine some of the ways in which we can help them comprehend more accurately the wonderful—but often confusing—world of sights and sounds in which they find themselves.

WE "LISTEN AND OBSERVE WITH OUR EXPERIENCES"

The trained musician is far more able to interpret the brilliance or ineptness with which a symphony is performed than is the person who enjoys music but knows very little about its technical aspects. Also, to the seasoned woodsman a forest may be full of significant sights and sounds which escape the tenderfoot's eyes and ears.

Everyone knows that great differences exist among

87

human beings in their ability to comprehend what is seen and heard. But *why* is this so—especially with respect to the five- through seven-year-olds whose human development is our professional and personal concern?

For one thing, children "hear and see" with their experiences. The stories they have heard, the televiewing they have done, the places they have been, and the richness or poverty of their home and school environments, for instance, have shaped their ability to interpret meaningfully the verbal and visual stimuli to which they are exposed.

What Is Listening? What Is Observing? We may interpret listening (technically known as *auding*) as "the process of hearing, listening to, recognizing, and interpreting or comprehending spoken language."[1] In terms of this definition, *listening* is much more significant than merely hearing.

One can *hear* a foreign language but, if not familiar with it, cannot *listen to* or interpret what he hears. For the very young child, and to some extent for kindergarten-primary children, English itself can be "foreign." That is to say, their native tongue can be unfamiliar in certain respects until experience has given it meaning. With the five- through seven-year-olds, an important task for the teacher is that of guiding language experience so that boys and girls are increasingly capable of *auding*, of listening with a steadily increasing grasp of what they hear.

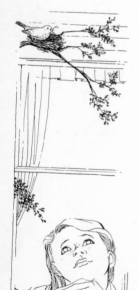

Observing, as distinct from *seeing*, may be defined in a manner similar to *listening.* Observing is the process of seeing, recognizing, and interpreting or comprehending one's visible environment. The general comments made above with reference to listening also apply to observing.

There are levels of listening and observing ability through which children progress. Consider so familiar an item as a table. At the most simple level of observation —the level of *identification*—a child recognizes the object as a table. Next there is the level of *interpretation*. The table is interpreted in terms of its function as a card table,

[1]This definition is Dr. John G. Caffery's and appeared in his article "Auding," in *The Review of Educational Research* for April, 1955.

dining room table, end table, and so forth. Finally, with more mature powers of observation one reaches the level of *description*. The object, in our example a table, is (1) *identified*, (2) *interpreted* as a certain kind of table, and (3) *described* not only as to use but also with respect to such concepts as its material, age, color, or location.

The power to listen develops through analogous levels at which a child can (1) identify a sound (e.g., an automobile horn), (2) interpret the sound (an auto horn as distinct from the more feeble honk of a bicycle horn), and (3) describe the sound (as a honk, beep, musical tone, etc.).

The Importance of Listening and Observing during the Kindergarten-Primary Years. In the kindergarten-primary classroom a methodical attempt should be made to help children advance from one level of listening/observing ability to another. It is especially important for the teacher of young children to emphasize these powers because in the pre-reading and early-reading years much of what children acquire in the way of information and concepts is made meaningful to them through listening and through observation. Also, readiness for effective language arts experiences in their many forms is largely the outgrowth of parent-teacher co-operation in the unending task of making what is seen and heard as completely clear and understandable as possible.

There is no single dramatic method or device for strengthening listening and the talent of observing. Rather, astute guidance in many little ways provides the foundation of experiences which seep under the skin of the child and gradually enable him to make sense out of things and events, people and places, that are a part of the world that buzzes about him. Pages 155 to 177 should be especially helpful to the reader as sources of suggestions for superior practices that lend accurate meaning to the classroom environment of the child.

THE LISTENING-OBSERVING SPECTRUM

We have already indicated that the power to listen and to observe passes through various stages. In addition to recognizing these levels it is important for the teacher to be aware of the fact that children in the average classroom group are spread over a "spectrum" of listening-observing skills. This point is illustrated in the following drawing.

Note how, in the first grade used as an example, there is an appreciable range in listening-observing ability and how general suggestions are made as to the kinds of experiences which may help children progress from the left end toward the right end of the spectrum.

As we have frequently pointed out or implied in earlier pages, the individuality of children is an exceedingly important consideration in promoting communication skills. The "spectrum" again illustrates this point as it applies to progress from seeing and hearing to observing and listening.

How Much and How Well Do Children Listen? In addition to the fact that young children obtain a great deal of their information through auding, the ability to listen is important because children are expected to listen during so much of the school day. One research worker visited schools in forty-two states in order to ascertain how much of the elementary pupil's day was spent in listening situations. It was learned that children were expected to listen to one thing or another 57.5 per cent of the school day![2] At the kindergarten-primary level the median amount of time presumably is well over 60 per cent since so many of the daily activities revolve around the spoken word.

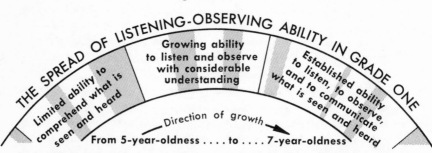

THE SPECTRUM OF LISTENING-OBSERVING POWER IN CHILDREN

In order to move forward, *all* the children symbolized on this spectrum need readiness experiences to carry them to higher levels of listening-observing power. They require a "classroom climate" that stimulates and motivates; they need parental interest and the guidance of an able teacher. They need experiences with language and literature and refreshing, exciting "adventures" in fields other than communications — adventures that bring into their lives things that are *worth* listening to and observing.

Granted that youngsters spend much if not most of their school time in listening situations, it is almost inevitable for us to wonder how *well* children listen. Here there is little that can be said specifically. We do know that some children have greater auding ability than others do, however, as illustrated in the drawing of the "spectrum" presented above. General intelligence, vocabulary, and language aptitude scores are known to be related to listening ability, but it is likely that skill in listening

[2]Miriam E. Wilt, "A Study of Teachers' Awareness of Listening as a Factor in Elementary Education," *Journal of Educational Research*, 43:626-636, April, 1960.

increases the child's vocabulary and language aptitude (which in turn influence I.Q. scores) approximately as much as the child's vocabulary and language aptitude increase his ability to listen.

Some years ago a research study, made at the intermediate grade level, indicated that children understood only about 75 per cent of the material presented to them orally. However, the skill and sensitivity of the kindergarten-primary teacher as well as the nature of the material being shared with her group have so great a bearing on comprehension (or its absence) that no arbitrary figure can be used to suggest how well the average child listens.

How Long Can We Expect Children to Listen or Observe at One Time? Years ago educational writers sometimes made rather definite recommendations with respect to teaching methods and children's attention spans. It was assumed, for instance, that a spelling lesson in grade three or four should last only so many minutes—often twenty or twenty-five—if the teacher wanted to "hold children's attention." This kind of arbitrary statement simply does not make sense when applied to observing or listening—or to any other kindergarten-primary communications experiences for that matter.

Differences among children and among observing and auding situations make it literally impossible to prescribe how many minutes children can be expected to absorb information without squirming. When it comes to gauging how long and how well the fives or sevens are able to observe and listen, teaching enters the realm of art. Creative teaching ability. the *un*common good sense of the skilled professional, remains the best means of determining when a point of diminishing returns has been reached.

CREATING A GOOD ENVIRONMENT FOR LISTENING AND OBSERVING

An author of children's stories, speaking of what made a good book *good*, once said that, "It has grass and earth and familiar things on a level with the child's eyes; but it also has treetops and wind and stars to draw his gaze upward." So it should be with respect to a good language environment which helps children to observe and to listen with pleasure and intelligence.

Listening, Observing, and Retaining Ideas and Concepts. To observe and to listen well, boys and girls in early childhood need an environment which contains familiar and reassuring qualities but which also stimulates curiosity and contains challenge. Here are some general suggestions which may be helpful ones to the teacher who is deliberately designing a classroom setting "to draw the child's gaze upward" on the long trail he is climbing toward self-realization.

1. Study the group of children in your room in order to acquire a professional grasp of their individual levels of maturity. Look for clues in their questions and expressions which may help to reveal their under-the-skin interpretations of what they see and hear.

2. Recognize that the child's power to observe and to listen is likely to grow or to wither with the total language or communications experiences of children. We do not "teach listening" or "teach observing" in isolation from other language learnings. We create a classroom world in which total communication understandings assume new significance to the child with each passing day and fill him with a consuming desire to learn by listening and observing.

3. Temper your daily plans to suit the deepening insights you are accumulating with respect to the out-of-school life of each child. What are the experiences *in* school which you can guide so as to supplement the home environment from which he comes?

4. When feasible, link new classroom listening-observing experiences to the familiar and well-known. This enhances the speed with which new understandings are gained by children.

5. Examine your work for a week or two in the past. What have you included in your plans to encourage listening and observing? What have you done informally to appraise pupil growth in these regards? What are some of the opportunities you can use in the future to create ever better powers of listening and observing?

6. Bring *your own* powers of observation to bear on the classroom. Are there objects of interest to children which have been introduced *recently* to stimulate listening and observing? Are such items varied and "exciting" to youngsters of the age group with which you are working?

7. Make methodical use of features of the school day such as "show-and-tell" time and group planning both to appraise and to improve listening and observing.

8. Be sure that your classroom does not reflect *too much* of a "listening type" of instruction. It is not so much the *amount* as it is the *quality* of listening and of opportunities to observe that promotes children's ability along these lines.

To sum up, children best learn to listen and to observe when they hear and see things that are *worth* listening to and observing.

Mass Media and the Child's Interpretation of His World. It was pointed out in Chapter 1 that mass media such as radio and TV seem to be creating a "phantom curriculum." That is, mass media are introducing children to many experiences, ideas, and concepts that persons born a generation ago simply did not encounter so early in their lives.

The fact that mass media have such an influence on most children's lives has an important implication for the kindergarten-primary teacher interested in strengthening the power of the young listeners and observers in her classroom. We must recognize that the school is now competing with powerful forces for the attention of the child. A pallid program for the five- to seven-year-olds may have managed to pass muster when its only competition was the nickelodeon. Today, however, we are likely to have scant success if we attempt to motivate and to stimulate children with colorless fare in school. Academic pap is no diet for vigorous young minds that have been introduced by films, radio, and TV to the drama, beauty, and excitement of life found in every quarter of the globe.

Also, we need to sense fully that our old ideas as to what is suitable content for young children need to be reweighed. If they are found wanting, then significant changes are in order. Clearly, the "simplicity of the childish mind"—if it ever was anything more than a myth—is becoming a thing of the past. The fives, sixes, and sevens may well know at least some things about cabbages and kings, jets and rockets, dinosaurs and volcanoes that we do not. Let's capitalize on this interesting new era for youngsters—and for *us*—by pioneering in creating experiences that capture the ear and hold the eye of childhood.

Who can dream of what we may learn about what children can grasp through sight and sound as our electronic-atomic era begins to come of age?

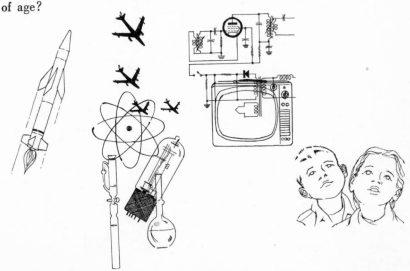

CHAPTER 9

Teaching a Second Language
in the Elementary School

Trends in the Teaching of a Second Language

The Growth of Programs since 1950
Some Reasons for the New Interest in Teaching a Second Language

When Should We Consider Introducing Children to a Second Language?

Questions to Be Studied before Foreign Language Experiences Are Incorporated in the Program
Some Concluding Observations regarding Foreign Language Instruction below Grade Six

Teaching a Second Language
in the Elementary School

There is a newcomer in the language arts family. The belated arrival is foreign language instruction in grade six and below. Strictly speaking, of course, the teaching of a second language in the elementary school is not an entirely recent development. A few schools in the U.S. and many European elementary schools have supported foreign language programs for generations. For practical purposes, however, most American elementary schools have yet to decide what steps, if any, they wish to take toward introducing a second tongue to primary or intermediate grade children.

At first glance it may seem somewhat impractical or even irrelevant for us to include a chapter on a second language in the elementary school in a book concerned with *beginning* language instruction. Yet the current interest in and development of foreign language instruction make the topic not only timely but one meriting careful study. Also, there are those proponents of the teaching of a second language who contend that the kindergarten or first or second grade is the most appropriate time to begin instruction.

TRENDS IN THE TEACHING OF A SECOND LANGUAGE

Within recent years there has been a marked increase in the teaching of a second language in grade six and below. Programs have been introduced so rapidly that many people—even some of those working in the field of elementary education—are unaware of the extent to which instruction has spread.

The Growth of Programs since 1950. In 1941 fewer than 5,000 children were exposed to a second language. Then, after 1950, came the flood of enthusiasm that began to sweep languages, notably French and Spanish, into the curriculum. By 1954 approximately 330,000 children in the K-6 range were receiving foreign language instruction. While this number represents a relatively small proportion of the total elementary school population, it is significant that 80 percent of the programs in which these 330,000 pupils were enrolled *had been begun within the three preceding years.* Also, the opportunity to learn a second language is being afforded to more and more pupils in early, middle, and later childhood. By 1955 nearly 400,000 children were receiving instruction, and by the school year 1959-60 the total enrollment probably had, at the very least, passed the half-million mark.

Some Reasons for the New Interest in Teaching a Second Language. The trend toward the teaching of a foreign tongue at the K-6 level began and flourished for a number of reasons. Some of these appear to be valid while others are difficult to support. Among the main arguments advanced by the proponents of a second language are the following.

1. Familiarity with a foreign tongue has cultural value. One does not fully understand his own language until he becomes familiar with another. Also, for generations, mastery of more than one language has been a hallmark or traditional characteristic of the educated man.

2. Learning a second language trains the mind and sharpens the memory.

3. Foreign language instruction provides a suitable challenge to fast-achieving and gifted children in the elementary school.

4. Children seem to grasp a foreign language quickly, as illustrated by youngsters who move to a strange land and acquire competence in a new tongue in a matter of months. Therefore, let us begin to instruct our children at an early age—say in kindergarten or grade one.

5. Improved communication and increasingly rapid transportation have made our world a very small place, figuratively speaking, when

the traveller can breakfast in Los Angeles, then dine in London ten or twelve hours later. This shrunken world is one in which we rub shoulders with and do business more and more frequently with people who speak languages other than English. As a result, there is a growing need for linguists in many lines of work. Furthermore, it is desirable for the tourist, too, to have a reasonable understanding of a foreign language. Such knowledge not only makes his trips more pleasant; peoples overseas are pleased when persons from the U.S. have learned their tongue and speak it with reasonable skill.

6. Knowledge of a second language creates sympathy and builds a feeling of understanding for the countries the backgrounds and cultures of which are introduced to our children through a knowledge of their languages.

7. An elementary school background in a second language, adequately presented, increases the opportunity for the study of this language in greater depth at the junior-senior high school level. Or it may permit the secondary student to begin yet another language.

Points in addition to those given above might be added, but the seven presented here are at least partly representative of the thinking and of the values of the large number of lay people and professional educators who have staunchly advanced the cause of foreign languages in our schools. However, it should not be inferred that a blanket endorsement can be given to the teaching of a second language at the K-6 level merely because seven items which purportedly justify such instruction are listed. Also, some of the seven points are the subjects of lively controversy. A great many people in elementary education would, for example, probably reject point two which states that the study of a second language trains the mind and sharpens the memory. Such a concept of mental discipline or training was becoming obsolete as far back as the late nineteenth century. It is also questionable whether learning a second language really builds sympathy and understanding for the people and culture of other lands as suggested in point six. Many Europeans are bi-lingual or multi-lingual, but the history of Western Europe has not always

reflected complete amity among its inhabitants. "Brotherhood" is based on attitudes more than on linguistic accomplishments!

WHEN SHOULD WE CONSIDER INTRODUCING CHILDREN TO A SECOND LANGUAGE?

In order to build more perspective with regard to the introduction of a second language, let us now turn to certain questions which the people in a given school district may wish to answer to their own satisfaction before launching, or discarding, a proposed program of foreign language teaching.

Questions to Be Studied before Foreign Language Experiences Are Incorporated in the Program. The problems which surround beginning instruction in a second language are particularly challenging because there is relatively little definitive research and but scant precedent to be followed. Conversely, the lack of tradition in this regard in the U.S. is also an asset. There is the opportunity for research afforded us as well as the freedom to work creatively without the limitations imposed by the hand of tradition which is often an iron one.

The following questions should be of help to teachers and administrators in the initial stages of program development. By "initial stages" we mean the period in which a local interest in the teaching of a second language has been recognized but during which no program has been begun or has been begun on a limited or try-out basis.

1. *What are our purposes or goals in offering a program? Do we want our children to develop the ability to communicate in a foreign language? To develop a foundation for high school or college? To communicate with minority language groups in the area? Merely to learn a bit about a foreign tongue or culture rather than to speak and to understand it?*

A discussion of the nature of the school's purposes in offering a second language is as good a starting point as any. Once the proposed goals of the program have been studied, a local staff should be able to decide whether to continue with the program, whether there are likely to be resources and support for the kind of program demanded by the goals sought, the nature of the program, and the age level at which it seems best to begin it. Generally speaking, if a second language is to be offered at all, it seems logical to expect that children will gradually be helped to speak, read, understand, and "think" in that tongue. There is little value in a loosely knit program that pleases a few parents because their children learn to mouth a few banal phrases.

2. *Does it seem likely that the learning of a second language can be made a functional experience for boys and girls in the local school situation?*

A foreign tongue—like any body of knowledge—should be learned for *use* rather than for mere *possession.* In *your* school are there reasons which children understand and accept that justify learning Spanish or French, for example? Can this linguistic experience be made *meaningful?* Will the majority of six- and seven- or ten- and eleven-year-olds ever put to real use the content of the language?

3. *What will we eliminate, decrease, or combine in the elementary school day to provide time for significant second-language experiences?*

The elementary curriculum has become increasingly crowded. Elementary science, art, music, and similar subject areas are competing vigorously for every minute of the school day. To avoid subsequent confusion and time problems it is desirable to have a clear-cut picture of how much time is necessary for genuinely effective instruction in a second language before a program is begun. Also, what classroom experiences can be eliminated, abbreviated, or combined in the school day to free the time that will be needed.

4. *What is the probable long-range cost to the school of second language instruction?*

Most of the other questions raised here will need to be answered before this one can be settled. However, since many elementary schools may lack linguistically competent teachers, it is not unreasonable to assume that one additional full-time teacher will be needed for every 300 to 500 children for a minimal foreign language program. A school with eighteen to twenty-one teachers in grades K-6 might well anticipate a 5 per cent increase in the faculty salary budget in order to pay a full-time foreign language teacher-consultant. A modest outlay would be required for teaching materials, too.

5. *Can the school locate and employ able teachers of a second language who also are aware of the nature of the elementary school curriculum and who understand young children?*

The fact that a person speaks French, Spanish, or a similar foreign tongue does not automatically qualify him to teach, nor does it insure that he can meet state certification requirements. Also, it may be a questionable practice to transfer a secondary school teacher to the elementary level without careful appraisal of such a person's adaptability.

6. *What language or languages shall be offered?*

At present, Spanish and French are most commonly offered in grade six and below in the U.S., with German a poor third and other languages trailing far behind. How shall the local school decide what language is "best"? Is widespread use a sound basis for the decision? Should a given school's geographical location be deemed more significant? Or should the second language be the one that someone who is available happens to be able to teach?

7. *For which children shall experience with a second language be provided? For those who want to learn it? For the fast-achieving or the gifted? For all children?*

The original decision to begin the study of a foreign language undoubtedly should be postponed until the local district has decided on the purpose of the program, as indicated in point one above, and then determined for whom the program should be designed. It is unwise, for instance, to jump to the conclusion that teaching French is a good way to challenge children with high I.Q.'s. Superficial or hasty decisions can quickly discredit even the best of ideas if these decisions prove unwise.

8. *At what grade level do we wish to introduce children to a second language?*

This query is so closely related to item number nine that the two points are considered at the same time below.

9. *What methods shall we use in presenting a foreign language and what organization of instruction do these methods suggest or require?*

Eight and nine are among the most basic questions raised here. As teachers decide what to do, they are also shaping the nature of elementary school foreign language programs in the years ahead. Practices at present are fluid ones and the judgment exercised today will, for better or worse, create the policies of tomorrow. Since research and precedent are scanty, it seems extremely important to reach whatever decisions to which discussion and study lead them by remembering that what we know about child development and the language arts in general is also applicable to learning a second language. Meaning, purpose, readiness, social adjustment, maturity, health, and all of the other components of human individuality that have a bearing on learning good English usage have implication for learning a language other than English. It is quite likely, therefore, that the "right" time to introduce a second tongue and the "best" methods to use can be decided only through study in each local district as the staff learns through experience what proves most effective. It certainly does not seem likely that what proves best in Laredo, Texas, will be equally suitable in Madison, Wisconsin.

10. *How shall we evaluate the success of our efforts to teach a second language?*

For twenty-five years or more specialists in evaluation have pointed out that a school program can be evaluated only in terms of its stated goals. Here again, we note the close interrelationships existing among many of the ten questions. Appraisal of "success" can be made only after a school has decided on what it proposes to accomplish through foreign language teaching.

The present section bore the heading, "When Should We Consider Introducing Children to a Second Language?" Apparently the safest response to make is "Only after careful local study." The writers' values motivate them to view the learning of a foreign language in the elementary school with considerable sympathy—but only after the ten questions above have been adequately considered and a carefully examined program appears to be feasible.

Some Concluding Observations regarding Foreign Language Instruction below Grade Six. Research that is available, and the experiences of schools that have introduced a second language in recent years, permit a few concluding suggestions that may prove helpful to teachers contemplating work along this line. They are offered with a minimum of comment.

1. If a program is introduced it should be so designed that children learn to communicate in the second language. It is wasteful of time to develop a program in which children only learn a smattering of phrases.

2. Consider introducing the foreign tongue as early as possible. The Modern Language Association has suggested that many children are ready at age five to begin such experiences if instruction is properly begun. In any case, the second semester of grade one (after children have become well acquainted with school) does not seem too soon to begin—if a program is begun in the primary years.

3. Instruction at the kindergarten-primary levels apparently should be based on the aural-oral (i.e., hearing and conversing) approach. Reading and writing experiences can be postponed until the intermediate grades (assuming that the second language has been initiated at the primary level).

4. In deciding which foreign language is to be taught, preference probably should be given to any major tongue which there is an opportunity for children to use functionally in out-of-school situations. Thus, Spanish is likely to be the best choice, say, in the Southwestern U.S., while Chinese or Japanese might conceivably be more appropriate in Hawaii at the elementary level. Because of available instructional materials and as a result of its prevalence as a second language in many parts of the globe, French is often suitable when no language other than English is prevalent in a given community.

5. When possible the public schools should co-operate with "language schools" maintained by many local cultural groups (Modern Greek, Chinese, etc.) when both are concerned with the same second language.

6. If a second language is offered it might well be offered to *all* children. There is nothing inherent in learning a second language at the elementary level which makes such learning a prerogative of the fast-achieving child. All normal children learn English in the U.S., Russian if they live in Russia, or Turkish if they are native to Turkey. *If it is made meaningful,* any American child can learn a second language at an early age and in a surprisingly short time if there is the proper motivation and opportunity to use it.

7. Only persons who are thoroughly competent should work with children in a second language. This is particularly important when the aural-oral approach is used with young children.

8. Instruction should be comprehensive and adequate or it should not be undertaken. Two thirty-minute periods of the routine or rote type of teaching per week are probably not enough to build a level of ability sufficient to justify teaching the second tongue. Ideally, there should be daily experience with the second tongue and, as soon as feasible, some regular classroom work (teacher-pupil planning, story time, show-and-tell time, etc.) should be carried on in the second language. If this level of application and use cannot be reached in from one to three years, there is reason to doubt the merit of beginning the program in the first place.

9. Many elementary schools must recognize that in their particular districts experiences with a second language are not educationally sound. Offering no program at all may be a better policy than attempting instruction that consumes time to little purpose.

PART TWO

Guiding Language Learnings During Children's Early Years In School

Practical suggestions for improving classroom practice in the language arts during the early school years.

CHAPTER 10

These Are the Children

The Delightful Fives: Their World of Wonders Ever New

The Lively Sixes: Their Uneven Growth toward Maturity

The Steady Sevens: Their Big Steps toward Effective Learning

The Growth Continuum in Language

Creating a Classroom Setting and Climate for Meaningful and
Functional Language Experiences

These Are the Children

One day a four-year-old we know was drawing a picture of a man. As his nursery school teacher passed his work table, he grabbed her skirt and said, "Hey, look-a tis. It's a hooman bean!" The dawning concept of human beings as distinct personalities was growing in this lively four as he moved toward developing a unique personality of his own.

Just three months previously he had displayed what seemed to be little more than the instincts of a healthy young animal when he expressed his feelings—for instance, by snapping his teeth together several times and punctuating his ideas with such comments as "I've got sharp teef for to bite you folks wif!"

Barbara Biber, a research psychologist, has said that "The pre-school child becomes a member of the human race, while the school child becomes a member of society."[1] The four-year-old we have mentioned illustrates this progress toward maturity. And we must understand him as a person to guide his language development.

Our pre-school child comes to many of our schools for the first time as a kindergartener, as one of the "delightful fives."

---

[1] Cited by Joseph L. Stone and Joseph Church, *Childhood and Adolescence* (New York: Random House, 1957).

111

THE DELIGHTFUL FIVES: THEIR WORLD
OF WONDERS EVER NEW

1. At this age children are at a leveling-off stage of rapid initial physical growth and development. To paraphrase a line from *Pippa Passes* by Robert Browning, "all's right with his world for the five."

2. Much of the time they are responsive to reason. Tears come easily but are short-lived.

3. They become increasingly free of the dependence associated with early childhood.

4. They begin to play well with others—but they sometimes like to play by themselves.

5. They are bursting with energy, have a well-developed sense of adventure, and are "action-packed." Rarely do they walk when they can run and seldom stay in one position very long. They need play equipment which gives them an opportunity for activity with a purpose. They need a balance of strenuous activity and quiet activity. They need freedom to move from one activity to another. Their attention span is increasing, but should not be overestimated. Both interests and attention should be given the chance to develop naturally.

6. The fives usually have ideas on how to carry out the activity they choose—finger-painting, let us say—and try to create, and seek to achieve a feeling of accomplishment.

7. They love dramatic play, rhythms and songs, stories and poems, art activities, play, blocks, animals—anything and everything it seems.

8. They are beginning to have improved control of their bodies, using them skillfully and with purpose. Larger muscular development is still relatively superior to smaller co-ordinations, however. The hand and eye do not work in complete co-ordination.

9. Dressing, toileting, and bathing are usually handled independently by the fives, although they need assistance occasionally—and they sometimes seek help they *do not need* in order to gain a bit of extra attention. They eat well, preferring fingers to spoons and forks whenever they

can elude the iron grasp of convention. Some fives are beginning to use table knives, too.

10. They are eager to do small jobs at home and school —running errands, for example.

11. *In the realm of communications*, they are beginning to handle language well; they talk freely, express ideas, and carry on conversations. Speech is beginning to be patterned somewhat more nearly in an adult manner. Pronunciation is generally clear. Five-year-olds ask innumerable questions, love to be read to, evaluate tasks like, "This is no fun," or "This is easy," define simple words, have difficulty distinguishing between fantasy and reality, are interested in using large and new words while seeking to capture their meaning.

The school-age child, as distinct from the *pre*-school youngster, usually enters our first grades as he joins the company of the "lively sixes."

THE LIVELY SIXES: THEIR UNEVEN GROWTH TOWARD MATURITY

1. The six-year-olds sometimes pass through a period of disorganization and apparently regress at times. This temporary upheaval is a harbinger or sign of an impending social-physical-intellectual growth spurt, with new growth elements not as yet incorporated as components of a well-balanced whole. In other words, the first grader is often in a transitional time during which he stands with one foot in babyhood and prepares, with the other foot, to step forward into childhood.

2. They may be over-sensitive, over-emotional, less cooperative and less sure of themselves than when they were five. This is normal and must be expected and accepted by the teacher.

3. The sixes fluctuate between the dependency of babyhood and a strong drive for independence, for identifying themselves with older children and adults.

4. The transitional phase between babyhood and childhood expresses itself in the play of the sixes, too, and they are torn between the individualistic play of

the early years and the team play of middle childhood.

5. Carefully guided activity is important as a means of helping the first grade child move in socially desirable directions. They are full of energy that they can release quickly and readily renew after brief periods of exhaustion. *Active* language activities are a great resource for learning and a physical necessity when their muscles and bones are developing rapidly. Boredom and restlessness may be indications of lack of activity in language learnings which are overly quiet and sedentary for too long a period.

6. Because of their exuberance, sixes frequently do not know when they are tired and have had enough. Adult guidance, with a minimum of necessary direction, can help balance their lives. Definite routines, however, are acceptable to them, and eliminate the necessity of making more decisions than they are easily capable of making while giving them a sense of security during a period of uneven equilibrium.

7. Sixes have an abundance of delightful intellectual curiosity which can serve as another resource for learning. They question, manipulate, build, and collect with zest. They start with their own environment but have ideas that can take them far afield. Fantasy in stories is of great interest to them. Their responses to language are rich and varied. They identify with the characters in stories, on TV, or in radio programs.

8. Large muscle development and co-ordination usually continues to be superior to the smaller muscle skills and, although eye and hand preferences are established, they may find it difficult to *co-ordinate* eye and hand movements. Their eyes are not yet fully mature in either size or shape, and this physical consideration has a bearing on initial success in reading. Generally speaking, physical growth is uneven at this time for the sixes and language skill development must be guided with due consideration for marked individual differences, say, in readiness for reading.

9. They may need a helping hand with personal routines accompanied with praise, encouragement, and sympathetic understanding.

10. They have an interest in identifying with adults and therefore are interested in accepting simple responsibilities related to adult-like activities: table setting at home, erasing the blackboard, feeding the pets, or cooking some simple dish.

11. *With respect to language they are very talkative.* Their intellectual curiosity leads them to ask swarms of questions. They use big words, slang words, many words, and use them from morning to night—sometimes with startling and amusing results. They use them at the lunch

table and on the telephone (some sixes still need help with dialing, by the way). Their pronunciation is usually good, and grammatical forms are fairly accurate if sixes have been exposed to good adult speech. They may begin to read and write.

After a fairly tumultuous year, the "lively sixes" become the "steady sevens."

THE STEADY SEVENS: THEIR BIG STEPS TOWARD EFFECTIVE LEARNING

1. By the time they move into grade two, most sevens have begun to develop more mature attitudes and feelings and are gaining appreciably more socio-emotional equilibrium.

2. They are responsive and eager to live up to adults' wishes—at least *some* of the time. Sevens are also anxious to have their age-mates like them. They are more critical of and sensitive to the results of their own actions. But they need support and encouragement rather than criticism and teasing. Do not make fun of their misadventures as they try to cope with big words! They are much more sensitive to the feelings of others than they were when they were six.

3. Sevens often are quite independent, but because of their sensitivity to others they may temporarily revert to dependency if the adults who work with them either do too much for them or are unwilling to be patient. Children who work independently need plenty of time to carry things out for themselves.

4. Boys and girls continue to enjoy group play together, but their interests now are leading them toward more peer friendships with others of the same sex. They are for a time increasingly competitive. It is a "me first" age. As they learn to defend their rights, they sometimes *over-*defend them—but on the positive side, they will at times defend a friend, too, from either real or fancied injustices.

5. Activity is still one of the best foundations for learning because the sevens, too, are full of energy and vitality. However, the balance between activity and quieter periods

is shifting. Desk work, reading, and other sedentary tasks can be sustained for a longer time. They may be pensive and dreamy during the quiet times. This is perfectly normal—but keep alert to help the child of seven who is *too* inclined to withdraw and dream.

6. They are interested in accomplishing things and may strive for a level of perfection that is as yet beyond the average seven's grasp. School work usually is a challenge. They are in an absorptive and assimilative phase. They also enjoy home responsibilities. Their "efficiency quotient" in regard to working independently is generally comparable to their experience.

7. They still like to lose themselves in dramatic play, and because they are broadening their interests, their dramatic and linguistic expression of adult activities draws from a bigger world than the "here and now" of the fives and sixes. Movies, books, TV, radio, and comics, we must recall, are furnishing experiences and vicarious adventure to an extent without precedent in the world of yesterday.

8. No great physical growth spurts are noticeable in the majority of the sevens. Smaller muscular skill is developing now, however, and is mirrored in their writing, art, woodworking, and other activities requiring fine manipulative ability. The difficulty encountered by the sixes in co-ordinating eye and hand movements is being mastered by the sevens, but care must be taken not to exploit this gain until the eyes are fully ready to adjust themselves to close work. This is also an extension of the "toothless age" which begins at six, and impressive gaps are evident in most seven-year-olds' dental equipment. This characteristic can temporarily affect speech development.

Fatigue remains a factor to cope with, for while the second grader usually has long since outgrown napping he needs opportunities to "recharge his batteries" during rest periods.

9. Their personal physical care, such as bathing, toothbrushing, and dressing, is usually handled by the children themselves.

10. The interest that fives and sixes show in working with and helping adults is retained by sevens. Because of their increased skill the number of job possibilities has increased. They are ready to handle a small allowance and often can do simple budgeting.

11. *In language they continue to be highly verbal,* frequently using the telephone as an added means of extending the range of their communication.

They frequently are reading at this stage with considerable independence. Storytelling and being read to by others is still highly acceptable, however, and some sevens continue to need patient and helpful guidance in reading.

They are often interested in the meaning and spelling of words and can note the similarities and differences between two simple objects.

THE GROWTH CONTINUUM IN LANGUAGE

The stages of development broadly reviewed above were chosen to accentuate some of the basic characteristics in the child's uneven progress toward maturity. The purpose of listing these points is not to stereotype youngsters, and seasoned teachers know that individuals cannot be neatly packaged in rigid age classifications. Rather, we have tried to show certain central tendencies in human development of which teachers need to be aware when they carry forward the important guidance functions which are theirs as they begin language instruction. Another concept which able teachers keep in mind is that the human organism is unique and reacts as a whole in learning situations.

Because of the interrelatedness of the elements which influence learning, a review of some of the more general developmental characteristics of children seemed necessary as a preface to further a deeper understanding of the nature and meaning of the language continuum concept diagrammed on page 12. As Chapter 1 suggested, good language growth is best achieved by the *active* sharing of communication skills with children, by making language *function* in their lives—not merely by talking *about* language. Surely it is apparent through the perusal of the young child's developing way of life that activity characterizes most of his learning.

Two other important qualities or elements in the learning processes of the five, six, or seven are his intellectual curiosity and his urge to interpret and understand his "world of wonders ever new" through play activities. These can be stimulating invitations to learning if the teacher considers them and incorporates them in the framework of her teaching methods and in the guidance of language learnings.

Since each child is a unique personality—one with an experiential background peculiarly his own—the teacher must *start with him where he is* on the path leading toward maturity. Obviously, she may find him at any one of a number of points on the Language Growth Continuum (see Chapter 1, p. 12). She needs, therefore, to determine through professional judgment the personal and group activities that will help him to gain new concepts and powers in the communication arts.

The second half of this book shares with the reader explicit suggestions and approaches which experienced teachers have used effectively to help children make progress along the language continuum. *All of our proposals, of course, will not apply in every school situation and they should not be used as patterns.* However, many of the suggestions have a general applicability to work with young children everywhere. They should provide ideas which the teacher can adapt creatively in the process of assisting an individual child or a group of children along the path to the ultimate goal of mature understanding and responsible use of both receptive and expressive communication.

CREATING A CLASSROOM SETTING AND CLIMATE FOR MEANINGFUL AND FUNCTIONAL LANGUAGE EXPERIENCES

The child's developmental characteristics and drives noted in the last section are spontaneous and creative ones which, if given an opportunity for expression, greatly facilitate the achievement of language power. The classroom should have stimulating centers of interest and activity which foster good communication and which are deliberately established in the light of what we know of child development, including language development.

Suitable types of classroom learning centers are discussed in the following part of *Beginning Language Arts Instruction with Children*. They include science centers, book corners, musical centers, play areas, and construction and art centers. These centers should be designed so as to "trigger" or to create ideas and questions in each child's mind and to encourage him in manipulation and experimentation with the many materials which are made available. Such stimulating clusters of learning materials aid language growth by providing experiences for the child to think, to talk, and to write about in the school environment. Constructive activities that further the child's knowledge and provide opportunity for the oral and written expression of his feelings and attitudes should, in short, be the foundation for the kindergarten and primary language program.

The early school years are exciting and influential ones. For most children they are the first really extensive experiences with the world outside their homes. It is the responsibility of the adults who guide our fives-to-sevens to keep this world fresh and inviting. In such a world of the classroom they have the best possible opportunities to use language in its many forms in ways that will help them become mature, contributive adults.

CHAPTER 11

Activities That Help Children
Use Oral Language Functionally

Group Activities and Experiences Which Foster Oral English Usage

Group Planning and Discussion Periods
"Show-and-Tell Time": Individual and Group Sharing
Reporting to the Class
Examples of Kindergarten-Primary Projects or "Units"
*   Involving Opportunities for Oral Language Growth*

Individual Experiences in Oral English Usage

Teacher-Pupil Conversations as Means of Guiding Individual
*   Language Growth*
Giving Explanations
Giving Directions
Using the Telephone
Making Introductions

Dramatic Play, Puppetry, and Dramatization as Channels to Effective Expression

The Nature of Dramatic Play and Some Suggestions for
*   Providing Adequate Motivation for It*
How Simple Puppets May Be Used in the Kindergarten and
*   Primary Grades*
Dramatizing Familiar Stories with Simple Plots

The Teacher's Role in Guiding Oral Expression

Diagnosing Language Needs
Providing Individual Help in Oral Expression
Guiding Group Growth in Oral Expression

Activities That Help Children Use
Oral Language Functionally

The ebb and flow of oral language, by means of which so much learning takes place in the early school years, is a vital consideration for the teacher.

In the exciting and educationally interesting classroom, "the world is so full of a number of things" that are designed to make children eager to begin their adventures in learning. Happiness and enthusiasm are important to boys and girls as they busily engage in *seeing, exploring,* and *talking about* experiences which have real meaning.

It is therefore necessary for teachers to provide breadth, incentive, direction, and outlet for the flow of communication so that each individual may progress along the continuum of language skills according to his degree of readiness and his level of abilities. Within a given group readiness and ability are likely to vary over a wide range indeed, as is indicated in the following examples.

Bill in the kindergarten cannot understand simple verbal directions such as, "Sit on the chair in front of Ann," but responds to, "Please sit here, Bill," as the spot is *pointed out to him.* Don, however, in the same group, discusses simple concepts of aerodynamics and jet propulsion with considerable understanding.

Sharon, who is shy and has a limited vocabulary, rarely if ever contributes

123

in first grade group discussions, whereas Roger volunteers information on subjects ranging from dinosaurs to air pressure and continually asks perceptive questions.

Paul and Jane, in the second grade, exhibit little evidence of meaningful association with the names *George Washington* and *Abraham Lincoln* as the group discusses Presidents' Day, but Jim rattles off the names of a dozen presidents, scarcely drawing a breath as he does so, and knows some background information about the lives of three or four of them.

Recognizing the varying abilities in her group, the teacher needs always to be ready to make use of those opportunities arising in daily school living which promise to increase the language power of each individual as well as the group as a whole.

In the pages which follow are examples of kindergarten-primary activities through which oral language can be helped to flourish both naturally and functionally. Although these are typical activities at each grade level, the *range* within every group must be kept in mind as well as the developmental progression from the *simple* kindergarten abilities to the increasingly *complex* second grade skills. Good activities for *all* children cannot be assigned arbitrarily to just one grade level, and teachers should be alert to the need to exercise judgment in adapting our suggestions to their classroom situations. A mature first grade, for instance, may profit from oral language activities which we have associated with the second grade level.

GROUP ACTIVITIES AND EXPERIENCES WHICH FOSTER ORAL ENGLISH USAGE

Before the young child comes to school, his oral language is for the most part the product of his interaction with family and playmates. In the kindergarten and primary grades, then, one of the important learning tasks is that of mastering the art of communicating with others in a group —taking turns speaking, grasping the ideas of others, and so on. In these years the child gradually emerges from his preoccupation with "me" and "my" to a consideration of "we" and "our" as he learns techniques of listening and contributing effectively in group discussions.

Group Planning and Discussion Periods. "Does anyone know what kind of food the rabbit needs?" "Which end of the playground is ours?" "What things must we think about in planning our first grade supermarket?" "What are the things we want to look for at the dairy?" Through discussion questions such as these children can be encouraged to:

1. Assume an active part in planning.

2. Express their ideas and opinions.

3. Have some share in making the decisions which will govern group activities and behavior.

When they are adroitly encouraged, classroom planning and discussion periods become truly vital experiences. Children under such circumstances are involved in a thinking-listening-speaking process which fosters growing skill in communication.

Planning and discussion are likely to be two sides of the same coin. Active pupil-teacher planning almost inevitably involves a discussion of ways and means of solving group problems. Clarification and extension of concepts usually precipitate planning.

Some situations which involve group planning and discussion are:

1. *General plans for the day—the role of oral discussion in planning daily programs.* Group planning in relation to daily activities and routines develops the readiness which precedes sound learning and provides a foundation necessary if children are to become efficient in going about their daily tasks.

"Talking together," "Group meeting," "Planning time," "Conversation time," and "Morning meeting" are some of the names which are given to the early morning period when a group thinks together about plans for the remainder of the day. With younger children it is helpful to have a designated meeting place where children may sit on the floor in a close-knit group, perhaps near a chalkboard, chart-holder, or bulletin board. Upper first grade and second grade children, however, often prefer chairs. It is helpful, also, to have a table or shelf conveniently near at hand on which may be placed books, pictures, exhibits, objects, and other materials which may be used during a discussion.

The kindergarten teacher usually can encourage children to talk about plans for their work by using verbal approaches or questions similar to those listed below:

Who has woodwork to finish today?

Who would like to have a turn at building with the big blocks?

What people are waiting for a chance to paint a picture at the easel?

Who are our helpers with the pets? What do we need to do for the rabbits today? Yes, we need pellets. Do you know where to get them? When will be a good time for us to go to the store to buy them?

Can you think of something you might do when you finish your work? This question often elicits such responses as:

Water the plants; play with puzzles; dust the shelves; play with the musical instruments; look at books.

After the work period the teacher may call the group together for a short evaluation or review of their activities. This provides more opportunities for the use of oral language. "What a fine boat, John! Tell us how you made it." "Let's look at some of the clay work." "How many have work to finish tomorrow?"

This short evaluation can often lead to additional planning for the next activity. "Who remembers what comes after work time?" "Do you remember what we said we would do at music today?"

Some kindergarten teachers, especially early in the year, prefer to plan the work period with each child individually as he arrives. This provides an opportunity for the child to express himself more freely as the teacher aids him in his choice and planning.

Step-by-step planning is usually necessary at the kindergarten level since children's attention at this age is generally limited to the immediate job at hand. In first and second grade, general plans for the day can often be discussed the first thing in the morning with specific planning and more detailed guidance preceding each subsequent activity.

First Grade Play
Act One

The first and second grade programs may be written on the chalkboard or on a chart and used for reference during the planning time. Picture clues are frequently used with the words in the first grade. As daily classroom routines become established, early morning discussion often focuses on changes in the program and on special events: "Do you notice anything different in our plans for today?"

"Yes, today we will see the second grade puppet show." "Who remembers the name of the show?" "Can anyone tell us something about the story?" "How can we be a good audience?"

Following this type of oral discussion of the "special event," the teacher may direct the children's attention to immediate work plans: "What ideas do you have for the new page in your booklet about the planets?" "What important news do you have for our 'Class News' this week?" These are typical questions which stimulate children's thinking and channel discussions relating to their daily activities.

2. *Making plans for effective group living.* When children are given an opportunity to express their opinions and have some voice in making decisions about sharing materials, use of equipment, safety measures, and other problems involved in daily group living, they understand and accept these agreements more readily. At the same time they are inevitably increasing their facility in oral expression. Problems such as how to share the school tricycles or bicycles on the playground, play on the jungle gym, take turns at using the big blocks, choosing between free play and organized games on Tuesday, and who will deliver the thank-you letters to Mrs. Williams' group, are of importance to children and they want and need to express their ideas and feelings about them.

3. *Making plans for special events—excursions, visitors, parties, programs.* Oral language experiences in planning for special occasions are common to all groups. Motivation always seems especially keen when a party or program is on the horizon and the planning involves talking over *what, when, how, why,* and *where.* However, if maximum growth in oral language is sought, it is necessary that the teacher's preconceived plans are not thrust down the children's throats. Children stop thinking and planning for themselves when they sense that the teacher has already decided what the group will do *before* she invites the children to "plan" with her. A teacher who understands the values of planning will accept the workable ideas of children and thus maintain a planning situation that is a mutually co-operative one. And in "*mutual* co-operation" the children are not the *mutes!*

4. *Planning related to specific group interests.* Discussions of group projects, as in primary-level social studies, may involve discussion of questions similar to these:

What do we need to know?

How can we find out?

Where can we find out?

Who might be able to come to tell us more about airplanes?

Danny thought we might be able to build a super-market in our room. Do you think we can? Who has some ideas?

Group activities and the evolving interests of youngsters can be used to launch careful pupil-teacher planning and lively discussions. After an initial exploration of possi-bilities in, for example, a study of the post office, and some general planning, the class may often be divided into smaller groups, each of which carry responsibilities for various jobs to be done in connection with the activity. Planning and discussion in the small groups rather than by the entire class is often more efficient and effective in-sofar as language growth is concerned. There are relatively more chances for each child to speak out in small groups, and more opportunities exist, too, for cultivating unique, personal interests.

5. *Other forms of discussions: extending and clarifying concepts.* Many group discussions are initiated for the purpose of broadening and clarifying concepts related to a major class interest.

Sidney, a seven-year-old, brought a leaf fossil one morning which stimulated the group's curiosity about fossil formations. The children were encouraged to express their ideas and the interest broadened to a simple study of prehistoric animals. "Dinosaur," "brontosaurus," "stegosaurus" became familiar words on the second grade lips. Vocabularies were extended as when Bill, who said dinosaurs were "extinguished," learned the true meaning of that word as well as of the word "extinct." Visual aids became essential elements, too, in this learning about early life on earth and helped to stimulate discussions. Teacher and children brought books and pictures which were pertinent and illuminating. Large sketches were made suggest-ing the "hugeness" of these creatures. Bulletin board back-grounds were put up on which children placed their cutouts of these "monsters." Film strips and slides were also useful teaching tools in helping children to increase their fund of word meaning.

Discussions such as the one described not only extend the vocabulary; they stretch the imagination of children as well. Children will think creatively and talk freely under such stimulation.

6. *Evaluations*. The merit or value of experiences and activities must be talked about: (a) *beforehand* in planning stages; (b) *during* the experience to clarify concepts and do further planning; and (c) *after* the event. This weighing or appraisal of learning *as it occurs* is the evaluative process at the child's level.

Evaluative discussions offer opportunities for children to judge procedures and weigh values according to their abilities at different age levels. "Do you think the first grade understood the program we gave?" a second grader may ask. "How could we have made it clearer?" Did we get the answers to our questions on the trip we made to the museum?" "What did we learn today that will help us in planning our next trip?"

Helping children, even at the five-year-old level, to begin to think critically will extend their thought processes, contribute to their growth in language usage as well as to their general growth and development. "We'll never get through talking this morning—we've got so much to talk about," said Karen. To this we would hope most teachers would respond with an enthusiastic, "Yes, and isn't it wonderful!" In the kindergarten and primary groups there are innumerable interests from which to choose for planning and discussion.

"Show-and-Tell Time": Individual and Group Sharing. "I'm going to the football game on Saturday with my father!" announced seven-year-old Tommy. "Today is my birthday," said Gail as she entered the kindergarten room. "Let's show our movie about the volcano to Miss Carlson's first grade," suggested Linda. In a classroom with a homelike, inviting, and comfortable atmosphere the amount and variety of sharing is always abundant. Life is an exciting adventure to the five-, six-, and seven-year-old child in the right kind of environment, and he will *want* to talk about his experiences. This desire to share may be utilized most advantageously by teachers in guiding language development.

1. Spontaneous sharing. The manner in which sharing takes place varies from day to day and depends upon the particular nature of school situations and the needs and abilities of the boys and girls involved. Much spontaneous sharing occurs as children arrive in the morning with a new football or doll, toy tractor or jet plane, with books, phonograph records, flowers, leaves, grasshoppers, marbles, and the endless variety of things which children bring to school. Others will have tales to tell about seeing the fire truck, of meeting grandmother at the airport, of how they acquired the bandaged finger, about the arrival of new kittens, of eating dinner at the restaurant, or about Mommy's birthday. Often language activities involve children in chatting with the teacher, in visiting with a small group of friends, or in demonstrating the operation of a toy jet plane from the top of the jungle gym for a small audience during recess period.

2. Sharing with the group. The alert teacher frequently suggests that an article or event be shown or explained to the class when she believes it is of common interest or when she senses that a particular child needs the experience, attention, or recognition. "Sandy brought something interesting this morning," one may hear an observant teacher say. "Will you tell us about it, Sandy?"

Most children are eager to share with the entire group and grow in language skills in the process: "May I show my book, Miss Palmer?" "I want to show my boat." "Look, I have a new bracelet." While it is desirable to try to find an outlet for each child's request, the teacher also must use discretion with respect to the group's attention span and interest. She may ask some youngsters to share their "treasures" at a later period in the day. Again, guidance is needed to ensure that a few children do not talk on and on to a point where they are wearying their listeners.

It is good practice to have a special table or shelf in the classroom where articles brought from home may be displayed, examined, and talked over at children's leisure. The teacher may direct attention to these and encourage children to converse among themselves in this manner: "How many of you noticed the tadpoles and the toy nurse's kit on the sharing table? Ask Mike and Jane to tell you about them when you have some free time." Discussion of the care and use of others' property is a good verbal experience, too!

There are children at each grade level who need encouragement and even direct aid from the teacher as they learn the knack of speaking before the group. In the kindergarten, especially, the teacher must frequently assume a definite role if "show-and-tell time" is to be a success. At this level, for instance, some children can be expected to stand before the group clutching an article firmly but unable to say a word. The teacher may wish to speak for such a five-year-old who has "lost his tongue" by asking questions and making a few comments. "What a beautiful moving van! Was this a present for your birthday? Do you think you could use some of the small blocks as furniture to put in the van? Show us how it runs."

The temporarily mute child at first may participate merely by nodding and demonstrating. Later on the words start to flow. Also, many children at the kindergarten level *are* capable of speaking both audibly and expressively as they explain about their article or tell a story growing from their experiences.

As children mature, the group itself assumes a more dominant role in strengthening language power through discussion and sharing activities. "How does it work?" youngsters in the class may ask. "What does it do?" "Where did you get it?" "Let me see the picture." "That's a good book." "I went there, too." During the years between ages four and eight children become more and more interested in the contributions of others and are able to describe and explain with increasing clarity and precision.

Children continue to bring toys and "treasures" from home to share with their classmates throughout the kindergarten-primary years. In the latter part of first grade and in second grade the sharing frequently tends to be related to or an outgrowth of *group* interests—books, pictures, and articles which children bring from home because of topics, such as firemen, the farm, or weather, which are being studied in the classroom.

3. Inter-group sharing of individual and group activities. The teacher should keep on the alert for group sharing experiences that involve language. As the kindergarten class finishes a work period she may say, for instance, "Before you put your work away please come to the block corner for a few minutes." As the group gathers, she remarks, "I wonder whose building this is? Is it yours, Roy? Is there anything special you would like to tell us about it?"

Roy may be able to explain to the group's satisfaction the purpose of the building and how he did it. If Roy is somewhat slow in language growth, the teacher may help him by saying, "Your corners are so straight and strong, how did you do it?" Giving him support and suggestions such as these are necessary "helps" and nudge the child toward improved oral contributions.

When the first grade finishes drawing pictures of their families, they enjoy seeing one another's work. As they tell about their pictures, children comment and question. "Who is that?" "Were you having a picnic?" "Is that your baby sister?" All sorts of drawings, murals, booklets, and stories may be shared with profit.

Holiday programs, parties, the activities with which a study of the farm culminates, stories, reports, plays, experiments, and exhibits are among the experiences involving language which may be shared with other groups. Programs planned for parents or other classrooms necessitate thinking things through and planning what to say and do so that the "guests" may understand and enjoy their visit.

Reporting to the Class. The presentation of simple oral reports is basically a planned and organized form of sharing. Children's ability to observe and to describe accurately develops in step with the intensity of their interest and purpose.

Motivation for observing carefully is readily supplied through most of the activities likely to be found in a stimulating classroom environment. Excursions, experiments, exhibits, science displays, and the wide variety of visual aids which can be used to supplement real experiences are some of the means through which the teacher can guide observation, deepen awarenesses, expand concepts, and encourage children to *tell* about what they see and do. Here are some examples, from the kindergarten, grade one, and grade two, respectively, which relate to developing language power through *reporting*.

Kindergarten children are capable of simple reporting. For example, a group discussing firemen and their work wondered where the firemen got the water which they sprayed on the fire. After taking the fives in her group on a walk to the nearest hydrant, the teacher asked them to locate the one closest to their home and report back to the group. They also "reported" on how many hydrants they saw on the way to school.

Children love to collect things of every description, and many groups, even at age five, are intrigued by gathering such items as seeds, shells, leaves, flowers, and insects. Just what is collected—and when—varies of course with the season and with the location of the school. Kindergarten children's ability to report on where they found a seashell will vary from a terse reply such as "at the beach" to "Well, I found it when I went to my aunt's beach house on Saturday. The tide was low. We walked way out on the reef.

There were lots of shells. They had little animals in them. They die if you keep them out of the sea."

A first grade approached the study of community helpers through the occupations of their parents. Among their questions to be answered were, "How do our fathers help? How do our mothers help?" They planned to "interview" their parents at home and find out as much as they could about their work. The variation in subsequent reports gave the teacher clues to the children's motivation, confidence, and range in language ability. A sampling which suggests the variety of linguistic maturity in a *normal* group follows in an ascending order of complexity.

"I forgot."

"I don't know."

"I don't want to tell."

"My father is a carpenter."

"My mother works in an office."

"My mother teaches history at Roosevelt High School."

"My father works at the weather bureau. He checks the instruments. The anemometer tells wind velocity. The barometer tells about the air pressure. It looks something like a thermometer."

Before the second grade went on a trip to the supermarket, they were divided into groups, each group choosing one area for special survey — fresh vegetables and produce; frozen foods; canned goods; bakery; meats, and so on. In their planning sessions they developed criteria to aid them in their observation — for example, how is a particular product displayed, what varieties are there, what are the prices, how is it sold (1-lb. package)? On their return each group drew pictures and planned an illustrated verbal report to give for the class.

In reporting situations of this type the teacher usually should try to arrange to have children of varied language abilities in *each* reporting group. This improves the reports and creates a more effective learning situation. Spread your seven-year-old talent so that each sub-group has a few able youngsters to keep things going well.

Repeated reporting experiences of this nature throughout pre-school-primary years help children to strengthen their observation techniques and to gain skill in making their oral contributions more pertinent, precise, and eloquent.

Examples of Kindergarten-Primary Projects or "Units" Involving Opportunities for Oral Language Growth. Strong group interests, with their accompanying purposeful activities, provide the incentive for a wide and sound variety of oral language usage. The following synopsis of a group project suggests the scope of language experiences

which may be developed through these enterprises. Let us start at the five-year-old level.

Many kindergarten groups use the calendar as part of their morning discussion. Cards depicting the kind of day —windy, rainy, cool, or warm—may be put in a pocket under the date.

On one rainy morning a child asked, "What makes it rain?" This led the teacher to initiate a discussion about warm air rising and meeting cooler air. The children decided to become "rain-makers" by boiling water and watching the droplets form on a pie tin as the steam cooled. At lunch they observed the moist droplets form on the cold milk bottles as the surrounding air cooled. They begged for iced drinks at home "to watch the air *condense*."

"How does the air get warm?" "How does the earth get warm?" "How can they (the weather forecasters) tell if it's going to be rainy or sunny?" These were some of their eager questions.

Exclamations! Comments! Questions! There were so many things to see, do, think about and, of course, talk about. There were new words to try out — *condense, evaporate, experiment, forecast.* One thing led to another. Here is a sampling of the kindergartners' activities which were directly or indirectly linked to language usage.

1. Listening to weather reports on the radio and telling the class about them.
2. Finding pictures of storms, wind, rain, sunshine, and telling the class about them.
3. Listening to many stories with weather themes such as *The Wind and Peter,* by Alvin Tresselt.
4. Listening to poems and making up poems about wind, rain, and sun.
5. Singing songs about rain and sun and making up some dances.
6. Planning questions to ask the man who runs the weather station.
7. Visiting the weather station and seeing the anemometer, barometer, and a weather balloon.
8. Dictating a thank-you note to the weather bureau man.
9. Dictating a class story about weather.
10. Drawing and painting pictures suggested by the trip to the weather station.
11. Drawing or painting pictures about what we have learned.

12. Making a "movie" using our pictures pasted into one long strip.

13. Inviting the first grade to come and see the movie, hear our songs, and watch our dances.

Unified projects in first and second grades, though more extensive in scope, encompass essentially the same types of oral language experiences as were involved in the example given above: planning, sharing, discussing, reporting, listening to stories and records and talking about them, listening to poems and perhaps creating some, asking questions, searching for answers, observing and commenting and eventually attempting to arrange learnings in a logical or sequential order so that they have clarity for each individual and become part of his background of knowledge to be expressed and shared with others as the occasion arises.

INDIVIDUAL EXPERIENCES IN ORAL ENGLISH USAGE

Although speaking in group situations is usually a new type of language learning for the child entering kindergarten, the young child has already been talking to himself (thinking out loud), to the members of his immediate family, and to his playmates, during his pre-school years. Informal and individualized experiences in language continue to be an important avenue of learning for him in his school life and are the occasions for much of his "practice" in oral language through grades one and two.

Teacher-Pupil Conversations as Means of Guiding Individual Language Growth. Insofar as young children are concerned, sex is no determinant of verbosity. Boys and girls alike may be either inveterate talkers or somewhat on the quiet side. The teacher should recognize the importance of their oral communication as a pathway to learning.

Following are a few examples of the opportunities for individualizing growth in communication skills which are utilized by kindergarten-primary teachers.

1. *Early morning conversation.* Some children come to school in the morning so brimful of news that it

appears as if they have been away for weeks rather than just overnight. Here are some typical leads to conversations with boys and girls. "Miss Judson, guess what I did!" "Do you know what?" "Look, Mrs. Allen, look at my plane!" "My Daddy helped me with this model!" "Here's a picture of a volcano!" "My cat had kittens!"

The refreshing flood of comments that pour out may be expanded and clarified with subtle questioning. Yet the teacher must also be mindful of youngsters who loiter shyly, waiting for recognition. The ones who are shy may be drawn out with queries or comments such as: "What is in your bag, Sally?" "What a pretty dress, Jane!" "Did you have a fine time at the picnic, Bob?" "Did your Daddy get back from his trip yet?" or "When is mother coming home with your new sister?" Knowing what is happening in children's lives is, of course, a prerequisite for guiding progress in oral expression.

2. *Conversation during activity periods.* While building a boat of blocks, working with clay, or making a mural, children converse with one another or the teacher about their ideas and progress. You will want to build on children's comments and questions like these: "I need the red paint." "My clay is getting too dry." "I want to put a horse here but I can't—I don't know how." "How long should the paper be?" "Do you think this will fit?" "What do I mix to make a brown color?" Endless opportunities for conversation are present when children have a challenging task to perform, are encouraged to do their own thinking, and to help one another.

3. *Conversation during lunch time.* Conversations also may be brisk and flourishing at lunch time if the environment is conducive to lively but orderly chatting. If children eat lunch in their own room, talk can be facilitated by arranging furniture so that small groups of four, five, or six children may be seated together. Such small groups are suitable for kindergarten-primary children. The teacher will wish to provide variety in lunch-hour seating arrangements, permitting children to share a table with "special" friends though she takes precautions to see that each child has someone at his table who is friendly toward him. She

also varies grouping periodically. She, too, should join various luncheon groups either upon invitation, when she feels that the conversation of an individual or of a small group needs stimulation, or in some instances for the purpose of rechanneling the conversation if it becomes boisterous or too silly.

4. *Conversation during other periods.* Juice time, free time after lunch (before rest or the next activity), and outdoor times are other natural opportunities for conversations.

In planning the daily program a teacher should avoid the pitfall of rushing young children from one task to the next so quickly that any time for conversation is squeezed out. Since the oral use of language is an art to be nurtured and encouraged rather than eliminated, the young child must be helped to feel free to converse as well as to discriminate between those times during the day when *concentration* rather than conversation is of paramount importance.

Giving Explanations. The "why" and "how" of things are important considerations in life, and these are two favorite words in children's vocabularies. The adults in their lives do much of the explaining for them, but opportunities for the children themselves to assume responsibility for telling the *why* and *how* should be used whenever possible. Improving language power through giving clear explanations requires that the child "think his ideas through," use as clear and precise language as he can, and say what he has to say in a coherent, sequential pattern. This sounds like a large order for little children, but experience in giving simple explanations at an early age provides a background for the more complex skills which ripen with maturity.

Types of explanations children may be called upon to make include:

1. How some craft or art product was made by the child
2. How to play a game
3. How to do a trick on the playground equipment—an explanation that also may involve demonstrations
4. How to use art media such as clay, paint, or paper
5. How something happened
6. How to use a toy
7. Why some objects float and others sink
8. Why Jane can't eat chocolate pudding
9. Why a plant in the classroom died
10. What a turtle eats

If explanations are not clear, the children themselves are often helpful when they ask for clarification. The teacher, for her part, should be on the alert to help a child use *specific* language in his explanations. For instance, she might say, "What is the *name* of that 'thing' at the front of the plane?" when a child has not named the propeller on his model airship.

Giving Directions. Children can often be encouraged to "explain" many of their activities. "Giving directions" is a process similar to giving an explanation—how to do it or how to get there.

In the kindergarten, children are in the process of becoming acquainted with the physical environment of the school. Early in the school year oral language can focus on queries such as: "Who knows where the nurse's office is? Can you tell us how to go there?" "Who knows where to get our orange juice?" Since finding their way around the school is one of the learning tasks of kindergarten children, encourage them to direct one another. Later they may give directions to the nearest stop light, to the corner mailbox, or on how to cross the street safely.

First and second grade children, naturally, are more acquainted with the neighborhood and community. They may direct the class on "How to get to my house" if the class is invited for morning juice or a party. They may discuss directions for an excursion to a nearby park, store, or post office. Or they may be called upon to repeat directions for a game or for a class assignment. All of these experiences should be encouraged by the teacher to foster *definite*, descriptive language usage.

Using the Telephone. Since the telephone is an almost universal means of communication, children need experience and guidance in using it properly.

A toy telephone should be a part of the kindergarten and first grade housekeeping equipment. Many teachers have found that having two telephones provides a means to encourage realistic dramatic play involving language. "Ding! Ding! Telephone! Answer it, John!" and the conversation is on. If John is the grocer, he receives a big order; if he happens to be the pilot, he learns facts about his plane and an imminent trip to New York or San Francisco.

Some first grade children use a telephone competently. Many know their own telephone numbers and when necessary can call independently for a ride home or to remind mother about a program the sixes have planned for that day.

As first grade children learn to write, they are often delighted to be able to make "personal" telephone books with the names and telephone numbers of the children and their teacher. This often brings on an epidemic of telephoning after school and in the early evening, however, and can become troublesome. For this reason the teacher and parents both should guide children in understanding proper uses of the telephone— the purposes for which it is used and the need for limiting the time when making friendly calls. The teacher may suggest legitimate uses of the telephone by:

1. Asking a child to call another pupil who is absent and tell him about a particular plan.

2. Suggesting that children telephone to remind one another about bringing the sugar and eggs for cookies, bringing bus fare for the trip, the hat for the play, or some similar item.

Most second grade children are completely independent in making local phone calls. They can telephone their parents about changes in plans, dial their friends for a friendly call or reminders, and are beginning to be able to use the telephone maturely. One second grade even planned a plane trip around the city on a commercial airlines plane. Each child, by arrangement with the airline, was held responsible for calling and making his own reservation as a part of his oral language development.

Making Introductions. Making introductions properly is a language skill and a courtesy which can and should be learned in any group. On the first day of school the teacher introduces herself and asks children to tell who they are. In the kindergarten this may be done through a singing game or some similar device.

When a new child enters the group, there is an opportunity for children to introduce him to pupils in other classes, to the nurse, to the office secretary, and to other school personnel.

Visitors to the classroom are usually introduced by the teacher, or, if they come when the children are dispersed in various activities, guests may be encouraged to introduce themselves to individuals and small groups.

Visits by parents provide frequent opportunities for introductions. Teachers may offer encouragement and suggestion. For instance, when Jack's mother comes for lunch, the teacher may say, "Will you please introduce your mother to the people at your lunch table, Jack?"

Although the teacher has the responsibility for ascertaining that introductions are made properly throughout the kindergarten-primary grades, by the time children reach second grade a good many of them should have developed a certain amount of skill and poise in doing this on their own. In their dramatic presentations and programs it is desirable to choose a child as the "announcer" to introduce the various speakers who are taking part. Also, a child or group may be chosen to meet a visitor and introduce him. If the teacher is consistently thoughtful and gracious in making introductions, the children will imitate and learn by example during their very early years in school.

DRAMATIC PLAY, PUPPETRY, AND DRAMATIZATIONS AS CHANNELS TO EFFECTIVE EXPRESSION

Children respond physically, often with the whole body, to outside stimuli. Play and play acting, then, is a natural response in young children. Through this medium much "under-the-skin" learning takes place. At home and at school, children are listening, observing, and making associations and relationships. Some of these interpretations are then reproduced or "acted out" in school in dramatic forms. In this manner children deepen and reinforce their understandings, enlarge their vocabularies, and increase their powers of oral expression. Originality and creativity in oral expression are fostered especially well through dramatic interpretation.

The Nature of Dramatic Play and Some Suggestions for Providing Adequate Motivation for It. To the uninitiated who observe kindergarten-primary children playing with blocks or in the doll corner, digging in the sandbox, swinging on the jungle gym, grouping packing boxes, or playing with other equipment, it may seem that the children are merely having a pleasant play-time. But to the trained observer the opportunities for learning which are to be found in dramatic play are also apparent. Through creative, dramatic play children are "trying on life," attempting to experience how it feels to be a father, baby, storekeeper, postman, or pilot.

Spontaneity is the chief characteristic of this play. Children may assume roles at will and may change from one to another with kaleidoscopic speed—especially in kindergarten and first grade. Second grade children, on the other hand, tend to stay in the role of a given character for longer intervals.

"What's happening today?" asked Miss Logan as she approached the kindergarten doll corner and noticed the children all dressed up in gowns. "It's going to be a wedding," said Ann. "Will you come?" she asked as she busily began to set up chairs for the wedding guests.

"Is it almost time for the wedding?" Miss Logan asked as she returned in a few minutes.

"It isn't going to be a wedding. It's going to be a show," replied Ann. She promptly began to act as mistress of ceremonies, calling on people in the play to perform, as well as soliciting participation from the audience which had been attracted by the performance.

There are many opportunities for extending vocabulary in situations of the sort described above and below.

Paul and David seriously pilot their plane which is improvised from hollow blocks and a steering wheel. "Contact! Coming in for a landing! Roger! Over and out," they call. Pilot jargon is familiar to first grade children through firsthand experience as well as through movies, radio, and TV and they incorporate it in their play. "Check the landing gear! Watch out for the propeller!"—these are familiar terms to kindergarten-primary children in the air age.

The group playing in the boat use meaningful vocabulary as they *hoist* the *gangplank* (a board with cleats tilted from the boat to the ground) and call, "All hands on deck!" (knowing that this is not a literal phrase) or "Anchors away!" as they pull up blocks tied with rope.

It is fascinating to watch and to guide such co-operative dramatic play. Early in the kindergarten year many children engage in individual or parallel play in the doll corner, block area, or sandbox. Co-operative play gradually develops naturally as in the case of John, Mike, Danny, and Jack.

John had been very busy making a long boat in the block corner. Jack was impressed. "It needs a tugboat to pull it into the harbor. I'll make it," he offered. Mike and Danny thought that John needed some warehouses at the harbor and promptly began to work on this idea. "Let's put a bridge from your building to my building," suggested Mike who was at this point highly inspired. "Miss Young, look way down in the basement of my building," Danny commanded. "Why, I wonder what that is?" said Miss Young as she looked closely at the two cylinders. "It's the machine to print tickets —to ride on the boat," said Mike.

The teacher has performed a major portion of her function before dramatic play is instigated by: (1) providing the experiences and discussions which furnish ideas for the playtime, (2) supplying equipment and materials which stimulate the play, and (3) planning the program so that time is available for activities of this kind. During the creative play process she may enter into the play momentarily as she is invited for tea, for an airplane or train ride, or as her patronage is sought at the market, the post office, or the airlines ticket office.

However, her primary function during the activity is that of observer. She gauges children's clarity of concepts, ability to suit tone and inflection to the role, and their memory, understanding and accuracy in using vocabulary employed by the characters portrayed. This observation serves as a guide in future discussions to broaden concepts and clarify relationships as she sees the need. She also makes suggestions and helps children arrive at acceptable rules: "Build the wall of blocks only as tall as you are," or "We play with the trucks on this side of the room."

Clues to emotions and feelings may be gathered, too. Why is John never happy in a subordinate role? He invariably wishes to be pilot, not co-pilot; engineer rather than ticket taker. Why does Cathy prefer to sit and observe and offer suggestions rather than to dress up and take part in the doll corner play? Paul, a robust, somewhat aggressive young fellow, has been playing the part of the child or baby in the doll corner this week. Since he is the middle child among five boys, one a new baby, he is trying to decide which is more satisfying—following the pattern of the older or younger ones?

Clearly, dramatic play is a learning situation for both children and teacher and is an important aspect in the language arts experiences of boys and girls in kindergarten and in the primary grades.

How Simple Puppets May Be Used in the Kindergarten and Primary Grades. Children and adults take delight in puppet shows. Since children can "make believe" so readily, it is easy for them to invest their simple puppet figures with the human or animal characteristics which they are intended to portray. Children do this with dolls and toy animals from infancy.

Some teachers keep a hand puppet in the classroom, a well-worn figure which becomes an "old friend" of the class. He may tell a story to the class or "take over" group meetings on various occasions as he observes happenings in the room which he wishes to discuss with the children. This technique has been used successfully by teachers as an attention-getting device. When used sparingly, a puppet through which the teacher or children speak has the strong impact of novelty, captures their attention, and at the same time familiarizes children with the possibilities of puppet play.

Stick puppets (figures cut out of construction paper or tag board and glued to a stick), paper bag puppets (made by drawing a face on a paper bag, stuffing it with paper and tying it to a stick), and flannel board cutouts are particularly adaptable and very satisfactory for use with kindergarten-primary children. Many youngsters who lack the confidence or courage to assume a role in dramatizations are comfortable when crouched behind a table or box where they can "let the puppet talk and act for them" or when sticking figures on the flannel board. In other words, puppets help the shy child in particular to grow in oral language skills.

Teachers at each of these K-2 grade levels can motivate dramatization by using a flannel board while telling a story. *Ask Mr. Bear, The Three Bears,* and *The Five Chinese Brothers* are examples of stories adaptable to this purpose. In the retelling she may ask the group to "say the words" at appropriate parts as she manipulates figures on the flannel board, or she may invite children to put up the cut-out figures "when it is time."

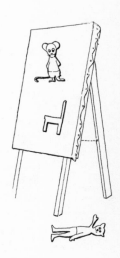

The flannel board and the figures (assembled in an envelope or box with an identifying picture and the name of the story) may be left in a convenient place and children are invited to play with them if they wish. When children have had sufficient experience with these materials, they may ask permission to create a flannel-board play themselves, or the teacher may suggest it.

"It would be fun to have a new story for our flannel board

today. Who can think of one we might make?" the teacher may ask. Children invariably suggest some of their favorite tales. The teacher, of course, will use professional judgment in making certain that the group's choices of stories are adaptable to the flannel board and not too involved. A group may volunteer for responsibility in choosing stories or, on occasion, the entire class may work on several stories. Note the excellent opportunities for oral language experiences in these examples.

In one first grade class *The Three Bears, Humpty Dumpty,* and *Tom Thumb* were chosen, while one group decided to "make up our own" and concocted an imaginative creation which they called *Mary and the Wolf.* After the stories were decided upon, the teacher checked each group, asking, "What is your play? What do you need?" She then suggested to a few stragglers, "Would you like to help this group with *Tom Thumb?*" "Could you make the wall for Humpty Dumpty?" "Would you make Mama Bear's bed?" Paper and small bits of flannel had been set out and the children worked busily. After outdoor time, when they were refreshed, they "presented" their plays. In the beginning this creative type of presentation is often a "community effort." That is, the teacher may say, "All the Humpty Dumpty people come up, please," and while the class chants the rhyme, the play group puts up the figures at the appropriate times. Or the teacher tells the story of *The Three Bears* pausing for each child to say the dialogue as he places his cutout on the board—"I'm the father bear," and so on.

One kindergarten group had been invited to a stick-puppet play, *The Three Billy Goats Gruff,* given by the first grade. The younger children were fascinated by the presentation and talked it over in the group and among themselves. Lunch conversation was predominantly about the play. "Who's that crossing my bridge?" could be heard time and again in their five-year-old voices.

The next day at work time the kindergarten teacher displayed professional creativity by setting out paper, crayons, glue, and sticks for work materials. A tall cardboard carton with a square cut out for the stage was nearby. In the beginning only one boy chose this activity. He made all the characters of *The Three Billy Goats Gruff* and took all the parts in playing it. The next day other children became intrigued and began to make stick puppets. Some did the "Billy Goats," but others began to make their own characters. Two or three at a time crouched down in the box and experimented with them. Dialogue in these early attempts, as may be expected, was somewhat limited: "Hello. How are you today?" "I'm fine. How are you?" "How is your baby?" "She's fine." "I guess I'd better be getting home now." However, a long stride toward improved oral expression was being taken by these five-year-olds.

First and second grade children grow rapidly in their ability to dramatize a well-loved play in which they use stick puppets or flannel-board cutouts. They may be stimulated to make up original presentations, too.

They also like to contrive plays based on experiences such as a visit to the zoo, the dairy, or a weather station.

The more mature children may become interested in painting back-drops for various scenes and trying out their play a few times before they present it to the class. This helps them in working out oral language sequence, but the teacher must guard against "over-practice" which can impair and even ruin the spontaneity of oral language in younger children.

Dramatizing Familiar Stories with Simple Plots. Dramatiza-tion, as distinguished from dramatic play, involves the child in the deliberate, conscious assumption of a role. In dramatic play the child *lives* the part, say, of a jet pilot. In creative dramatization, he *acts* the part of a pilot.

Younger children are engaged in dramatizing during even their simple finger plays such as "Eensy Weensy Spider" or "The Mouse Runs up the Clock." There is drama, in a sense, in their rhythms and singing games (being an elephant, raindrop, leaf, or soldier) and in their read-ing. ("How do you think father may have felt in this story?" the teacher may ask. "Read it the way you think he said it.") The young dramatize in the process of conversing, too.

If children are encouraged in dramatic expression, they may be stimu-lated—after hearing a particular story—to suggest, "Let's play it. May I be Bushy Tail?" Impromptu dramatizations of this nature help chil-dren to "loosen up" in their speech and to develop the poise which is a requisite for language usage in social and in audience situations. Com-prehension of a story or experience is also greatly enhanced through creative dramatics. Emotional reactions of characters are pointed up by the teacher who raises such questions as "How do you think he felt?" The gayety, happiness, fears, sorrows, mischievousness, and similar quali-ties of storybook characters can be discussed and reproduced with profit to the group.

Dramatizing poems or songs in pantomime accompanied by group choral speaking or singing is also a valuable and pleasing experience for primary children. A. A. Milne's "The King's Breakfast," Elizabeth Madox Roberts' "Firefly," and many others are well adapted to this purpose. Choral speech may be an "on-the-spot" activity or may be planned with some simple props and extremely simple costumes either for the children's own enjoyment, for another group, or for parents— depending upon the group's maturity, depth of interest, and the teacher's purposes.

Stories having a simple plot which have been read repeatedly and

have become well known to children are excellent for dramatization. *Bremen Town Musicians, The Cock, the Mouse and the Little Red Hen, Jack and the Bean Stalk,* and many others lend themselves admirably to dramatization. When children are familiar with the plot, characters, and story sequence, they should be encouraged to speak lines spontaneously and creatively in their own words. Memorization of lines is rarely if ever desirable for dramatization with kindergarten-primary children. They will, however, learn familiar verses and tales "by heart" in many instances through long familiarity.

When children wish to dramatize a story or poem which has too few characters to permit broad participation, two or more casts may be chosen. Each can then serve as an audience for the other. If the play is being presented to other classes or groups, the two casts may take turns— one presenting the play to a kindergarten and the other to a second grade.

THE TEACHER'S ROLE IN GUIDING ORAL EXPRESSION

In all of the language learnings, which are such an integral part of the fabric of the school program, the teacher's function is to supply maximum opportunities for *each* child to become more mature in his language achievement. To plan a program to meet these purposes she must be sensitive to the language needs of every *individual* in the group and of the status of the verbal powers of children spread over a wide spectrum of ability to communicate.

Diagnosing Language Needs. As the teacher observes her class in action, she should be aware of the various language needs and problems of individual children. These include:

1. The child who talks incessantly.

2. The child who rarely makes himself heard in group situations.

3. The child who has a restricted vocabulary—one with too few words with which to express his ideas.

4. The excitable child whose voice grows shrill with every utterance.

5. The child with physical speech defects.

6. The child with immature speech patterns.

7. The child who speaks so rapidly that he is often unintelligible.

8. The child who for psychological reasons stutters, hesitates, is shy, or becomes confused.

9. The poised child who speaks clearly and distinctly in both individual and group situations.

10. The child who possesses an extensive vocabulary and demonstrates a quick ability to grasp meanings.

As she pinpoints and analyzes the specific language talents or lacks of each child, the teacher should become increasingly able to plan a program with consideration of the particular guidance necessary for individual and group growth along the continuum of language skills.

Providing Individual Help in Oral Expression. After diagnosing the oral language abilities of her group, the competent teacher not only recognizes that each child has his own particular needs in the language areas; she also continually strives to see that such needs are actually met insofar as her resources permit. The nature of these needs, she realizes, may be physical or functional, and proceeds accordingly.

When speech defects seem to have a *physical* origin, such as enlarged tonsils, cleft palate, faulty teeth, or hearing loss, the need to solicit the aid of specialists is indicated. Such cases should be cleared through the school principal, nurse, or doctor so as to permit diagnosis and proper treatment. Many communities have speech centers or clinics where these children may be helped. It is wise for teachers to keep informed about the work being done with such children so that class experiences may follow up and supplement special therapy whenever possible.

Functional speech defects resulting from factors in the home environment, those which are emotionally derived or those due to arrested mental development, are more nearly in the province of the school than are severe physical problems. Even so, many functional disorders are beyond the school's power to remedy.

1. Common speech errors, such as substitution and omission of letters due to prolonged infantile patterns, carelessness, or inaccurate auditory perception, are being alleviated to some extent through many of the group experiences and activities discussed in the preceding section. Games and jingles designed for particular speech difficulties are among the devices that may be used. The following is an example from Barrows and Hall, pages 23-24.[1]

A Humming Top

A humming top am I,
　My voice is sweet and low,
M-m-m-m-m-m-m-m-m-m
　M-m-m-m-m-m-m-m-m-m-m

I spin around and hum
　My song so sweet and low,
M-m-m-m-m-m-m-m-m-m
　M-m-m-m-m-m-m-m-m-m-m

This poem is designed to develop nasal resonance.

Speech games may be played individually, in small groups, or with the entire group during short transitional periods. Since all children enjoy games of this nature, the child who needs the particular help may gain more through the group process than if he were singled out conspicuously—and with less embarrassment. Many teachers, moreover, are able to provide individual help with oral language subtly and artistically through carefully planned approaches which on the surface seem incidental or casual.

2. The child with a meager vocabulary and limited home background of experience should be stimulated and challenged in every way possible in a rich school environment. Concrete experiences and vicarious experiences through visual aids are an important means of expanding learning for him. He also should be given special attention to ensure that he clearly grasps ideas and materials presented in group discussions, and to check his comprehension of directions given verbally.

3. The shy child needs the encouragement and sympathetic aid which will help him develop confidence in oral language situations. The teacher

---

[1]Sarah T. Barrows and Katharine H. Hall, *Games and Jingles for Speech Development* (Boston: Expression Co., 1936).

may help him by discovering his interests, conversing with him about them, providing encouragement and aid in group situations, and helping him to feel that his contributions are important—as they often are once he has been drawn out of his shell.

4. Speech difficulties such as hesitancy and stuttering may stem from emotional causes. Individual guidance in these cases is directed toward recognizing and treating the problems of adjustment at their roots.

Guiding Group Growth in Oral Expression. Two major factors instrumental in developing the oral language powers of young children are *opportunity* and *example*. The importance of providing the opportunity for oral expression and encouraging children in this art has been emphasized in the preceding sections. It has been suggested also that the enthusiasm and interest of the teacher are important determinants of pupils' language power. As the pace-setter in the group she should strive to lend to learning that dynamic quality which stimulates the oral expression of children.

The influence of the teacher's speech patterns upon the group must not be minimized. Her enunciation, pronunciation, choice of words, inflection, and voice quality serve as an important model for the five-, six- or seven-year-old in her class for many of their waking hours, and they often adopt or mimic her speech and her expressions. Some teachers have found it helpful to tape-record various aspects of the daily program as a means of checking the quality as well as the quantity of their speech.

It is the function of the teacher to help children become *conscious of* but not *self-conscious about* their speech. Some procedures appropriate for developing increased awareness of various sounds are:

1. Imitating sounds: the "swoo*sh*" of the wind, "*ch*ug, *ch*ug" of an engine, "ti*ck*-ti*ck*" of the clock, or the "swi*sh*-swi*sh*" of rain wipers on the windshield.

2. The use of nursery rhymes, nonsense jingles, and poems. These are useful for developing keener auditory perception.

3. Using "ear pleasing" repetitions. These are numerous in the good literature available for children. For example:

The Seashore Noisy Book by Margaret W. Brown[2]
And he could hear:
Lapping, slapping,
Lap, lap, lap.

Encouraging children to "chime in" not only creates fun, it also affords a *natural* manner of "practicing" sounds.

4. Game devices may be employed. (Also see Chapter 15.)

Group growth in oral language may also be accelerated by the teacher who keeps the following general suggestions in mind:

1. Keep your vocabulary within the limits of children's comprehension. Guard against *talking down* to children and stretch their powers toward a continuously growing vocabulary.

2. Be constantly on the alert to clarify and to extend the meanings of words children already are using.

3. Foster increasingly effective techniques in group communication by helping children to:

    a) Have something to say and the desire to say it.

    b) Become more aware of *what* they say and *how* they say it. (Suggestions such as "Think about it for a minute" and "You have something interesting to tell—they all want to hear it" are helpful.)

    c) Become more discriminating in their judgment as to *when* to talk and *when* and *how* to listen.

---

[2]From *The Seashore Noisy Book* by Margaret Wise Brown, copyright 1941. By permission of Harper & Brothers.

To sum up, the teacher of kindergarten-primary groups has the responsibility for the continuous guidance of children toward mature speech skills: audibility, proper pronunciation and enunciation, correct speech patterns, pleasant voice quality, poise, and good posture. She understands that her own example is important. Finally, she recognizes that her encouragement of and creation of many language opportunities is of great importance in developing oral communication skills.

Children need experiences that give them something to talk about, a classroom atmosphere that encourages self-expression, and recognition for the progress they make. These are more important than repeated correction and drill in these early years. Free, accurate, and natural communications are both the *means* to progress and the *end goal* in oral language learning during the kindergarten-primary years.

CHAPTER 12

Ways of Helping Children Learn
to Listen and to Observe

Some Typical Listening-Observing Situations and How We Can
Put Them to Good Use

When Visitors or Consultants Come
Audience Situations and Their Use in Improving Listening
and Observing
Science Interests and Experiments as Examples of Resources
for Listening and Observing
Social Studies, Excursions, Discussions, and Exhibits

Using Teaching Aids to Improve Listening and Observing

Using Bulletin Boards, Flannel Boards, Charts, Pictures, Books,
and Exhibits Effectively to Command Interest and Attention
Using Slides, Film Strips, Motion Pictures, Tape Recorders,
Records, Radio, and TV to Foster Listening-Observing Skills

Listening and Observing Games for Use in the Classroom

Recognizing Individual Needs and Giving Help in Listening
and Observing

Identifying Pupils Who Need Help
Analyzing the Causes of Listening-Observing Problems

Guiding the Progress of Kindergarten-Primary Children in
Listening and Observing

Ways of Helping Children Learn
to Listen and to Observe

No one can tell the teacher exactly how to help children "stop, look, and listen." The steady stream of classroom experiences does, however, create many situations which the alert and sensitive teacher can use to help boys and girls see and hear in ways that are both meaningful and educational.

This chapter identifies some of the listening-observing situations that occur in most classrooms and points out how they can be used constructively in the process of guiding both individual and group growth toward higher levels of listening skill. Like the proposals made in Chapter 11, these suggestions are not offered as patterns to be followed. They are, however, examples of what *might* be developed with children as circumstances and the teacher's judgment dictate. No proposals for improving the teaching-learning process can replace *your* creative professional judgment. But these ideas should stimulate and extend your thinking just as ours has been extended by the good teachers from whom our illustrations have been borrowed.

SOME TYPICAL LISTENING-OBSERVING SITUATIONS
AND HOW WE CAN PUT THEM TO GOOD USE

Although listening is interwoven with all of the oral language experiences discussed earlier, many specific activities may be identified through which listening and observing skills in particular may be successfully encouraged. Among the school experiences which lend themselves to listening-observing are visits from consultants, opportunities to attend school programs, and social studies and elementary science discussions. Each of these areas of learning will be reviewed in turn to illustrate how they can be linked to the language needs and interests of children and to show how they can help to motivate purposeful listening and thoughtful observation.

When Visitors or Consultants Come. The school nurse, librarian, dietician, custodian, and similar school personnel may be invited to visit the group to explain their function or to answer questions which have arisen pertaining to their particular fields of work.

Musicians, firemen, policemen, scientists, geographers, pilots, and other workers in comparable fields are frequently among the kinds of persons invited by teachers to provide information and demonstration which will extend and clarify concepts relating to class interests. Parents often have talents or are engaged in occupations which make them suitable resources for kindergarten-primary discussions. Here are some actual examples of consultants who visited at these grade levels and helped to create good listening-observing situations:

David's father, a policeman, was asked to tell the first grade how policemen help in the community. On the appointed day he arrived in full uniform to talk about his work and brought his handcuffs, gloves, nightstick, and gun.

An artist who illustrated children's books visited each grade level and drew pictures to visualize a story which the children created spontaneously during his visit.

Edwin's father, a dentist, was invited to the kindergarten group shortly before the school dental inspection. He demonstrated proper brushing techniques and told how a dentist examines and cleans teeth.

Mrs. Grant, the school nurse, spoke to the second grade about foods in relation to their health study and brought charts and pictures to illustrate her points.

Mr. Jimpson, the trumpet player in a symphony orchestra,

was a guest of the second grade group when they were learning about the instruments in the orchestra. He played a composition, explained how tones were produced, demonstrated how to take proper care of the instrument, and played a few familiar tunes for group singing as a finale to his visit.

Brian's mother, a professional cake decorator, decorated his birthday cake for a kindergarten birthday luncheon, held in the classroom, as the children looked on in fascination. After she finished, each child had an opportunity to decorate a cupcake to take home.

Not all consultants need come to the school. Sometimes the children can visit the consultant. For example, Marcia and her mother invited her classmates to their home during Christmas festivities to hear Mrs. Reilly play the organ. She was beautifully gowned and five-year-old Anne said, "Mrs. Reilly looks like a lovely princess." She played several request pieces and then some familiar carols for group singing. Cookies and milk were served to the young guests as a climax to the afternoon visit.

Though these situations have strong inherent attraction for children, the teacher must be aware that listening capacity varies with individual children and make sure that their experiences with consultants and invited visitors are educative rather than merely entertaining. In other words, careful planning is necessary to ensure maximum effectiveness. The following suggestions may be helpful in this planning:

1. Introduce and explain to resource people the specific background and interests of the group and the approximate limits of their attention span. Encourage the consultant's use of visual aids whenever possible. Young children need visual reinforcement to aid them in gaining meaning from what they hear.

2. Suggest to the speaker or consultant that he allow time at the completion of the discussion for closer observation and handling of any materials he may bring with him—unless they are fragile or dangerous to touch. Remind him, however, that passing pictures and articles among the group during the talk can be distracting and that it interrupts listening. Ask if it is possible to keep the visual materials for a day or two so that children may have an opportunity to observe them at their leisure and to discuss them.

3. Be well enough informed about the contribution of the resource person so that you may guide and contribute to the listening and observing which accompanies his visit.

4. Adequate preparation of children is essential to develop the proper attitudes and readiness. "Who is coming to talk to us today?" "Where shall we sit?" "What will he need?" "What do you think he might bring?" "Who remembers some of our questions?" (In first and second

grade it is often helpful to have the questions written on a chart or chalk board so that the visitor and the group may be guided by them during the discussion.)

5. Plan the physical setup so that comfort, hearing, and vision for all children are facilitated.

6. Audience participation is desirable with kindergarten-primary children. If the speaker can develop a "talking with" rather than "talking to" situation by subtle questions —"Do you know what this is?" "What do you think will happen?"—the listening climate is enhanced. Singing with a musician and experimenting with a worker's tools are excellent techniques to increase attention span and maintain interest. Dr. Shaw, a pediatrician, demonstrated the use of his stethoscope, for instance, and then invited eight-year-old volunteers to test the instrument on one another.

7. Help children to develop good judgment with respect to participation by encouraging them to (a) "think along" with the speaker, (b) keep to the point of the discussion, and (c) use good judgment in their questioning. "Let's listen to what he says. He may be planning to tell us what you want to ask." Extreme or rigid listening rules stifle spontaneity and dull interest with a consequent negative effect on listening. Guidance should always be in the direction of more mature listening skills.

Audience Situations and Their Use in Improving Listening-Observing Skills. Simple sharing programs, as when the first grade invites the second grade to see a story creatively dramatized, offer opportunities for young children to participate in small, informal audience situations. Experience with simple programs also serves as an introduction to the more formal audience situations which children will meet in all-school assemblies. The preparation and planning which precede the exchange of programs between classroom groups are also important in developing a good listening climate.

A "preview discussion" by the children and the teacher as to what a forthcoming intra-classroom program will involve is useful to the young listener-observer for many reasons. It gives the teacher the opportunity to help children become more intelligent listeners and observers as well as serving to prepare them for the social amenities necessary for good audience participation.

The planning session can often be designed so as to bring out the purpose of an invitation to attend a program in an adjacent room. The children may review their background of experience in relation to the program planned and perhaps choose questions to ask if this is appropriate. Some previous knowledge of a forthcoming program sharpens a young child's expectancy and increases his ability to understand and to appreciate what he will see and hear. If the invitation is for a play, such as *The Boy and the North Wind*, a review of the simple plot and the sequence of action to be anticipated is desirable.

An example of such a planning session with five-year-olds preceded a visit to their neighboring kindergarten room.

One crisp autumn morning Jim's kindergarten group had two young visitors from another kindergarten room. They invited Jim's group to come to their room at juice time to share a treat of apple butter and crackers. The offer was accepted with pleasure and the prospective five-year-old hosts left.

"What's apple butter?" asked Jim, who had been one of the children most eager to accept the invitation.

"It's apples squashed 'til they're butter," said June.

"Oh no, not real butter," piped up Jim, " 'cause butter's made from cream and cream comes from cows. Apples come from trees. Anyway, butter's yellow and apples are red."

"Maybe they used yellow apples. Not all apples are red," stated Helen. "And cream's white. How come butter's yellow?"

"Jam, jam, jam, jam — it's jam," chanted Cheryl.

"We have many ideas about apple butter," said their teacher. "Cheryl seems to have a definite feeling that it is jam. Why do you think so Cheryl?"

"Because my grandmother makes it, and I helped her. She let me wash the apples."

With these comments to start them thinking, an ensuing discussion helped the children to focus their thoughts on the true identity of the product.

They still had many questions unanswered, however, and they decided to see if their junior hosts and hostesses would answer them in their presentation.

One question grew out of Cheryl's comment that the apple butter "smelled nice cooking."

"Hey, I'm a detective," said Blake. "I smelled a good smell yesterday when I worked in the block-corner of our room. Bet they made it. I'm a real detective!"

The group decided to check his sleuthing ability and agreed to be ready

to ask, "Where did you get the apple butter?" if the other
kindergarten group didn't tell them.
"Did you make it?"
"Was it easy?"
"What did you use to make it?"
"How did you do it?"
The following visits between classrooms are described
without reviewing the preliminary oral planning. They
were, of course, preceded by discussion planned so as to
make the children ready for careful listening and observing.

The first grade enjoyed the kindergarten circus. They
listened to the ringmaster as he introduced the acts: the
acrobats, who did intricate tricks with hoops; the tight-
rope walker, carefully maneuvering the rope (a board with
cleats supported by blocks); the animal trainer (the fero-
cious animals really were children, of course); the antics
of the clowns; the elephant act; and the circus music.

The second grade invited the first grade class to their
program to share "What we learned about volcanoes." One
group read the booklets, which were a compilation of their
learnings, and showed the accompanying illustrations. Another group explained the colorful mural of a volcano in
eruption which they had painted. Another group showed
samples of volcanic rock and explained the differences in
them. The climax was the simulated eruption of a minia-
ture chemical volcano which the fourth grade had made and
which the seven-year-olds had borrowed for their program.

When classes return to their rooms from experiences
such as those described, they should be encouraged to ex-
press their reactions. Skillful questioning may be used to
guide children in reviewing and evaluating the success with
which they interpreted what was seen and heard. Some
typical evaluative questions might include:
"What act did you enjoy the most?"
"Do you think it was difficult to do?"
"Did they plan it well?"
"Could you hear what they said?"
"How many kinds of rock did they show?"
"Do you remember the names of some of the rocks?"
In their thank-you notes (dictated or individual depend-

ing upon grade and individual abilities), children can be encouraged to be specific about what was seen: "I liked the part about . . . ." "I thought the elephants were good," and so on. These techniques foster discrimination in children's seeing and hearing and also enable the teacher to estimate individual abilities and to decide how to increase further the observing-listening phases of children's language growth.

Occasionally in the kindergarten, and increasingly in the first and second grades, children attend school assemblies. These often include plays, puppet shows, programs for holidays, programs for book week or fire prevention week, and educational films. When the presentations are within the experience and understanding of young children and the programs are of short duration, they provide another means of sharpening observation and developing listening abilities.

Kindergarten-primary children especially enjoy short dramatic presentations of stories with simple plots such as *The Story of Drakestail* or *The Golden Goose* (see Chapter 15). Holiday programs which usually involve singing, dancing, pantomimes, or short plays are also suitable for this age.

Science Interests and Experiments as Examples of Resources for Listening and Observing. Children's insatiable curiosity is nowhere more in evidence than in learnings related to science activities. Many a teacher encounters queries such as these:

"Why does the mercury rise?"

"Why does the balloon float up in the air?"

"How does the caterpillar make its cocoon?"

"How do they make a rocket go up?"

The creative teacher keeps this curiosity alive by encouraging and stimulating children's natural interest in the world about them. She pro-

vides opportunities for care of pets, for setting up a science corner with plants, fish, insects, or shells and other collections, and for planning experiments which help children better understand natural phenomena. Few activities, she realizes, are more useful than science-centered ones in developing the intellectural powers of children through observation.

The field of elementary science serves especially well in helping the teacher meet individual differences. Such topics as weather, sound, heat, plants, insects, or planets may be discussed in simple terms with the fives, sixes, or sevens. The level of difficulty and complexity of the science concepts presented can be varied with the needs and abilities of the group, and tailored to fit the background of experiences which they bring from the home.

The following are a few examples of experiments which have been used with young children in pointing up concepts about weather.

1. While some five-year-olds in Hawaii were resting on their sleeping mats after a strenuous play period, Nelson saw the wind moving the tree branches and he asked for "that poem about trees bowing their heads."

> Who has seen the wind?
> Neither you nor I:
> But when the trees bow down their heads
> The wind is passing by.
>
> CHRISTINA ROSSETTI

This same poem and its artfully expressed concept of air movement were recalled on several other occasions by this group—for example, when a hurricane buffeted the islands and lifted the roof from the school gym, and when there was no wind and the Boys' Day kites would not fly.

Awareness of the change in temperature afforded by air movement was also observed through a simple hand waving experiment and a "walking quietly" and then "running quickly" experiment to illustrate air resistance.

2. The first grade children wondered what happened to the water in the aquarium during the holidays. Some of it had disappeared. One lad even suggested, "Maybe the fish drank it!"

To find a tested answer, the teacher encouraged the group to put some water in an open glass jar and mark the level. They observed the level each day, noticing that it slowly lowered. They discussed this *evaporation*. The group continued with their experiments. At the suggestion of the teacher, they filled two pans with water placing one in the sun and one in the shade and eventually observed that "heat makes water evaporate faster." They also moistened two equal areas of a blackboard and fanned one, thus discovering that water evaporates faster when air moves past it.

3. What happens to the water that evaporates? A second grade group of children watched the steam rise from the teakettle spout. They learned that

water which evaporates is called *water vapor*. Their attention next was directed to the two or three inches between the
spout and the visible cloud of steam. (When water cools it
forms steam. A cloud is made up of tiny drops of water.)
A cold pan was held in the cloud of steam. (Drops of water
formed.)

There are many simple experiments of this type which
teachers may use to demonstrate science concepts. (See
Chapter 15.) Such experiments are powerful motivating
factors in developing listening and observing skills.

**Social Studies Excursions, Discussions, and Ex-
hibits.** The curriculum or program designed for kindergarten-primary children in most schools suggests a good
many firsthand experiences. These often take the form of
field trips or excursions. When careful preparation and
planning precede the excursions so that children are
helped to anticipate their seeing and hearing, they become
highly motivated and will *want* to observe and listen to
explanations.

The occasions and purposes of these excursions are innumerable, depending upon the needs and interests of the
group. Trips to the zoo, fire station, aquarium, airport,
dairy farm, dairy processing companies, post office, harbor
or railroad station, may often be arranged at the kindergarten-primary level. What children *look* for, and how
long such an excursion *lasts*, are dependent upon their
age level and their depth of interest. On a trip to the zoo
or aquarium, for instance, a group may go to observe one
species or perhaps *one* animal or fish in particular. Another group may wish to concentrate on the *varieties* of
fish or animals, their foods or their habits.

When children are taken on an excursion, it is desirable,
whenever possible, to disperse them in small groups—
each, of course, properly supervised by an adult. Opportunities for seeing, touching (when safe and permissible),
hearing, and questioning are more readily provided in
smaller numbers. Herding children in large groups from
one zoo animal to another, or from one phase to another
of a dairy's processing of milk, more often than not defeats
the purpose of the excursion. Children may even return

to school overfatigued and overstimulated having heard or seen little that was of lasting value to their intellectual growth.

Many teachers have found it helpful to invite parents, or school personnel, who plan to accompany the group on a trip to be present at a pre-planning session. This enables them to become familiar with the purposes of the trip. Thus they are better prepared to guide and to contribute to children's observations.

Staff members or guides in government institutions and industries who conduct school tours should be given clues to children's probable questions, their comprehension levels, and their listening limits before a trip is made. It is usually more effective to have kindergarten and early first grade groups spend most of their time *observing*. Some few words of welcome and short explanations or directions when necessary are usually sufficient. If elaborate verbal explanations are required the trip may be a poor choice for five-year-olds.

When there are many operations or processes to be observed, as at a bakery or ice-cream plant, for example, teachers may be wise to plan to make several trips or to divide the responsibilities of observation among small groups. Individual interests and abilities can be recognized most effectively in this manner.

Discussions and exhibits which children may experience after a field trip become more meaningful because of concrete experiences of the sort described above. Also their language power grows in direct proportion to the meaningfulness of what is seen and heard by the class.

USING TEACHING AIDS TO IMPROVE
LISTENING AND OBSERVING

Using Bulletin Boards, Flannel Boards, Charts, Pictures, Books, and Exhibits Effectively to Command Interest and Attention. The kindergarten-primary teacher who understands the learning needs of children employs a wide variety of visual materials when concrete, firsthand experience is impossible or not immediately available. She understands that lengthy verbal descriptions and explanations are often too abstract for most young children to grasp. Visual materials are, for this reason, an important supplement to verbal presentations in helping children relate meaning to words. When used artistically by the competent teacher they become invaluable aids in *gaining* and *retaining* the attention of children, an achievement which leads to more effective listening skills.

Using Slides, Film Strips, Motion Pictures, Tape Recorders, Records, Radio, and TV to Foster Listening-Observing Skills. Especially in the past several years, children have been provided with widening opportunities and incentives for listening and observing through mechanical and electronic devices such as the record player, radio, television, slides, and motion pictures (both sound and silent). Much has been written about the negative aspects of these mass media and the heavy toll in time which they exact. However, as indicated in Chapter 1, there are vast possibilities for broadening children's horizons through the vicarious experiences which such media offer.

So much knowledge, which was formerly available only through reading and speaking, may now be reinforced and made more meaningful by their use! The teacher of kindergarten and primary grades will want to make a point of becoming acquainted with the available visual and auditory material in her school and community, using it with good judgment as it meets the needs and purposes of the group by enriching the educational experiences of the children. Her adroitness in choosing material and in motivating and guiding the listening and observing which result are directly related to children's growth in listening-observing skills.

In primary grades the *record player* affords tremendous possibilities for pleasurable and valuable listening experiences. Music is a part of the daily living of these children and is a wonderful vehicle for fostering their listening skills. Children respond to pleasing melodies in instrumental, song, and musical-story forms, *Peter and the Wolf* being a first-rate example of a story told through the

medium of music. Of course adults should first listen to the music to be sure that it will not be overwhelming to the particular group or individuals for whom it is intended.

Kindergarten children enjoy responding to music in many ways, sometimes clapping and tapping, sometimes moving their bodies in various ways in time with the melody—and changing the volume and speed of their responses with the changes in volume and speed of the music. They quickly learn to discriminate rhythmic patterns at this age—to recognize a walk, march, run, skip, gallop, or slide—and to change their movements to match the cues which the music gives them.

Five-year-olds are also strongly motivated to imitate the actions suggested by the words of many songs and by the "sound pictures" created by the music. Children *become* the steam shovel, the train, the fire engine, or the tug boat as they duplicate movements and sounds in a most realistic way. A large repertory of these "action songs" is available for use with children. (See Chapter 15.)

Youngsters in the first and second grades become increasingly able to follow more complex patterns in music. Singing games such as "Bingo" and "Hokey Pokey" and simple dances like "Chimes of Dunkirk" and "Kinder Polka" require careful listening to both the verbal directions and music clues.

Well-balanced record libraries should contain singing, story, and instrumental records as well as selections with a strong rhythmic beat which may be used in expressive dance and dramatic activities. Children may also be encouraged to bring records from home to share with the group.

Burl Ives's recording of "I Know An Old Woman Who Swallowed A Fly" is an example of an amusing singing record which has strong appeal for primary children. Its nonsense and the lovely choice of words—"it wriggled and jiggled and tickled inside her"—promote both sheer enjoyment and strong sensory impressions. The repetition is excellent for children of this age and they are quick to join in repeating the phrases which tickle their own insides.

"The Caissons Go Rolling Along" and other rousing songs of this type are especially loved by the more active and extroverted element in the groups. Children are inspired to sing lustily and march with vigor by pulse-stirring tunes.

Though radio and TV programs are most often heard and seen in the home, some programs are broadcast expressly for school listening and observing. As these programs are made available to more and more schools, they offer possibilities for guiding children's listening and observing through the preparation which precedes the actual programs and subsequent discussions.

"Today you will hear the story of Rumpelstiltskin," the teacher may say to make children ready for a scheduled program. "How many of you have heard this story? Only four of you, I see. Well, let me tell you just a little about it."

Following the program the class and teacher may "talk it over" by retelling parts of the story or play. This affords the teacher the opportunity to verify her ideas with respect to both individual listening skills and pupils' abilities to sense a sequence. Some of these programs may stand on their own as a "complete experience." Others require interpretation. Spontaneous comments give the teacher an index to the understanding and interest which exist. When a program seems to be well understood and appreciated, do not dissect it. Didactic over-discussion may mar a truly esthetic and pleasant experience.

It is important for the teacher to keep herself informed as to the content and nature of the TV programs which most children see. Occasional sharing and discussions of favorites may help to improve children's tastes and stimulate them to view some of the more suitable TV fare for their age group.

Simple homespun stories such as those built around the adventures of a boy and his dog, for example, may well be stressed in lieu of the more overstimulating, adult type of western, problem play, or murder drama. There are also public service presentations which some of the mature first and second grade children may enjoy. The possibilities for valuable educational experiences in this electronic medium are vast. Since young children often average from twenty to twenty-five hours per week in televiewing, let us try to help children develop powers of critical listening and observing which lead to socially desirable interests and tastes.

The tape recorder as a listening device for school use has many potentialities. In the kindergarten, a recording may be made of a group as they engage in block play, work with clay, or participate in any of the various work groups. Conversation will be freer if children are unaware that their voices are being taped. During the play-back children may comment, "That's Paul," or "Mary is talking now."

Familiar sounds which may be heard about the school may also be recorded: the whir of the power mower, the library book cart rolling along the corridor, the tap-tap of a typewriter, a telephone ringing, an airplane flying overhead, the snip of the yard man's pruning shears, a

pile of blocks toppling to the floor. Children enjoy trying to identify these sounds—and their listening ability is likely to improve accordingly.

In the first and second grades, group singing lends itself very nicely to recording. The class may record some of their favorite songs and enjoy hearing the sound of their own voices on the play-back. The tape recorder may also be used as a teaching device in developing reading skills.

Slides, 16 mm. films, and film strips on numerous topics are available to reinforce children's learning through visualization. Some examples of the use of these aids in building the power to listen and observe are found in the following anecdotes.

Ann, a second grade child, was to go to Japan where her father, a Navy man, was stationed. The children naturally were curious about Ann's future experiences—what she would see and do, what her school would look like. Miss Lovatt, the teacher, told the group that her friend, Mrs. Bartels, had some slides of Japan which she had taken on her travels there during the previous summer. The group invited the lady to show her slides and everyone was keenly interested and observant since this was helping them to understand what Ann would experience.

Since the local zoo was new and had no elephant, many of the kindergarten children were unable to develop a clear conception of the size and habits of one of the animals. They wanted to learn more about the huge creatures. Mrs. Jackson, their teacher, was able to supplement their background by showing a film strip on elephants.[1] It gave the two children who had seen elephants in a circus a clearer conception of the pachyderm, who by storybook reputation had a " 'satiable curiosity," and made him a reality through visualization to the others.

As a part of her reading readiness work with a group of first graders, Miss Powers worked on story sequence. She found that films were a helpful source of promoting awareness of story sequence. Later the children composed a simple story and drew pictures to illustrate the order of events. Miss Powers borrowed the opaque projector from the school's audio-visual room and showed the story to the whole class as the six-year-old authors recited the text to their classmates.

[1]*Animal Friend Series*, Encyclopedia Britannica Films (See Ch. 15).

Reinforcing educational concepts presented verbally with visual and auditory materials is part of the instructional task of the kindergarten-primary teacher. She will undoubtedly wish to keep abreast of developments in new equipment and media which promise to enhance the listening and observing skills of youngsters.

LISTENING AND OBSERVING GAMES FOR USE IN THE CLASSROOM

Frequently during the school day a change of pace or a time for relaxation is highly important. Many teachers grasp this opportunity to "kill two birds with one activity" by using recreational and relaxing games through which listening and/or observing skills may also be taught. Games and play elements motivate strong interest and attention and are excellent approaches to learning in a variety of situations. The following list suggests some of the numerous possibilities in the use of games which may foster listening-observing skills. Most of these may be used with five-, six-, or seven-year-old children depending upon the teacher's ability to adapt them to her particular group.

1. *Jack in the Box.* Children curl up in a ball as if in a box. The children and/or teacher sing or say "Jack is quiet down in his box until someone opens the lid . . . POP." Children jump up on the "Pop." Variation in the pauses before the *pop* necessitates careful listening and is more fun, of course! (This is an example of many such "action songs." See bibliography.)

2. *Horses and ponies* (you may wish to substitute other animals). Children choose to be a horse or a pony. When the music is played in the higher octaves the ponies prance. When the low octaves are used the horses trot. Occasionally the teacher "plays a joke on us" and uses both high and low octaves and all trot or prance. This develops sensitivity to high and low sounds and heavy and light tones.

3. *Which is gone?* Display three, four, five, or more articles, depending upon the grade level. Ask children to observe carefully and then close their eyes. Cover or remove one of the articles. Which is gone? A variation of

this is to change the order of arrangement. "Who can put them back the way they were?"

4. *Playing statue to music.* Children run, skip, or twirl depending upon the rhythmic pattern used. When the music stops, everyone "freezes." In older groups this may be played as an elimination game—those who are in motion after the music stops are "out."

5. *Musical chairs.* Arrange chairs in one, two, three, or more rows depending upon the number of children playing. Twelve to fifteen in a group is a good number for first and second grades. Seats and backs are faced alternately along the row. The number of chairs is always *one less* than the number of children. The children march around the chairs until the music stops and then scramble for a chair. The child left standing is "out" until the next game. He removes one chair and the game continues until one of the last two is seated. Most children have a hilariously happy time playing the game and listen intently during the marching. On occasion, a more immature child may find it difficult to accept being "left out." Giving him the responsibility of "chair remover" and the assurance of having another opportunity to play usually reconciles him to the situation. Variations of musical chairs may be played with large cutouts taped to the floor at various points in a circle. Children march around the circle and *must* step on each cutout as they come to it. (Pumpkins are fun to use at Hallowe'en.) When the music stops those whose feet— one or both—are on a "pumpkin" or "turtle" are eliminated.

6. *The drum guessing game.* The teacher beats out syllables on a drum. Children listen for the number of syllables of their name. Boom, boom— *Ma ry, Ca thy, Bil ly.* Boom, boom, boom—*Cath er ine, Mar gar et.* Boom —*Bob, Ann.* As listening skill develops, first and last names may be used. *Har ri et Ben nett.* As children gain skill, they enjoy taking turns beating the names on the drum.

Names of songs or first lines of familiar songs may be sounded out on the drum or clapped. *Ma ry had a lit tle lamb.* The auditory training in this type of game is excellent and children become very adept in associating rhythm pattern with the name of the song.

7. *Completing rhymes and jingles.*

Jack and Jill went up the _____.

Little Jack Horner sat in a _____.

As children's ability to distinguish rhyming words increases, the teacher may make up rhymes asking the children to complete them. The little boy sat holding his _____.

Children are encouraged to make up rhymes for classmates to complete.

8. *Which one doesn't belong: sit, mit, kit, fat, or hit?* Recognition may be shown in various ways. Stand, sit, or clap when you hear the one that is different. Numerous adaptations of this type are usable in later first and second grades. Classifications, initial consonants, and final consonants may be used depending upon children's abilities. All of these are designed to develop auditory perception and are important in beginning reading skills.

9. *Discriminating colors or sounds.* This may be played just for fun with a group or used as a device for gradual group dismissal. The teacher may say, "All those who are wearing red may go." "All those whose names begin like Bill's may go." Many varieties of this type may be employed. Using colors is suitable for kindergarten and early first grade. Children are able to discriminate beginning consonants sometime during first grade or early second grade. As children gain skill in auditory perception, first letters in last names may be used, also.

10. The *"Color Game"* is very popular with fives, sixes, and sevens and demands both recall and listening. All class members save one are seated in a circle. This one child stands in the center. He is "It." The children who are seated previously have been given the name of a color either by the teacher or (with the more mature groups) by a child. The color is a secret so is whispered in each individual child's ear. The number of colors given is also controlled by the group's ability to handle few or many—four colors are enough for very young children. The child who is "It" calls any color name that comes to his mind. If it is one of the "secret" colors, the children who have been given this color get to their feet, step to the outside of the circle and begin skipping around it in a given direction. "It" also goes to the outside of the circle and begins skipping. He must tag the individual he is chasing in order to eliminate him. As he eliminates one, he proceeds to chase another, until all but one have been caught. This last one may be "It" for the next game.

The eliminated skippers drop out of the game as they are tagged, moving quickly to the side of the room and settling down so they do not impede the progress of the other players. As a new game resumes, they rejoin the circle. This game can become a bit noisy and teachers often prefer to play it in a multi-purpose room or in the gym.

11. *Irrelevant Sentences Game.* The teacher tells a simple story. It is, of course, more fun and more meaningful if it deals with someone in the group. She puts in one irrelevant sentence. The children pick out the sentence that is unrelated to the story. For example:

Sandy brought his kitten this morning.

His name is Rocket because he shoots around so fast.
There is a red car in the garage. (Irrelevant)
Rocket likes to eat, play, and sleep.
Isn't it fun to have him at school?

As a rule this game works best with children above the kindergarten level or late in the kindergarten year.

12. *The Dog-and-Bone Game.* This old favorite is another circle game requiring careful listening. The children sit in a circle. One chair is placed in the center with a ball, toy bone, or some object representing a bone under the chair. One child plays the role of the dog and sits on this center chair with his eyes closed. The teacher points to one child in a circle who tiptoes up with the objective of getting the "bone" from under the chair and creeping back to his place without being detected. If the dog hears the burglar he says, "Bow-wow, who has my bone?" The burglar must answer, "I have." Dog tries to identify the burglar. If he can, he takes the burglar's circle spot and the burglar becomes the dog. For younger children it is more feasible to have the dog sit up in front of the room with his back turned because children this age frequently find it difficult to keep their eyes closed for any length of time.

13. A game similar to Dog-and-Bone is called *Little Tommy Tittlemouse* and also calls for listening and observing skills.

"Tommy" (one child) sits on a chair at the front of the room. His back is turned to the audience. Another child goes quietly behind the chair. The other children recite:

> Little Tommy Tittlemouse
> Lives in a little house.
> Someone's knocking—me, oh my!
> Someone's calling, "It is I."

When the clue about the knocking is recited, the visitor knocks and after the group's words, "Someone's calling," says, "It is I." "Tommy" has three chances to guess who has spoken, and if he cannot guess, someone describes the visitor. When the visitor is identified, Tommy joins the group and the visitor takes Tommy's role.

RECOGNIZING INDIVIDUAL NEEDS AND GIVING HELP IN LISTENING AND OBSERVING

There are some children in every group who invariably have more difficulty in listening than others and whose powers of observation and concentration are often equally limited. Although what may be expected with regard to listening ability at each grade level, as well as *within* a group, depends upon the particular activity and the individuals who make up the group, certain developmental trends may be identified.

The attention of kindergarten children normally is quite brief and is often spasmodic in situations which are highly verbal, such as sharing, planning, and discussion times. Ten minutes is a long period for discussion for the young fives. First grade children typically can concentrate for somewhat longer periods when well motivated—sometimes fifteen to twenty minutes. By the time children are in second grade their ability to "think along" with the discussions has grown considerably, and most seven-year-olds may be expected to attend for even longer periods.

No rigid time limits may be set on the attention span in any group, however, since attention and listening vary appreciably with the type of situation and the degree of interest and of motivation which are present. It is wise, nonetheless, to plan to keep listening periods brief for all kindergarten-primary groups. It is more effective for the development of children's skills in listening and observing to plan several periods during the day, depending on need, for "talking together" rather than one extended time which strains children's ability to listen and sometimes actually fosters the habit of inattention.

A few children in each classroom group seem to have specific listening difficulties beyond the limits of expectations for their developmental level. How most of these boys and girls may usually be identified is suggested below.

Identifying Pupils Who Need Help. In group situations the restless bodily movements, diversion of attention to a toy or some other personal possession, literally wandering off (as some kindergarten children are wont to do), chatting with those sitting nearby, and similar signs of inattention are readily detected by the teacher. It is more difficult to detect the inattentive child who remains fairly immobile, often with the outward appearance of listening, but whose thoughts may be roaming the universe.

Some children whose facility with language suggests that they should possess adequate or more-than-adequate ability to concentrate occasionally have difficulty in following even the more simple, routine procedures in the kindergarten or in following specific directions in academic work and other assigned activities at first and second grade levels. Others are observed who remain listless and apathetic throughout the daily program, rarely contributing or evidencing enthusiasm. Recognition of lapses in the ability to listen and to observe is fairly easy. The big problem is how to help such youngsters.

Analyzing the Causes of Listening-Observing Problems. After recognizing differences in listening-observing skills, the teacher's task is to determine the possible causes of deviations from expected performance.

Any *physical impairment* of hearing obviously creates listening problems for a child. Such a young child often finds it difficult enough to sit relatively still and listen even when he is highly motivated. The child who cannot hear clearly and thus cannot understand what is happening becomes bored, restless, retires into his own thoughts, or compensates in some other manner. To illustrate:

Bob, a very active first grade youngster, seemed alert and able in many situations, both indoors and outdoors, and in all of the art activities. In group discussions, however, Bob's attention was very limited. He giggled, played, tried to distract others, and was most unco-operative. He also seemed overly sensitive and worried about tasks related to beginning academic learnings and displayed difficulty in understanding and following directions.

The teacher suspected that Bob might have a hearing impairment. Under such circumstances, checking health cards and records with the school nurse is the first step in discovering if any hearing loss can be verified. Asking the child to listen to a watch-tick, addressing him softly when his back is turned, and other simple tests may help the teacher to decide whether it is likely that a hearing defect exists. She also must bear in mind that sometimes there is a temporary hearing loss due to congestion following colds and sinus conditions. Any suspected physical handicaps should be reported immediately through proper channels. Also, in all discussion situations children with hearing difficulties should be placed in an advantageous position near the speaker. The use of visual materials is important in working with such children and individual attention should be given to ensure their understanding.

Lack of *readiness* is another factor which frequently interferes with listening and observing. In discussion activities which involve the entire group there are often a few boys and girls whose backgrounds of understanding are limited or whose interests are less mature than those of others in their age group. Again it seems helpful to offer an illustration:

Mary, Cathy, Sally, and Ellen were usually capable and co-operative group members in the first grade during the work periods and they followed directions quite successfully. During the discussion periods, however, they were prone to giggle, to visit, or to explore the contents of a handbag. The teacher suspected that these girls lacked the readiness required for attentive listening, that the social and natural science concepts which had so much appeal for most of the members of the group were beyond their "little girl" interests. She felt that working on a project at their own level of interest might help to command their attention and listening and accordingly asked them to assume responsibility for some needed renovations in the doll corner as a step toward the goal of more appropriate six-year-old participation.

Home background problems may explain the difficulties of children who display strong interest in the science table, film strips, puzzles, and other visual materials but who are restless and inattentive during oral planning and discussion periods. These children may come from bi-lingual homes or from an environment where the use of language in the home is limited and incorrect. Emphasizing visual material with these children, keeping directions simple, and checking carefully on their understanding of word meanings generally helps such culturally deprived youngsters to develop greater facility with language and in turn enhance their listening power.

Emotional problems are the basis of some listening difficulties. The child who is involved with problems of personal adjustment often has difficulty in concentrating on or participating in group interests. The following descriptive statements may help to cast some light on the nature and effect of emotional problems.

Jack, a kindergarten boy, was a worried, frustrated youngster who was too preoccupied with his own problems to listen to anyone for any length of time. He was always desirous of being in the choicest spot for any group meeting or viewing, and anyone who touched or nudged him in the group or circle was likely to receive an unfriendly punch. It was, however, difficult for him to sit in a relaxed manner. He jostled others and changed places frequently. He constantly questioned, commented, and interrupted the proceedings since he was too involved with himself and too impatient to attend to the discussion long enough to form logical associations and to follow the gist of the matter under discussion. The teacher suspected that Jack's basic emotional problems (the rejection by his father and his mother's overprotection to compensate) were affecting his behavior and that growth in observation and listening skills would be dependent upon the alleviation of some of his anxieties and tensions.

Joseph's vocabulary was extensive, and his hearing was unimpaired, but he dreamed and his mind wandered continually, and as a result he listened intermittently. Why? What could the teacher do? Joseph had entered first grade the year before and, after having an unsuccessful time of it for a half year, dropped back into the kindergarten group. Now, in his second start in first grade, he was quite happy with the situation, since no one was pressuring him into all sorts of things which he thought he couldn't do. He preferred to maintain this status quo and not become enmeshed in any of those things which he had already decided were going to be too difficult. *So he didn't listen.* However, in spite of himself, he sometimes became intensely interested in discussions about boats, planets, or some other ongoing interest and offered contributions from his good background of knowledge. He had made some boats at the workbench and some drawings and paintings about planets. He listened more and more frequently and became increasingly productive.

Pat, the new boy in the second grade, had fine capabilities, but he was so busy working through his problems of adjusting to the group that he had little time or inclination to listen. He was noisy, boisterous and wished constantly to call attention to himself. The teacher was busy, too, trying to help him gain prestige and friendship. She realized that when his social problems were eased, he would probably be able to settle down and listen more attentively.

GUIDING THE PROGRESS OF KINDERGARTEN-PRIMARY CHILDREN IN LISTENING AND OBSERVING

Guidance of the child's progress toward listening power is the responsibility of all persons who seek to help children become more mature. The teacher needs to bring herself to an awareness of the situations in the classroom, both planned and incidental, which foster the development of listening skills. It is well for her to ask at frequent intervals, "What is the listening environment of the classroom?"

In evaluating the listening which occurs in the classroom, and as an aid in future planning for experiences which increase children's listening-observing powers, the following proposals should prove helpful.

1. Keep your expectations with respect to listening (both the quantity and frequency) well within children's ability to attend:

  a) Give simple and precise directions.

  b) Present concepts which are within the experience and understanding of the class. Keep them simple, forceful, and uncluttered by irrelevant detail.

  c) Use visual aids to reinforce verbal presentations.

  d) Alternate quiet listening times with active periods of participation.

2. Determine and make use of the types of situations which invite listening. Stories, poems, social studies, or science discussions and activities, and many musical experiences usually fall in this category.

3. Remember that children are motivated to listen and observe:

  a) When backgrounds of experience and preparation by the teacher have created a *readiness* for this listening.

  b) When they feel a *need* to hear or see so that they may more ably cope with an immediate problem.

  c) When the material presented *challenges* their imagination and intelligence without being overwhelming.

4. Arrange physical conditions under which the listening-observing takes place so that they permit concentration:

  a) Ensure comfortable seating.

  b) Remember that all children may not have the physical resources of vision and hearing that are such essential factors in effective listening.

  c) Keep distractions to the unavoidable minimum.

5. Recognize that the teacher must use her voice effectively:

  a) Voice quality should be pleasing.

  b) It is desirable to change inflection, pitch, and tone to fit the needs of the situation, being dramatic, dynamic, or soothing, as the occasion demands.

Good guidance in listening and observing requires of teachers that they exercise self-control in speaking to children. They must be able to tell *enough* but not *too much*, sorting out the essential things to be learned from among the mass of material available. They must understand that children interpret what is seen and heard in the light of what they know and feel.

CHAPTER 13

Reading Activities That Help to
Build Language Usage Power
in Children

Reading Readiness as a Consideration in the Development of Facility in Language

Reading Readiness Activities Which also Help to Develop Maturity in the Use of Language

Phases of the Total Reading Program Which Lead to the Development of Language Power

The Basal Reader Program as a Part of the Total Reading Experience
Reading Experiences as a Means of Developing General Language Powers
The Importance of Spontaneous Reading as Involved in such Helps as Signs, Charts, Notices, Labels, and News Items
Building Motivation for Recreational Reading in the Kindergarten-Primary Program

Individualizing Reading Instruction to Meet Children's Needs More Adequately

Enjoying Books with Children

When and Where Do You Use Prose?
How Do You Use Prose?
What Prose Do You Use?

Enjoying Poetry with Children

When and Where Do You Use Poetry?
How Do You Use Poetry?
What Poetry Do You Use?

Choosing Books with and for Children

Evaluating the Young Child's Language Growth as Reflected in Reading and Literature

Evaluation as Especially Important in the Early Grades
Suggestions for Keeping Anecdotal Records

Reading Activities That Help to
Build Language Usage Power
in Children

The purpose of Chapter 13 is to offer down-to-earth advice regarding ways in which classroom activities involving reading can help to strengthen younger children's total grasp of language. The sections which follow are devoted to descriptions and explanations of some procedures in the kindergarten-primary grades which improve language understandings through reading skills and activities.

READING READINESS AS A CONSIDERATION IN THE DEVELOPMENT OF FACILITY IN LANGUAGE

Learning to read is a continuing process, a lifelong task. Children progress along the reading growth continuum at various rates, as noted on page 36. Each stage creates a readiness for the following one. The teacher who understands and accepts the developmental concept of reading growth will plan a program that enables each child to progress at a rate which affords both personal satisfaction with his present achievement and a challenge to continued improvement. The suggestions which follow are based on a recognition of the fact that all children will *not* be performing the *same* reading tasks at the *same* time or in the *same* way.

READING READINESS ACTIVITIES WHICH
ALSO HELP TO DEVELOP MATURITY
IN THE USE OF LANGUAGE

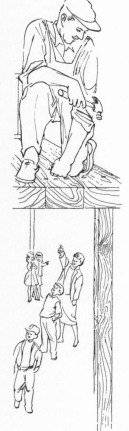

In the kindergarten-primary years, many phases of the program as a whole provide the background of experience which fosters language growth. Indeed, it would be difficult to isolate any specific area or activity in the well-directed kindergarten-primary program which did *not* serve to increase facility in using language, as well as to accelerate readiness for reading.

Here are some examples of readiness activities which have been tried out by teachers and found to be effective because they provide the raw material of experience on which both oral language and reading are based:

1. *Providing backgrounds of direct experience which increase children's fund of language meanings.*

   a) Orientation trips to various parts of the school at the kindergarten level (e.g., the nurse's office).

   b) Trips in the immediate neighborhood to locate the nearest mailbox, to see a house under construction, or to a nearby park to see the swans in the lagoon. (Kindergarten or grade one level.)

   c) Trips to the farm, zoo, aquarium, harbor, and similar places in the community which appeal to six- and seven-year-olds.

2. *Music activities.* Well-selected songs and singing games provide opportunities for using and interpreting language in rhythmic movement and developing auditory acuity. To give an illustration, readiness for "book" reading was fostered by a kindergarten teacher through an ingenious musical activity. Colored paper was fitted to the piano keys found in one octave. A book of songs was then prepared by pasting in it squares of paper forming patterns with colors which coincided with the notes for certain simple songs as in this example:

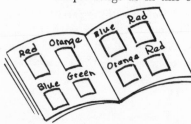

As the child played the music, this old favorite evolved, "Are You Sleeping, Brother John?" Note the left-to-right eye movement involved here for accurate interpretation of the color clues to the music.

3. *Poems and literature.* An inviting reading corner where children may browse is highly useful in developing interest in books and reading. Children are encouraged to choose books for the teacher to read and to discuss their favorites. In the process of reading stories to children the teacher is developing the idea that the printed text is telling the story. She may occasionally pause and let the children "read" a word, words, or phrases, in large print which are suggested by the context—such words as "Bang" when the firecracker goes off in *Shhh . . . Bang!* a book by Margaret Wise Brown, or a repeated phrase such as "Red Light—Stop" in *Red Light Green Light* by Golden Mac-Donald.

The latter part of this chapter is devoted to a discussion of the use of stories and poems with children. Such experiences are important in developing both interest and the desire to read.

Dramatic play, dramatization, "show-and-tell" time, and other oral language activities are also important in increasing language facility. See Chapter 11, pages 124-146.

Teachers can also plan experiences related to probable interests of children which help them to associate meaning with word symbols. Some of the effective activities found in many schools at the kindergarten-primary levels are as follows:

1. A large booklet may be made with the title *Our Pets.* In preparing such a booklet, children may dictate stories about their pets which the teacher writes down in their words to help children begin to sense the linkage between the spoken and written word. It is also a pleasant activity to have children draw pictures or bring in photographs as illustrations for a book about pets. Upon completion, such a book can be kept and enjoyed as part of the room library. Beginning readers who consult it learn to recognize the word "Pets" and the names of specific animals, even without the aid of the picture clues.

2. A trip to a nearby supermarket, planting a garden, discussion of the school lunch menus, or a physical examination by the school nurse are among the things that may inspire discussions on foods, their kinds, and their health values. Children may browse through magazines, choosing representative foods—vegetables, meats, fruits and desserts—and arrange them in labeled categories. These may be assembled on a large chart, in group booklets or in individual booklets.

3. Children like to talk about their families. They learn to recognize family words such as *father, mother, sister, brother, baby,* or *grandmother* through a variety of activities. These words are introduced early in basal reading series; hence six-year-olds should be familiar with them. Experience with these words—even at the five-year-old level—*before* children meet them in books, or *after* reading begins to reinforce learnings, is desirable. After an "interview" at home with his father, the child may contribute an illustrated page for a classroom booklet on "How My Father Helps." Written explanatory captions may accompany each picture depending on the grade level and individual ability.

4. Individual pictures may be painted or drawn of family groups with a caption such as "This Is My Family." In addition to observing the child's degree of language readiness, the teacher may obtain clues to his feelings and attitudes through the medium of his art work. One first grade boy drew an interesting picture of a family group—father, mother, grandmother, and grandfather. "Where is your baby brother?" asked the teacher. "I didn't put him in," he replied through clenched teeth. The teacher did not pursue the subject by questioning "Why." But she did make a mental note to see whether the lad was having difficulty in accepting the new member of his family.

5. "What things do you think about when you think of Christmas?" asked Miss Lovatt, an imaginative teacher, early in the holiday season. Ideas from the kindergarten children poured forth. Santa Claus, wreaths, bells, holly, toys, Baby Jesus, shepherds, presents, ribbons, Christmas trees, and ornaments were among the things mentioned. The teacher suggested that children look for pictures of these ideas in a stack of magazines which she had on hand. (She had been careful to bring in only the *seasonal magazines* in which Christmas pictures could be found.) Miss Lovatt then made a cut-out picture book with the group, their ideas being woven together into a simple but delightful script which the children dictated and which she wrote on each page of Christmas pictures.

6. A group of children became interested in cattle brands because of TV "westerns" they had seen. After discussing these symbols and their

uses, they created their own. These were assembled on a bulletin board under the caption "Our Brands."

Booklets, charts, bulletin boards, and other teacher-made reading materials of this nature help to develop readiness for the printed word in the pre-reading stage as well as reinforcing and increasing skills for the beginning reader.

The games and puzzles listed below may be helpful in developing *specific* visual skills necessary for success in reading.

1. *Mother Goose puzzles and similar story puzzles of sturdy wood-cut design.* These should be introduced by reviewing the story portrayed. *(The Three Bears, Jack and Jill,* and *Little Red Riding Hood* are examples of puzzle types.)

2. *Other jigsaw puzzles.* There is a variety of puzzles available related to many subjects such as transportation, community helpers, animals, etc.

3. *Sequence puzzles, both commercial and teacher-made.*[1] Children must know the stories well and understand the plot sequence to master these puzzles. The puzzle board contains pieces which must be inserted in order of the plot development. Frequently they are based on old folk tales. Observing children work these games gives the teacher clues to children's stage of readiness for beginning reading.

4. *Matching games.* "Old Maid" is a familiar example of the kinds of games in which pictures are paired. The teacher may devise a variety of these matching games with pictures cut from magazines. The children begin with simple picture-matching games and later progress to matching words and pictures. Eventually they are able to match words or phrases or even short sentences without the picture clue.

5. *Lotto.* There are many picture lotto games available commercially or the teacher may devise her own sets. As reading skill develops, children are ready for lotto games using words and phrases.

6. *Story games.* Some teachers devise games which are played in the manner of such commercial games as "India" and "Parcheesi" in which little figures or counters move along a path. The game board may be an original one—say, about Hansel and Gretel or Cinderella. These games are helpful in developing number readiness and color discrimination as well as reading readiness. Such terms as "Stop," "Go," "Go ahead 3 spaces," "Go back 4 spaces," "Go to the witch's house," or "Stop at the pumpkin coach," are used. Cards with numbers or verbal directions

---

[1]Commercial puzzles and similar items which teachers may wish to obtain are listed in the bibliography. See page 276.

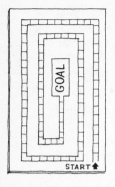

may guide the player in his progress from "Begin here" to the "Goal," or a large die or spinner may be used.

7. *Miscellaneous picture clue games.* Many games may be devised for fostering picture interpretation and classification skills. Games may be made which are helpful in developing children's ability to organize and categorize. Game boards with pockets are constructed (similar to the pocket charts used in word and phrase study). A picture clue is inserted at the left of each pocket and a stack of cards is provided to the player. The player places cards in the pockets according to the category picture clue. Endless varieties of this game may be devised—categories of foods, pets, zoo animals, transportation, etc.—and used as these interests are explored and discussed by the group.

8. *The picture file.* Picture files are useful to the kindergarten-primary teacher. While waiting for lunch, for the cars to go on the excursion, or during comparable brief "breaks" in the school day, the teacher may place three, four, or five cards in the chalk tray or pocket chart. "These are pictures of some animals you know. Which ones did you see at the zoo?" she may ask. Or she may ask:

a) Can you find two things that rhyme? (A child chooses the picture of the *house* and the *mouse.)*

b) The teacher (and later children after they "catch on" to the game) may make up jingles.

"I dropped the plate
When I slipped on the _____."

(Child chooses the picture of the *skate.)*

See Marion Monroe's book, *Growing Into Reading*[2] for further suggestions of games which may be played with children to develop visual and auditory acuity.

Games, activities, and routines which involve comprehension of directions increase skill in vocabulary and the ability to interpret oral language. With growth in reading skills, the ability to understand simple written directions is acquired.

Art media such as finger paint, woodworking material, housekeeping equipment, blocks, or science exhibits are

[2]See bibliography for complete reference.

all an integral part of stimulating language learnings in these early years and have been mentioned earlier.

PHASES OF THE TOTAL READING PROGRAM WHICH LEAD TO THE DEVELOPMENT OF LANGUAGE POWER

Children today are growing up in an increasingly literate world in which the need to understand language is appreciably greater than in 1900. For this reason concepts regarding the reading program have changed in recent decades. Reading is no longer taught *merely* as a skill with major emphasis on the mechanics of reading. The concept of the reading program has changed so as to foster an ability to read competently in many varied situations, to interpret what is read, and to make language development as a whole occur more rapidly.

The Basal Reader Program as a Part of the Total Reading Experience. A basal reading program introduces and develops the specific skills necessary for mastery of the mechanics of reading. The young reader progresses through a series of graduated reading materials in his progress toward ultimate independence and effectiveness in reading.

As children show signs of their readiness to understand the meanings of written symbols, they are introduced to the pre-primers of the basal series. Because of the differences in levels of readiness which normally exist in a group, the teacher may introduce one small group at a time to a pre-primer. The number of groups in a particular classroom depends upon the range of ability displayed by the children as well as the teacher's own readiness to adapt her methods of instruction to the individuality of children. Also, she may combine groups upon occasion for some specific phase of instruction such as recognizing stem words and their variants, like *toy, toys* or *ball, balls.*

Irrespective of the number of reading groups in a class there will be some pupils who will need personalized instruction in learning reading skills. The teacher also must endeavor to work with *all* children individually as often as possible. (See comments on individualizing instruction, pages 194-197.)

At the end of the first grade, some children are often reading above grade level, a few even being able to handle simple third grade material. Conversely, there are those boys and girls who will be reading primers, some working with pre-primers, and a few may still be engaged in developing the readinesses necessary for initial success. This range of reading ability commonly widens in the second grade.

If a particular basal reading program is used in your school, it is desirable to have several complete or partial sets of co-basal readers available for use. Then, as children finish a pre-primer, primer, or other volumes in the series, other books may be placed at their disposal to provide additional contacts with stories. This enables them to enjoy more stories, acquire more information, and consolidate their learnings before they proceed to more difficult material.

If children are encouraged to proceed at their own rate in the development of reading skills, and if their achievement is met with encouragement and approval by teachers and parents, they are likely to find satisfactions and enjoyment in their reading activities—and to read more than ever!

Manuals which accompany basal reading series have been painstakingly developed and often are helpful guides for the teacher. However, the teacher should use her professional judgment in adapting commercial materials to meet the specific needs of her group. Most basal series include expendable workbooks which also may be used to extend or reinforce reading learnings. The teacher of insight analyzes the needs of her group carefully and uses these workbooks as supplementary tools rather than as the focal point for the reading program.

The basal reader program should be conceived as *one* aspect of the reading program. However, it invariably needs to be augmented by many other available opportunities for reading in co-basals and in the supplementary books found in the rich classroom environment. In short, the teacher uses the basal materials; the materials do not dictate her program. The good reading program in the primary grades is four-fold: basal and co-basal, experimental, spontaneous, and recreational.

Reading Experiences as a Means of Developing General Language Powers. Stories, reports, news items, and questions which reflect or stimulate the lively interests of children provide an inexhaustible supply of reading material in the kindergarten-primary program. The neophyte reader may recognize the words *Saturn, volcano, gravity, rocket, sugar,* or *cookies* because of the importance of these words in his quest for an understanding of the world about him. Reading activities which flow from the child's stream of experience and his growing fund of meanings must also be varied in their degree of difficulty as individual needs and purposes dictate.

Here is an example of an experience—a simple one that might have occurred in *your* class—and a review of the reading and language activities to which it led.

When Mrs. Wilson brought an Easter basket, a slotted can for coins, some gummed seals, and a poster to the first grade for the Easter Seal drive, a discussion ensued about the purpose of the drive. Concepts of what "Crippled Children" were like, what they and non-handicapped children *could* do (sing, listen to records and stories, read, play games like checkers and puzzles, work with clay, and paint—depending upon the handicap) were established. What we can do that they often *can't* do (run, jump, etc.) was also brought out.

"Why do they need money?" "What do they do with the money?" were among the questions raised. The group became quite conscious of the need to help others and invited Mrs. Wilson to come again. Interest was high and it was decided to have a cookie sale and to contribute the money to the Easter Seal Drive at the time she returned.

This incident serves to illustrate how a commonplace happening can open wide the door to many language growth channels—including reading—at the six-year-old level. The seventeen points which follow suggest the possibilities in a situation like the one described which arise from children's strong desire to *find out* and to *do*.

Actvities involving reading and writing:
1. Letters of invitation to Mrs. Wilson to come again.
2. Thank-you notes to Mrs. Wilson.
3. Letters to parents (also see Chapter 14) asking for their help and inviting them to come to the cookie sale.
4. Posters announcing the time, place, date, and purpose of the cookie sale.

Reading activities:
1. Charts for group responsibilities (for example, basket-making committee, poster committee, baking committee, etc.).
2. Study of several recipes in order to make a choice among the several types of cookies that might be baked.
3. Chart explaining how to make "Snickledoodles," the group's choice of cookie recipes.
4. Charts and news items about progress. A typical chart might read, "We need 100 cookie baskets. We have made 43."
5. Daily reminders of work tasks.
6. Chart of questions to be asked of a guide during a forthcoming trip to the bakery.

7. Group story about "Our Trip to the Bakery."
8. Reading stories about cookies which are to be found in some basal readers and in supplementary books.
9. Stories about cookies made up by the teacher, shared, and placed in the room library.
10. Stories read aloud to the children for their enjoyment, such as *The Duchess Bakes a Cake.*
11. Coin charts devised to help boys and girls learn about making change.
12. Keeping a bookkeeping chart depicting sales and profits.
13. Group and individual stories, placed on reading charts, which tell about the sale.

The curiosity of children is boundless, and their interest encompasses a wide range of subjects. Here is another example of a language experience which was infused with reading experiences for seven-year-olds.

A second grade group used a globe to locate Alaska because one girl had received a letter from her uncle, in the Air Force, when he was stationed there. The teacher helped the children to locate it on a flat (Mercator projection) map of the world. A discussion ensued about the shape of the earth. Suddenly Kenneth said, "Well, how did the earth get here, anyhow?" This curious child triggered one of the most exciting interests the group had explored. Questions poured out of the children. They needed the help of the librarian, their parents, and resource people from the community. The teacher had to reinforce her background of knowledge with some intensive reading to keep abreast of the scientific discussions. Among the meaningful language experiences which developed were the following.

A bulletin board was arranged showing a large diagram of the solar system. Each "planet committee" of seven-year-olds cut out the planet assigned to them and placed it in its orbit, with an appropriate number of moons. Each "planet group" (with the help of the teacher) also worked to find out all that it could about what was known of their planet and reported to the class.

The intensity of the group interest was illustrated in this incident.

The class had discussed space trips and decided to take an "imaginary trip to the moon." They were aware of some of the problems and had discussed what the lunar terrain and climate might be. "Let's get into our space suits and take off," suggested Mac. Children began pantomiming the action. "Wait," called Sally excitedly, "I've got to get my shoes," and she rushed to her small locker to get her shoes. (In Hawaii, where this incident occurred, many elementary school children go to school barefoot or shed their shoes soon after arriving in the classroom.)

Saturn, Jupiter, gravity, gaseous (the sun is a large *gaseous* mass), *orbit*, and many other words became part of the vocabulary of the group as they acquired some simple concepts about their solar system.

Thus it is that oral vocabularies expand and concepts are deepened and clarified, as children reach out to explore their world. The reading activities (charts and booklets) which retell these absorbing experiences not only build reading vocabularies; they also lead toward the development of many of the reading skills which are a part of the quality we call *competence* in reading.

The Importance of Spontaneous Reading as Involved in Such Helps as Signs, Charts, Notices, Labels, and News Items. Ours is a "reading world" and the young child has been exposed to the printed word long before he enters school. The pre-school-primary child discovers a world of reading in his classroom, too, however. The astute teacher capitalizes on the abundant opportunities in the classroom living for *functional* reading—reading which serves the immediate purposes of the child and which makes sense to him as he works his way toward *his* personal goals.

In kindergarten and early first grade, readiness for beginning reading skills may be the cultivation of the potential reading experiences which lie at hand in every classroom if the teacher will but take them up.

Some examples of "reading-for-a-reason" which may be introduced in the kindergarten-primary classroom range are listed below.

1. *Use of the calendar.* The idea of the sequence of days, and the ability to recognize names of days, months, and their related number symbols, are fostered through daily

use of the calendar in these early years. Weather symbols may also be used to depict the kind of day—cloudy, sunny, windy, or rainy. A large calendar can easily be made by the kindergarten teacher or by children in the primary classrooms.

2. *Attendance charts.* Teachers often devise various kinds of attendance charts. In kindergarten and first grade, figure or picture clues are usually used. For example, clowns with a child's name on each may be posted on a large sheet of oak tag. A slit above each is made so that a hat can be inserted. When the child arrives in the morning, he finds *his* hat and slides it in the slit to signify that he is present. Some teachers have used snapshots of each child which they have pasted on a large chart next to a pocket with the child's name. The child places his name in the pocket next to his picture to denote his presence.

3. *Helper's charts listing room responsibilities.* Children may refer to the helper's charts to determine their room responsibilities on a particular day or for the week. Picture clues of juice, housekeeping, library, sweeping, or lunch aid the young reader in interpreting the word symbols and in "finding the place to put my name." Picture clues should be used less frequently in second grade. A picture at the top of the chart may suggest the purpose of the chart but the tasks can be listed without identifying pictures.

4. *"News" items center.* Items *a* and *b* below are suggested for the first grade.

   a) As an example of a first grade "news" item, "Happy Birthday, Malcolm" may be manuscripted on the chalkboard or a bulletin board when the children arrive. A large and colorful birthday cake may be sketched below the announcement with the appropriate number of candles. Even the most immature child understands that the words represent a birthday greeting. As children are able to cope with more advanced reading material, some sentences such as "Today is Malcolm's birthday. He is seven years old" may be added.

   b) "Cottontail [the group's pet bunny] needs carrots,

lettuce, and cabbage greens. He will be hungry." Here we have a second representative bulletin board item. The youngsters see Cottontail's name written frequently and many begin to recognize the word.

Second grade "news" items are often similar to these:

   a) "Six people from the Symphony Orchestra will come to play today. The concert is at 1:30."

   b) "We will give our play about *Snow White* for the first grade tomorrow. Remember to bring what you need for your costume."

5. *Schedules for the day*, menus, lists of reminders, and other aspects of routine business matters can create opportunities for reading in the classroom.

6. *Science displays and exhibits* may be labeled to indicate the donor or point out an interesting fact—for instance, "See Leigh's goldfish," or "Cathy brought her bird. Listen to him sing."

7. *Teacher initiative at an opportune moment.* A combined reading and writing experience may arise from a transient interest. Malcolm's birthday and his birthday wish combined with the reading of "Mr. Topple's Wish" prompted his teacher to make a large cover for a booklet. She wrote the title, "If I Had a Wish," in bold manuscript with a brush pen and taped a wishbone on the cover. "What do you think it says?" she asked.

"Something about wishing because of the wishbone," guessed Jim. The children were given clues and aids in deciphering the title. Soon they were eager to reveal *their* wishes.

"Let's draw pictures of our wishes and see if we can guess what they are," suggested the teacher. The children wrote, "I would wish for:" then drew a picture of their heart's desire. In the process of sharing their wishes children had the opportunity to read and say, "If I had a wish, I would wish for" many times, and the guessing was good fun. Later the teacher assembled the pictures in the booklet and put it on the classroom library table for a few days.

Children also enjoy reading and then guessing the answers to riddles dealing with familiar objects such as a caterpillar.

What Am I?

I am black and yellow.

I live in this room.

I live in a jar.

I cannot run.

I like to eat leaves.

In the later months of grade one and in grade two, children enjoy copying these riddles and drawing a picture of the answer.

Building Motivation for Recreational Reading in the Kindergarten-Primary Program. An inviting room library acts as a magnet on the kindergarten-primary children who are being introduced to the pleasures and the possibilities of "finding out" through books. Many of the "early birds" who arrive twenty or thirty minutes before class begins may be encouraged to browse through favorites, and one soon finds them chuckling over *Curious George*, by H. A. Rey, or experiencing the thrills in *The Duchess Bakes A Cake*, by Virginia Kahl. New additions to the library collection are grasped avidly and examined. If one book in particular suits the "young reader's" fancy, he often requests, "Will you read this today, Miss Marshall?"

As children finish an activity, or during transitional and other uncommitted periods of the day, they can be encouraged to use the library corner or to examine the "books about insects" on the science table and the "books about airplanes" on the display table under the bulletin board. The importance of such recreational reading in the kindergarten-primary program cannot be overemphasized.

INDIVIDUALIZING READING INSTRUCTION TO MEET CHILDREN'S NEEDS MORE ADEQUATELY

We now direct attention to effective ways of making full use of stories and poems with *individual* children. Individualized reading is an approach in which a child is encouraged to self-select books on his own level of interest and ability. Instructional aid, of course, is given by his teacher as the need arises.

Many teachers have heard the term "individualized reading" and have inferred that it is "something new under the sun" in the educational world. Actually, individualized reading is not a new idea at all, and has been an integral part of good programs for teaching reading for almost half a century. Current widespread *interest in* and *use of* the term are, however, relatively new.

The basic ideas behind individualized reading have been simply and intelligently presented in two easy-to-read publications. The first of these is a four-page monograph written by Willard C. Olson. This leaflet, *Seeking, Self-Selection, and Pacing in the Use of Books by Children*, is available without charge.[3] The second is a 1958 pamphlet published by the

---
[3]Address requests to D. C. Heath & Co., Publishers, Boston, Massachusetts.

Bureau of Publications, Teachers College, Columbia University, New York. Written by Leland Jacobs, *et al.*, and edited by Alice Meil, the booklet is called *Individualizing Reading Practices*. Helpful references are listed in the bibliography.

A psychologically powerful quality of individualized reading is the fact that it starts *with the child*. It capitalizes on his normal, healthy drive to explore his environment. From this environment the child seeks those experiences that are consistent with his maturity and his needs. This supports the contention (since children grow at widely varying rates) that it is impossible to say exactly when a given boy or girl will be ready for a particular reading experience. Rather, his developmental pattern will be found on a continuum or range of growth toward maturity as suggested by our diagram in Chapter 1.

Although one might conclude that a child must have acquired a fairly extensive basic vocabulary before an individualized program is started, this is only partly true. Of course, until the child is an independent reader he needs instruction and cannot successfully read many *words* with no guidance. Nonetheless, there is a great deal of pre-reading activity, both in picture reading and story telling, that comes before the printed word. The child's habit of selectivity in perusing books for home and school use can be stimulated in the kindergarten and first grade both by an enticing classroom library and by the teacher who offers the children opportunity for developing their skill of critical selection. Procedures for developing children's self-selective abilities are discussed later in this chapter under the heading *Choosing Books With and For Children*.

Let us turn now to early first grade experiences in selectivity. To begin an individualized reading program the teacher should keep the following points in mind.

1. A child has established his basic vocabulary and has some ability in attacking new words.

2. The teacher provides books appropriate to a given child's particular developmental stage and which she feels will appeal to established interests or help to create new ones. She may have these books on a specific table or shelf and invite him to choose one that promises to interest him. She does not *limit* him to this shelf but suggests that it might include what he is after.

3. Once a child chooses a book the teacher spot-checks parts of the reading content with him to ascertain whether it is within his ability to comprehend and enjoy. Also, she anticipates his need to know new

vocabulary words before he reads independently.

4. As a child begins to read independently, he continues to need some help. There are several ways to provide this assistance:

a) Urge him to ask the teacher for needed help, or to ask another child who reads well. The frequency of his requests for help is an additional check on the difficulty of the material. Caution must be observed, however, lest boys and girls who read well be exploited by their classmates who make too many requests for help from others. Some teachers and children work out "buddy" systems where two people of somewhat similar reading abilities read next to each other and rely on one another for help.

b) The child may write difficult words he encounters in his reading in a notebook or card file that the teacher might see when she is free to help.

5. The young individual readers should periodically be asked to read with the teacher for a considerable span of time.

6. It is desirable to evaluate the individual reader's progress with him. This enables the teacher to isolate needs he has for specific learnings and to help him master them —for example, if he is having difficulty distinguishing between the words *know* and *knew*. Appraisal of this sort also reveals growth in oral language as he reports on his readings, suggests power of comprehension, sense of humor, sense of beauty, his interests, and his judgments.

7. The child and the teacher can also agree on independent activities which the former can do in connection with his reading. Some suggestions are:

a) Through *art* he might:

(1) Paint or draw a picture to depict an event or a character in the book.

(2) Make a puppet patterned on one or more of the characters.

(3) Finger-paint a picture of a part of the story.

(4) Model characters with clay.

(5) Make a mobile depicting the characters.

(6) Make a paper-roll movie with another child

who read the book too.

b) Through *science* he might:

    (1) Do some simple experiments if the book deals
with science.

c) Through *dramatization* he might:

    (1) Pantomime a part of the story.

    (2) Work out a play with other children who have
either read the same book or who want to take
a role after they have heard him tell the story.

    (3) Give a puppet show.

    (4) Make up a flannel-board story.

    (5) Dress up as one of the persons in the story.

b) Through *writing* he might:

    (1) Keep a record of the books he reads either in
a notebook or on mimeographed forms which
the teacher devises.

    (2) Compose a story or poem stimulated by the
original story.

In most situations these suggested activities are feasible
for a few first graders and for most second graders.

ENJOYING BOOKS WITH CHILDREN

Chapter 5 suggested why literature is such an important
offering in the language arts program. This section moves
ahead from this point by concentrating on prose and poetry
that are a part of the young child's heritage. Let us examine:

1. *When* and *where* do you use prose and poetry?

2. *How* do you use them?

3. *What* prose and poetry can you use?

When and Where Do You Use Prose? There are
times when the entire group will want to share a story,
and there are times when only a small group may be involved. These groupings will, among other things, be
dependent on programming and pupil interests. While
there should be no "forced listening" to stories, this is
rarely a problem. Like the Pied Piper of Hamelin, during
the story hour the teacher usually finds that she has a
"magic song."

It is quite usual for the teacher of young children to read a story almost every day. The seating arrangement for these sessions should be as informal as possible and many young children like to sit on the floor at the teacher's feet when circumstances permit. With the older sixes and sevens there is a more general pattern of sitting on their chairs at their own places.

When story telling "just happens," it may take place almost anywhere —on the playground, on the bus, at the lunch table, or in a transitional time as when the group is waiting for a special teacher to arrive. It may also be precipitated by something unexpected.

Some second grade children were waiting for the school bus to pick them up after their trip to the dairy. The driver was late and the group sat under a tree. "Oh, I wish Mr. Jordan would come; I'm hot." "We'll never get to school for lunch!"

Mrs. Anderson said, "Did you ever hear the story about the old woman who had a pig that wouldn't jump over a stile and she wasn't sure she'd get home? Well, once upon a time . . . ." and so a folk tale eased the restlessness of the group and provided a good fill-in for an unexpected wait.

How Do You Use Prose? What are some practical ways in which a kindergarten-primary teacher may use stories to enrich the young child's reading and language environment? Although much emphasis should be put on planning a program where the young child has firsthand experiences, the vicarious adventures found in a literature program can help acquaint him with his surroundings and help him to interpret the world in which he lives. Most frequently boys' and girls' listening and comprehension levels forge far ahead of their reading ability. This is a clue for us.

They are ready to learn from books even though, perhaps, they cannot yet read. *They have ideas* on which we can build with our stories of facts, feelings, and fantasy. *It is these ideas we need to capitalize on,* for through them we can enhance the child's imagination and thinking power. As James Hymes notes:

> Reading stories to children is not "building" readiness; it is capitalizing on readiness. It is not a technique for getting children ready for something that will happen tomorrow; choose good books and it becomes teaching now. Reading good stories can be one of your best means to help young minds cope with people, with problems, with human relations, with science, with man's past and present and future.[4]

The following situations are only a few of the many which occur daily

---

[4]James L. Hymes, *Before the Child Reads* (Evanston, Illinois: Row Peterson and Co., 1958), pp. 48-9.

and which suggest how prose can be used in furthering human development.

1. *How a story can help to dispel a child's fears.*

Five-year-old Skippy had been restless for two days. He wandered from job to job, cried easily, and frequently questioned when his daddy would call for him. This was unusual behavior for him, for he generally found it hard to leave the school grounds at dismissal time until everyone was gone. Miss Osgood noticed that he frequented the doll corner during play time and work period, concentrating on play centering around a toy nurse's kit which someone had donated. He would play with another child sometimes but often was alone.

He had told the group his mother was sick. He asked many questions about sick people and when he got up from his nap he told that they had taken a picture of his mommy and that "she had bones in her." This statement was accompanied by a rush of tears.

Skippy's father happened to arrive during this episode since it was near dismissal time. He was distraught because of his wife's incapacity and burdened with additional duties. As Skippy went to get his coat, the father said, "Poor Skippy. He hasn't had much attention lately. I showed him his mother's x-rays but I guess I didn't explain enough. The doctor is trying to locate a point of an old break in her leg. She has been having severe pains. Apparently Skippy doesn't understand about the real problem. I'll visit with him tonight and try to explain things again."

After everyone had left, Miss Osgood went to the school librarian with a request for some books that might be helpful to Skippy and his dad. She found Herbert S. Zim's book illustrated by Herschel Wartik called *What's Inside of Me* (see bibliography, p. 256) and *My Body and How it Works*[5] by Dorothy Baruch and Oscar Reiss and dropped them off at their house on her way home.

Next morning Skippy arrived bright and cheery, fed the guinea pigs, played on the slide, and came eagerly to conversation circle. He could hardly contain himself and finally burst out, "Say you guys, you know we're all skeletons!"

2. *How stories were used to answer seven-year-old's questions on dinosaurs.*

Jim brought a plastic model of a dinosaur to school. It was a well designed, accurate model.

Mr. Zeller asked him to show it to his second grade classmates. Jim's conversation indicated that he had quite a knowledge of prehistoric lore and when asked where this interest stemmed from Jim said, "My uncle's a geologist and he tells me all this."

---

[5]Dorothy Baruch and Oscar Reiss, *My Body and How It Works* (New York: Harper & Brothers, 1934).

When the children asked him some questions related to more specific points, however, Jim was unable to answer their queries. Jim said he'd like to ask his uncle but he was gone to South America for two years!

Mr. Zeller suggested that Jim, with other interested class members, could check with the librarian on possible books that might help them. They followed through on the project and used such books as *Book of Big Beasts*, by Bettina Kramer, *Dinosaurs*, by Herbert S. Zim, and the *True Book of Dinosaurs*, by Mary Lou Clark, and made a final report to the rest of the group.

Radio and TV impinge on the home life to a greater degree than they do on the in-school life of the very young child, but their importance in the classroom is increasing. Phonograph records for young children do, however, have an established place in the home and school. They may be used in addition to the personal story-telling experience but should never be used to the exclusion of stories told by the teacher herself. There are many good recordings and schools frequently have a record library where the teacher may borrow materials and occasionally one finds a room record library. The advantage of this medium over radio or TV, for classroom use, is that the teacher and the child have more choice in making and timing the use of selections. Also, the teacher can review a recording, judging its merits for classroom use, before deciding whether or not to use it.

Sources for some of the better story records are found in the latter part of this book. (See pp. 273 to 275.)

Weather permitting, the playground is another place in which story reading and telling can provide pleasant hours during the year as we seek to use prose effectively.

One day a group of boys and girls were seated under a tree resting after some strenuous play. They were perspiring, and their features were grubby because they had wiped their hands over their faces. "We sure don't look like 'The Clean Pig,'" said Dale.

"What's the clean pig?" asked Lenore. "It's a story. I'll tell you about it," said Dale and paraphrased Leonard Weisgard's whole story to the delight of the other six-year-olds resting with him. The teacher, too, can take time to tell a short tale on the playground to give youngsters time to cool off after strenuous play.

The reader will note that while this chapter is concerned with *reading activities* that build language power, at the kindergarten-primary level these *reading* activities are closely related to *oral* communication such as reading aloud to children and telling stories. Patently, in the pre-reading and early reading phases of human development much "reading experience" (readiness activities, the building of perceptual and aural acuity, helping children find enjoyment in literature) extends beyond the covers of basal readers to the new co-basal "story readers" and the charming children's stories, old and new, found in our libraries.

What Prose Do You Use? This topic was introduced in Chapter 5, under the heading of "What Books Do Children Like?" Generally speaking, youngsters find joy in books that have:

1. Ideas that answer questions, like:[6]

   a) Elephants, by Herbert S. Zim

   b) Song of the Swallows, by Leo Politi

   c) Bits That Grow, by Irma E. Webber

   d) Follow the Sunset, by Herman and Nina Schneider

   e) All About Eggs, by Millicent E. Selsam

   f) The Big Book of Cowboys, by Sidney E. Fletcher

2. Ideas that inspire and stimulate the imagination, like:

   a) Millions of Cats, by Wanda Gág

   b) The Quiet Book, by Helen Flynn

   c) I Can Fly, by Ruth Krauss

   d) Stone Soup, by Marcia Brown

   e) My Mother Is the Most Beautiful Woman in the World, by Rebecca Reyher

   f) Patty Paints a Picture, by Laura Bannon

3. Ideas that are funny, like:

   a) Mop Top, by Don Freeman

   b) Story of Ferdinand, by Bunro Leaf

   c) Georgie, by Robert Bright

   d) Magic Michael, by Louis Slobodkin

   e) Caps for Sale, by Esphyr Slobodkina

---

[6]Publishers and other information may be found in the bibliography.

4. Ideas that come from story illustrations, like the pictures in:

  a) *The Little Island*, by Golden MacDonald, pseud. (Margaret Wise Brown) and Leonard Weisgard

  b) *Village Tree*, by Taro Yashima, pseud. (Jun Iwamatsu)

  c) *Farmer in the Dell*, by Berta and Elmer Hader

  d) *Johnny Crow's Garden*, by Leslie Brooke

  e) *Boats on the River*, by Marjorie Flack

  f) *White Snow, Bright Snow*, by Alvin Tresselt

  g) *The Little House*, by Virginia Lee Burton

ENJOYING POETRY WITH CHILDREN

When and Where Do You Use Poetry? Poetry has the same versatile qualities that characterize story-telling. Both use literary forms that are desirable for bringing the beauty and the delight of our language into the everyday world of the learner, giving him the opportunity to assimilate good language patterns and to base his own upon them.

Poetry may be used at almost any time during the day as shown by the following illustration.

Usually the children in Mrs. Hatton's second grade voiced requests for a variety of poems during their "Singing Words" or poetry time. However, the several days of spring rain prompted them to suggest, "Let's do just rain poems today." They heard their old favorite *Little Rain*, by Elizabeth Madox Roberts, helped chant *Raining*, by Rhoda W. Bacmeister, and Mrs. Hatton introduced a new one, Rose Fyleman's *Very Lovely*.

Later in the morning the sevens were lined up in the corridor to go to assembly hall. As they were waiting for several other groups to enter the auditorium, Mrs. Hatton turned quietly to her group and said, "Isn't it interesting the way we get places? Do you know this poem?" She recited *Jump or Jiggle*, by Evelyn Beyer. By the time she was finished with the verse, the other groups had arrived and the second graders entered the hall and took their places.

Poetry, like prose, involves considerations for seating except where (in the example above) it is used spontaneously. The important issue is really one of comfort during a good listening session. Distracting noises and objects should be eliminated and a pleasant "tone" should predominate.

How Do You Use Poetry? There are several successful methods of "using poetry" with children. A basic point is that it takes *preparation* by either the neophyte or the seasoned teacher to make full use of verses. With this prerequisite in mind you may wish to note that the following items are important.

1. Have a knowledge of *what* children like in poetry. Suggestions are made below (see pp. 208 to 209) in the section "What Poetry Do You Use?" The appended bibliography (p. 245) will be helpful for further general information.

2. Equip yourself with several selected volumes of poems, find an isolated, comfortable spot—your own room, the beach, your attic if it's as good as Jo March's in *Little Women*—any place where you can read aloud and "play actress." Read poems that appeal to you—have fun with them—read them again and yet again. Make them yours! Then share them with your fives, sixes, or sevens.

3. Select the poetry that appeals to you. Judge it by what you know about your children's interests and what authors of anthologies choose.

4. Take your selected treasure of verses to your young customers.

5. The really astute teacher works at "getting to know" her group, as recommended by the teacher in the Broadway musical *Anna and the King of Siam*. She will be sensitive to the varying backgrounds of her children.

Two of the writers, whose roots were deep in the middle west, eventually became teachers in Hawaii, islands of many cultures. Some of the children we worked with had early "singing words" from other than European sources. Akiko, a second grader we know, used to say this charming bit of poetry and the rest of the children joined in on the refrain of *Tanton, tanton, tanton ton.*

> *Kasan, okata wo tatakimasho*
> *Tanton tanton tanton ton.*

Mother, shall I pat your shoulder?
Tap on right and left shoulders.

Kasan, shiraga ga ari- *masu ne*	Mother, you are getting gray, aren't you?
Tanton tanton tanton *ton.*	Tap on right and left shoulders.
Oengawa ni wa hi ga *ippai*	The sun is shining brightly out on the porch.
Tanton tanton tanton *ton.*	Tap on right and left shoulders.
Makkana keshi ga waratteru *Tanton tanton tanton* *ton.*	The red poppy out there is smiling. Tap on right and left shoulders.
Kasan, sonna ni ii kimochi *Tanton tanton tanton* *ton.*	Mother, oh, how you're feel- ing so fine. Tap on right and left shoulders.

If the verses you select stand the test—if children like them—repeat them more than once. Children like to hear favorite verses again and again. The use of poetry spontaneously to fit at situation is another technique and "comes easy" if the teacher has enthusiasm for using it.

Examples of the spontaneous use of poetry are reflected in the following situations.

The school had purchased some surplus army shovels. The kindergarten group were given the tools. They sanded and painted the wooden handles, put nail pegs up in the corner to ensure their proper storage, and, when the shovels were in usable order, some children happily took off to their play yard to dig a hole to test their new equipment. Harbor construction was the immediate imaginary project. The digging hole was therefore done in a corner where there was access to a water faucet. The bridges, quays, buoys, and lighthouses were built and water was poured in to float the boats. Although they appeared almost motionless as they paused to survey their work, little ripples around the fives' legs indicated that their toes were digging into the mud. Mrs. Marshall, the teacher, started to chant Polly Chase Boyden's: [7]

Mud is so very nice to feel
All squishy-squash between the toes!
I'd rather wade in wiggly mud
Than smell a yellow rose.

[7]"Mud" by Polly Chase Boyden. Published in *Child Life*, April 1930. Copyright by Rand McNally and Company. Reprinted by permission.

> Nobody else but the rosebush knows
> How nice mud feels
> Between the toes.

This was an old favorite taken from their poetry time, so after Mrs. Marshall said the first few words, several children stopped their play and joined the chant, wiggling their toes in delight.

As the children rested after play-time, Mrs. Marshall reported the experience to the other children and said, "I have a poem about an animal who also likes mud." She read:

The Hippopotamus [8]
by Georgia Roberts Durston

> In the squdgy river,
>   Down the oozely bank,
> Where the ripples shiver
>   And the reeds are rank.
>
> Where the purple Kippo
>   Makes an awful fuss,
> Lives the hip-hip-hippo
>   Hippo-pot-a-mus!
>
> Broad his back and steady;
>   Broad and flat his nose;
> Sharp and keen and ready
>   Little eyes are those.
>
> You would think him dreaming
>   Where the mud is deep.
> It is only seeming—
>   He is not asleep.
>
> Better not disturb him,
>   There'd be an awful fuss
> If you touched the hippo,
>   Hippo-pot-a-mus.

The preceding discussion deals with the teacher's direct presentation of verse. There are other ways to use poetry with young children. Several teachers and children have had experiences like the following.

1. *Using a verse for rhythmic expression.* Some kindergarten children galloping to *Ride a Cock Horse*, skipping to *Hippety Hop to the Barber Shop*, swaying to *Brooms*, by Dorothy Aldis, clapping to *Hot Cross Buns*.

2. *Using verse for dramatic action.* Five-year-olds playing *Little Miss*

---

[8]Reprinted by permission of *Junior Home* and Child Training Association, Inc.

Muffet and the Spider, or *The Elf and the Dormouse* being
enacted by the first or second graders. If poetry has been
a real part of young children's daily living, the older sixes
and sevens find pleasure in pantomiming a favorite verse,
inviting the audience to "Guess our riddle."

3. *Using verses for choral speaking.* This often begins
naturally in the poetry-oriented room because even your
youngest children will begin to chant parts of favorite
verses with you as they hear the familiar refrain. One of
the five-year-old groups we know quite unsolicited joined
in the "Ah-choo's" in Mary Louise Allen's *Sneezing* poem.[9]

Sneezing

Air comes in tickly
Through my nose,
Then very quickly—
Out it goes;
Ahhh—CHOO!

With every sneeze
I have to do,
I make a breeze—
Ahh—CHOO!—Ahh—CHOO!

Another time we observed a kindergarten teacher who
suggested that a child give the initial two lines and the
closing two lines of Rose Fyleman's lovely poem *Mice.*
This required listening and observing skills, and although
poetry is essentially for joyful listening at this early stage,
a limited amount of memorizing "just comes naturally"
to the learners. A little later some children can take a one-
line-per-child role in choral speech. *One, Two Buckle My
Shoe* is an easy beginning poem for this work. This should
not be required memory work but offered as a means
of enjoying participation. Second grade children frequently
like experience in the choral area.

Poetry is sometimes used effectively in building positive
attitudes, too. However, we must be cautious not to be
moralistic, but rather take the responsibility of promoting new ideas.

A delivery man walked past the first graders' porch. Sev-

---

[9]From *A Pocketful of Rhymes* by Mary Louise Allen, copyright 1939 by Harper
& Brothers. By permission of Harper & Brothers.

eral boys shouted, "Look at the fat man! Look at the fat
man! Look at the fat man!" Later in the morning Mrs. Peacock was reading poetry and at the very end she said, "Our
new poem today is called *People*. It's by Lois Lenski—you
remember she wrote the stories you like about Mr. Small.
Let's hear what she has to say."

People [10]

Tall people, short people,
Thin people, fat,
Lady so dainty
Wearing a hat.
Straight people, dumpy people,
Man dressed in brown;
Baby in a buggy,
These make a town.

"Now let's think of the people we know who are different
sizes." The ensuing conversation brought up thoughts about
their families, friends, etc. Alice asked what "dumpy people"
meant. After Mrs. Peacock defined it, Alice said affection-
ately, "My mother's dumpy." "You love her, don't you, Alice?"
said Mrs. Peacock.

When poetry has been a natural part of the language
growth continuum, children begin speaking rhymes, riddles, and verses. This is encouraged by the teacher's own
enthusiasm for words and her establishment of a climate
for the children's creation of verse. As you read the examples below, notice how sensory-centered many of their
creations are. [11]

A five-year-old:

I went swimming
Without any trimming.
—Mary

The six-year-olds visited the kitchen:

The doughnuts warm my tummy,
Yummy, yummy, yummy.
—Virginia and Catherine

A group poem:

Doughnuts are good,
Good! Good! Good!

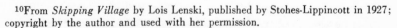

[10]From *Skipping Village* by Lois Lenski, published by Stohes-Lippincott in 1927;
copyright by the author and used with her permission.

[11]We are indebted to Miss Isabel Snow, Instructor in Pre-school- Primary Education at the University of Hawaii, for these children's original verses from her collection.

Doughnuts are brown,
Brown! Brown! Brown!
Doughnuts are fat,
Fat! Fat! Fat!
Doughnuts are round,
Round! Round! Round!

Seven-year-olds:

What has wings
And flies in the air
And carries people
Everywhere?
                                    —Nancy

I carry worms.
I live in trees.
I fly in the air
Wherever I please.
                                    —Catherine

The People's Feet
Pitter, patter! Pitter, patter!
Goes the rain.
Pitter, patter! Pitter, patter!
Go the people's feet.
Pitter, patter! Pitter, patter!
They are running home.
Pitter, patter! Pitter, patter!
Go children's feet.
They are running home.
The trees shake.
The leaves fall.
Pitter, patter! Pitter, patter! Pitter, patter!
Into the gutter they fall.
                                    —Audrey

What Poetry Do You Use? Perhaps the first reply is "good poetry."
But such an answer says everything and nothing. For the beginner it is
often a good idea to review some of the choices of specialists in the field,
choices to be found in anthologies. The final chapter of *Beginning Language Arts Instruction with Children,* by the way, offers a list of books prepared by people experienced in the realm of poetry. With these suggestions
as a basis for choices the novice in using poetry with children will be able

to test the response and later can go further afield in making personal
selections with some sense of security.

An important asset to teachers is a personal poetry library. This usually
consists of at least one good anthology, a book of the poems of one's
favorite children's author, and/or a personal index or loose-leaf file of
poems in the teacher's own collection. A good *Mother Goose* book for the
younger child is an example of the kind of volume that teachers use often
enough to justify its purchase.

Fives, sixes, and sevens, with whom we are most closely concerned,
enjoy the following qualities in poems.

1. Humor and nonsense poems, that tickle your ribs—found in favorites
such as:

Hey, diddle, diddle!	Mother Goose
The Little Kittens	Eliza Lee Follen
Only My Opinion	Monica Shannon
Grizzly Bear	Mary Austin
Eletelephony	Laura E. Richards
Jonathan (Dutch)	Rose Fyleman
Nonsense Alphabet	Edward Lear
Mrs. Snipkin and	
Mrs. Wobblechin	Laura E. Richards
Old Quin Queeribus	Nancy Byrd Turner
Bursting	Dorothy Aldis

2. Lilting melodies, found in poems such as:

Higgledy, Piggledy,	
My Black Hen	Mother Goose
The Cupboard	Walter de la Mare
Hoppity	A. A. Milne
Jabberwocky	Lewis Carroll
Momotaro (Japanese)	Rose Fyleman
Felicia Ropps	Gelette Burgess
The Pirate Don Durk	
of Dowdee	Mildred Plew Meigs

3. Verses with sensory appeal, found in poems such as:

Mud	Polly Chase Boyden
Silver	Walter de la Mare
Animal Crackers	Christopher Morley
The Big Clock	Unknown (See May Arbuthnot's
	Time for Poetry)
Little Rain	Elizabeth Madox Roberts

CHOOSING BOOKS WITH AND
FOR CHILDREN

The matter of choosing books with and for children is, first of all, controlled by the *availability* of such books in a particular school collection. Schools in the United States vary considerably with respect to their school libraries ranging from those which have few or even no facilities to those which have both classroom book collections and a central library collection. Realistically, therefore, we must examine several considerations when dealing with book selection.

1. Some suggestions for the teacher in the school with few if any library facilities.

   a) Develop a small but select book collection of your own, including items of many uses such as *The Arbuthnot Anthology of Children's Literature,* which includes three books: *Time for Poetry, Time for Fairy Tales, Old and New,* and *Time for True Tales and Almost True.* (See bibliography, p. 253.)

   b) Enlist the help of parents and children in beginning to build a room library together. They might raise money to buy a small collection like the one mentioned above.

   c) Try, in co-operation with the local public library, to work out a system allowing teachers special borrowing privileges if they have not yet been arranged. For example, a specified number of books might be borrowed on a long-term basis, thus creating greater variety in the room libraries available in smaller schools. Or a bookmobile might serve more isolated areas. Many counties have them!

   d) Make more use of the story-telling techniques described in Chapter 5.

2. Some suggestions for the teacher in a school offering a limited room library and no central collection.

   a) If the room library is limited, the public library collection might supplement it as noted in part *c*, item 1 above.

b) Periodically switching a few books with other classroom groups should help to improve the variety in your available titles.

3. Some suggestions for the teacher in a school with a good room library.

a) Blessed are the teacher and the children in this situation! The question of who should choose the books may rest with a central curriculum committee, a school library specialist, or in the teacher's own hands. It is generally best for all three to meet periodically to select volumes to be purchased.

b) If the teacher is to be the selecting agent, she would do well to consult several references such as a periodical guide like *The Horn Book*, a publication on distinguished books such as May Hill Arbuthnot's *Books too Good to Miss* and *The Children's Catalog*, edited by Ruth Giles and Dorothy E. Cook, published by H. W. Wilson Company. See the bibliography for further suggestions. Caution should be exercised in using publishers' book lists since they are limited to one company's offerings. The individual publisher's educational research services frequently publish professional material such as *Enjoying Poetry with Children* by Mabel Snedaker.[12]

c) Stimulating young children's interest in books is significantly influenced by the teacher's story-sharing skill. In addition it is well to consider the display of books as an invitation to the child. It is sometimes unfortunately true that *too many* books are shelved in a classroom library or small central school library. This practice generally attracts little attention to the good individual volumes in a classroom library. A book table or center, attractively featuring a dozen or so volumes, perhaps with a plant or flowers added, and/or some colorful pertinent illustrations of merit from either book jackets or magazines, serves as a magnet to draw the child's attention. "Center attractions" on the library table should be changed frequently.

4. Some suggestions for the teacher in the school offering a good central book collection.

This system brings up the moot question, do the young children go to the library or does the library come to them? A variety of solutions is possible, but in the final analysis the school's interpretation of the best plan for its members must be made in accordance with consideration of such points as: plant size, class size, disposition of the group, etc. We

---

[12]Mabel Snedaker, *Enjoying Poetry with Children* (Chicago: Ginn & Company, 1958).

have observed the following plan in use by the teachers, librarian, and children of the younger groups in one good school.

a) The teachers in the kindergarten and first grades went to the library every two weeks and replaced about one-half of their room book collections with new volumes.

b) When the books were brought back to the classroom, the teacher took a few volumes and showed them to the children saying things such as: "Here's another good book by Robert McCloskey. Remember his book *Make Way for Ducklings* that was such fun? This one has a good story called *One Morning in Maine*. It is about a little girl with a loose tooth. This is a very different kind of a story but try it and see if you like it." This gave the children a guide in choosing what they wanted read in school or what they wanted to take home.

c) The children went to the library in small groups for story periods with the librarian. These were scheduled about once a week, and sometimes the librarian came to the room for story time, bringing a new book or books she knew the group would enjoy.

d) The librarian kept the teacher informed of new books she felt would be of interest at some time to the group.

e) The teacher and children kept the librarian informed of their interests. With the younger child this had been handled in a conversational way when the librarian visited with the children —either casually during story time or during occasional observations of them and their room interests. The sevens were able to work out a written report check list to keep the librarian informed. It was a simple but helpful communication of interests and needs. They had mimeographed a form that looked like this:

Room:
Name:
I would like some books about:

Sometimes the group sent one copy of this form to the librarian or an individual used the form. This procedure was helpful to the librarian in locating materials for the group or individual to use.

f) Many sevens were quite ready and eager to choose their own books in the central library. This was done with the regular borrower's privileges and responsibilities. The group of children continued to have a room collection, but the selection of books for this section was shared by the teacher and the children.

Even the youngest child can learn to handle the books in a room library with respect, thus earning the privilege of borrowing them for home use on a short-term basis. Several kindergartens we have observed have worked out systems for overnight borrowing. For example, one kindergarten class had a large manila envelope in which books could be carried home. There was one such envelope for each child with his first name, group number, and room number printed in bold manuscript on it. When the child wanted to draw out a book, he found his own envelope, or the teacher got it for him if he could not yet identify his name.

The teacher had a five-by-eight card with the child's name. These were kept in alphabetical order in a "charge box." The name of the book to be withdrawn was written on the card along with the date. This was filed and was to be checked in the next morning when Jim returned the book. When he *did* return it to the checking table, the teacher located his card and had him cross out the name of the book and date. He then returned the envelope and the books to their respective places while the teacher refiled his five-by-eight card.

Other suitable book lending schemes are possible and need only a creative teacher and children to devise the system most feasible for their purposes. As the child grows in his ability, he may want to take over the role of the librarian. Some sixes and sevens usually begin to show such an interest.

This chapter has sought to stress the point, cited in

Chapter 1 of *Beginning Language Arts Instruction with Children,* that good language instruction is not made up of a few fixed teaching methods but is made up of many and varied practices which are associated not so much with the exact grade level as with the stage of development of individual children.

EVALUATING THE YOUNG CHILD'S LANGUAGE GROWTH AS REFLECTED IN READING AND LITERATURE

Evaluation as Especially Important in the Early Grades. Continuous teacher appraisal of group language growth is a necessity in the early years. Appraisal or evaluation begins long before conventional testing and measurement is possible with five- to seven-year-olds. No teacher, however seasoned and well prepared, is able accurately to remember enough specifics pertaining to a child's growth to permit her subsequently to give an objective evaluation *unless she keeps some form of written records.* Such notes help to guide the course of her teaching in two ways.

1. Written records will give the teacher help in discussing progress with the child himself. For example, book-borrowing cards are one form of record that may be talked over with a child. In a first grade, as the teacher checks such cards, she might note that Anne took home very simple picture books early in the year but toward April was borrowing more complicated stories and was reading them herself. You can use such information to encourage Anne to even greater effort. This is a simple but a basic example of how a teacher helps a child sense his own growth. And Anne's learning, as in the example given, should include opportunities for self-appraisal to guide her self-direction.

2. There are other adults in the child's life who need specific data from us to help them to guide children. Both parents and the child's next teacher need more than vague written or oral reports as they share in directing his reading and general language development.

Here is an example of an anecdotal entry that was used to supplement a teacher's memory when she saw a five-year-old's parents:

October 10th: What a wonderful surprise! Charles talked to the group for once at sharing time. He volunteered to show his painting offering no explanation and as usual hid his head behind it. Jim said it looked like an "Indian hat" and Jon said it looked like a "turkey tail." Suddenly Charles said, "It's a picture of my busy little mind!" and hurried and sat down.

It surely is a busy little mind. This may be the beginning of lots of talking! Must call his mother tonight.

Other notations on October 15 and November 11 preserved additional evidence as to Charles's slowly growing oral language skill.

Suggestions for Keeping Anecdotal Records. The anecdotal note described in the last episode is representative of a technique employed by many teachers. There are several ways of recording these notes. One procedure in rather general favor is that of making notations on five-by-eight cards. Several tips on how to preserve and use them are:

1. Have a sturdy box in which to store the cards. Keep it in a place where the confidential contents are secure.

2. Use an individual card for each child.

3. Keep the cards in alphabetical order.

4. Be sure to indicate the date when you record an incident.

5. Record behavioral notes that indicate the possible *nature* and *causes* of problems, lacks, needs, and significant signs of growth. Sometimes several days will go by when there is nothing of merit to record; again you may make several entries for a child on the same day.

6. Be sure you record enough of the circumstances or information so that you will have no trouble interpreting the report at a later date.

7. Remember that a quick note jotted down on the spot will be enough to remind you to record an observation or comment later in the day. Be sure to record your data as soon as possible after a significant event occurs.

8. Do not make children self-conscious by recording information in a conspicuous manner.

Observation records kept by the teacher are invaluable in helping to gauge a child's reading progress. Certainly the report on Charles cited above was indicative of his maturing oral language pattern and his progress toward readiness to read. The teacher can also observe and keep records on *specific* items related to visual and auditory abilities and to social-emotional development—all factors related to language growth in the area of reading.

Tests and similar data compiled by other school workers should be recorded—e.g., eye examinations including telebinocular-type check-ups and tests for far- and nearsightedness which are prerequisite for thorough study of the young school child. Audiometer tests, too, are helpful in locating the hard of hearing child.

Parents can be helpful during conferences by contributing to the teacher's appraisal of socio-emotional maturity. They also can give information about the child's experiential background. Another check on background knowledge can be made through the use of commercial reading readiness tests. (See bibliography.)

CHAPTER 14

Activities That Pave the Way
for Skill in Written Expression

Planning Effective Writing Experiences in the Kindergarten
and Primary Grades

Procedures That May Prove Helpful in Developing Creative
Writing

Fostering a Classroom Climate in Which Creativity May Flourish
Teacher Leadership in Providing Pre-Writing Experiences Which
Motivate Creative Expression

Considerations in Beginning Handwriting

Opportunities for Meaningful Writing
Stages in the Development of Writing Skills
Mechanical Aspects of Handwriting

Spelling in the Primary Grades: Procedures That Help Younger
Children Learn to Spell

Learning to Spell through Speaking
Learning to Spell through Reading
Learning to Spell through Writing

Activities That Pave the Way for
Skill in Written Expression

Kindergarten and primary teachers have a unique opportunity to encourage not only *readiness* for, but also a positive *attitude* toward, written expression. Children need both if they are to progress at a normal rate along the language continuum in the thinking-speaking-writing process. If he has lived in a stimulating classroom environment—one which has given him "experiences to think with" and to talk about—the child should be ready to write as soon as he has the physical co-ordination which is necessary when he takes pencil in hand to put his ideas on paper. Let us now examine some ways in which we can build readiness and also help boys and girls capture a part of themselves in writing.

PLANNING EFFECTIVE WRITING EXPERIENCES IN THE KINDERGARTEN-PRIMARY GRADES

Teachers with a talent for understanding children are as much concerned with *what* these boys and girls write as with how they write it when this form of expression first begins. In the course of the daily living of busy kindergarten-primary groups there are many occasions when individuals or the whole group may wish to employ written expression to serve an immediate purpose. At first, of course, this is done by inviting the kindergarten and beginning-first-grade children to *tell* the teacher what should be written on a chart or chalkboard. As the youngsters see the purpose and use of the written word thus demonstrated, understanding and readiness grow, and writing begins to become a functional process for children.

Opportunities for functional writing are often quite similar at all grade levels throughout the kindergarten-primary range. The frequency, the flavor of, and the approaches to situations involving writing vary with the grade levels and with the individual abilities of children. Typical situations which involve some form of written expression are suggested below. The youngest children, of necessity, will tell the teacher what words to write.

1. Writing names to identify possessions.

2. Captions for bulletin boards, exhibits, displays, collections, and individual or group projects.

3. Letters and notes to parents: requests for materials such as foodstuffs for a baking project or permission for a trip to the aquarium, news items about "Binker," the class pet bird, or reminders to parents about the forthcoming P.T.A. meetings.

4. Letters to absentees to express the wish that they will soon be back in school.

5. Invitations and thank-you notes to other classes, parents, and consultants before and/or after programs or presentations.

6. Greeting cards for a holiday, a birthday, on Mother's Day or Father's Day, for a child going on a trip, and so on.

7. Individual and group stories, both factual and imaginative.

8. Group records of:

   a) Information gained through excursions, discussions, or visits with consultants.

   b) Observations of science experiments and phenomena such as the growth of plants, the life cycle of the moth.

   c) Class agreements such as those reached in governing playground use.

   d) Listings of such group responsibilities as watering plants, feeding animals such as a pet turtle, or caring for the appearance of a library table.

9. Writing numbers: pages of booklets, telephone numbers, home addresses, pupil-made calendars, for instance. When counting lunch or juice money, or collections for the Red Cross, Community Chest, or simi-

lar fund drives, and bus fare for excursions, number writing also "comes naturally."

In the kindergarten in particular, *readiness* for written expression should be stressed since early in the year many children have yet to learn to write their names. Though very little writing is done by individual kindergarten children, even late in the year, they are introduced to the *idea* of writing and are becoming aware of the purposes for which writing is used. They like to have their pictures and art products identified, for instance. Many a kindergarten teacher has heard a child say, "I'm finished. Write my name on it, Miss Jamison."

Some time during the kindergarten year, nearly all children try repeatedly to write their names. At this stage they often become so intrigued with this newly—or at least partially—acquired skill that their names overshadow in size and importance the theme of their paintings or drawings. Practice in writing such things as one's name should be purely voluntary. Easels, large eighteen-by-twenty-four sheets of newsprint, thick crayons, chalk and chalkboard space should be kept available for these beginning scribes. Reversal of the whole name or individual letters within the name may be expected since the child's sense of left-to-right movement in writing has not been established. Suggesting to an individual child that he "begin here" is helpful, but the teacher should not make such an issue of this that the five-year-old child's initial enthusiasm for writing is dampened.

In most writing experiences in the kindergarten, as we have noted above, the teacher assumes the burden of the mechanics, acting as "secretary" for the children. Hers is the opportunity to help a group begin to sense needs for writing when direct oral expression does not suffice. Here is an example of a situation—comparable to those which present themselves in any classroom—which illustrates how simply and naturally writing can be used to good purpose in the kindergarten.

When Judy brought her guinea pigs to school, she was obviously disappointed to learn that Jack was absent. "Jack wanted to see my guinea pigs. When is he coming back?" she asked. Mrs. Angstrom said she didn't know, but said that they could send a letter home with his brother, Allan, in the third grade, telling about Judy's pets and the other kindergarten news. "Let's ask the rest of the group to help us plan the letter," she concluded. The group was glad to write to Jack and tell him about the recent happenings. Mrs. Angstrom aided them in composing a letter, and, of course, "took dictation."

Many other approaches to the use of writing with kindergarten children can be found in every classroom. For instance, children often have a story to tell about the pictures they draw. The teacher may write such little stories for them and later help them to share both drawing and story with the class in oral conversation. Again, invitations and thank-you notes from the fives which are directed to consultants and resource people may be dictated to the teacher.

A kindergarten-primary room that is "alive" will contain many labels and signs, although few, if any, of these should remain in place unchanged for more than a week or two. Children may keep the teacher busy writing "Wet Paint—do not touch" for the newly painted woodwork, and "McCully Station" for the fire-house which they built. When children bring in objects of interest, the teacher may label them, "See Sarah's turtle," or "This is Mike's jet." The kindergarten teacher should, however, avoid over-labeling such obvious objects as the faucet ⎣ *faucet* ⎦ , paste ⎣ *paste* ⎦ , door ⎣ *door* ⎦ , chair ⎣ *chair* ⎦ . A better way of labeling a chair is to identify it with a child's name ⎣ *Joe* ⎦ .

In the first grade, children become able to do more writing on their own, but individual abilities vary enormously. In the early part of the year many youngsters are still grappling with mastering the skill of writing their names. Although the teacher continues to play the major role as "secretary" in the written expression of the first grade, children do more and more writing for themselves as the year progresses. Some boys and girls of six do not pass the level of copying, while there are a few who may gain a considerable degree of independence.

First grade children frequently can be encouraged to request that the teacher prepare words or phrases for them to copy for their dramatic play. These may be signs to identify the ‖ Bus Station ‖ , ‖ Airport ‖ , ‖ Stop-R.R. Crossing ‖ , or signs dealing with tickets for rides on the many vehicles which they build: ‖ One Ride: 10¢ ‖ and names and prices for their market ‖ Cookies – 20¢ a box ‖ or names for their caged animals ‖ Camel ‖ or ‖ Beware of the Lion. ‖ .

Making greeting cards of all types and descriptions is a good activity for most first grade children. Here are some hints on procedures:

One first grade teacher kept a large and sturdy box with materials for making cards. One compartment contained an assortment of plain and colored paper cut in a variety of lengths and widths. Other sections contained bits and scraps of colored papers, crepe paper, gold and silver paper, paper doilies, ribbons, and other materials which might be used for decorations. Children were encouraged to use these materials whenever the need arose.

At appropriate times conventional greetings such as "Merry Christmas," Happy Easter," are available for the children to copy.

Making cards is great fun for the six- and even the seven-year-old child. Most of the first grade children are dependent on the teacher to supply the sample of writing to be copied on their cards. Many second graders are able to write their own captions or to reproduce familiar phrases without using a model.

PROCEDURES THAT MAY PROVE HELPFUL IN DEVELOPING CREATIVE WRITING

Some language arts specialists classify written expression under two major headings, (1) *creative* and (2) *functional*. "Creative" writing emphasizes self-expression, and "functional" writing is done for purposes of basic communication. Although these labels are artificial ones, they do make the point that children write for different reasons.

Daily school activities provide numerous experiences through which writing skills may be developed in a func-

tional manner, as suggested in the preceding pages. Opportunities for
and encouragement of creative expression are, however, often neglected
at the kindergarten-primary level. Capturing the child's "free spirit" of
expression in the oral and written word is, nonetheless, a responsibility
of all who guide young children. Perhaps in no other area can teachers
do *so little* or *so much* depending upon their approaches, their sensitivity,
and their appreciation of vitality and beauty in children's language.

It is important to *avoid* conventionalizing children's oral and written
expression by being concerned with molding it prematurely into patterns
and usage which anticipate adult skills. Premature emphasis on usage
makes children self-conscious and dilutes the blithe spirit of fresh, original
expression before it has had time to develop a rich flavor of originality.
Correct the spelling and grammar for young children so that they are
exposed to proper form, but do not *drill* them on matters of usage when
they are just beginning to write.

**Fostering a Classroom Climate in Which Creativity May
Flourish.** The ability to express himself creatively in writing does not
appear automatically as the child develops independence in the mechanics
of writing. As has been noted earlier, effective expression both oral and
written, *is dependent upon previous experiences which create the raw
materials out of which vivid language comes.* Thus the sum total of
kindergarten-primary living is the measure of the child's readiness and
ability to express his ideas in written form. A favorable framework for
the development of language power is established when a teacher provides a classroom climate which is characterized by:

1. A friendly and relaxed atmosphere which is conducive to good
human relationships

2. Freedom to speak and encouragement to express one's thoughts

3. Many appealing firsthand experiences

4. An introduction to the child's heritage of stories and poems

5. Varied play equipment and materials such as blocks, paints, clay,
housekeeping center, or musical instruments which motivate artistic and
dramatic expression.

**Teacher Leadership in Providing Pre-Writing Experiences
which Motivate Creative Expression.** It is the teacher's responsibility
to stimulate, to encourage, and to preserve the imaginative and original
quality of children's expression. The following are some specific suggestions which may be explored at the kindergarten-primary level, both to
develop greater awareness of the nuances of language and to increase
effectiveness in children's appreciation and use of words.

1. Encourage originality in expression by becoming more sensitive to children's speech. Respond to unusual, descriptive, and imaginative language of children through appropriate comments and subtle sharing of the individual pupil's vivid remarks with the entire class whenever possible. Here are some examples of ways in which teachers can tune their ears to children's phrases:

Ann, a kindergarten child, arrived at school all wind-blown from her ride in an open convertible. *"The wind was brushing my hair,"* she announced.

"It certainly was!" her teacher responded. "What a big brush! You might like to paint a picture about the wind brushing your hair this morning."

Keith, in the first grade, told about a new bush in his yard which had just burst into bloom. "We thought they were going to be big, but they are tiny, *as tiny as a penny.*" The teacher encouraged the children to think of other things which were tiny. They took a few moments to share their thoughts:

"... as tiny as an ant."
".... as tiny as a flea."
"... as tiny as a dot."

The second grade discussed a wind storm which had arisen on the previous night. "The wind was *bumping* the windows," said Vic. "It *whacked* ours," said Bob. "The wind *pushed against the wood* and made the glass rattle," offered Margaret. The teacher had an anthology handy and chose this opportune moment to read Christina Rossetti's "Who has seen the Wind?" and "The Wind is a Cat," by E. R. Fuller (see bibliography, Chapter 15).

During art work later in the day many children painted pictures or made chalk drawings of the storm. Some gave the pictures a title and others wrote stories about them with the teacher's help in spelling and writing, depending upon their individual needs.

2. Because firsthand experiences of children are the sources from which oral and written expression most easily flow, teachers should encourage the spontaneous and un-fettered "telling" of simple adventures as an oral foundation for subsequent writing ability:

"What I did on Saturday"
"My vacation"

"Mice in Our Garage"
"My Ride in the Airplane"
"Our Trip to the Pumping Station"
"Why I Like to Swim"
"An Exciting Day"

However well or ineptly the child tells his story, it is his personal creation, his manipulation of verbal symbols, of words which convey his thoughts and feelings. The child's initial creative attempts in school should be enjoyed for what they are and exempt from criticism of flaws in form. Bear in mind that the spirit of self-expression soars with encouragement and recognition, and that it may plummet, broken-winged, to earth if sharply criticized or if derided. The quality of expression grows as the control of the use of words and language forms matures. Later, when the child has become more familiar with the mechanics of writing, he should be able to adapt himself comfortably to writing effectively on paper if he has found initial satisfaction and recognition in oral expression.

3. Although firsthand experiences provide the most provocative and useful material for developing children's expressive power, pictures which "tell stories" also may be introduced to good purpose in the classroom to stimulate creativity. The teacher will find it easy to free a controlled flood of conversation by displaying appealing, interesting drawings or photos about which she asks such questions as:

"What do you think is happening?"

"Who can tell a story about this picture?"

As a rule, pictures of the familiar and of the near-at-hand object or scene are most appropriate with younger children.

4. Another approach which may be employed is the telling of a part of a story and using the device of stopping at a crucial point and asking children:

"What do YOU think might happen now?"

"What would YOU have done?"

"How do YOU think it will end?"

The suggestions given in points 3 or 4 above provide an opportunity for the imagination of children to spill forth through the teacher's subtle guidance.

5. Rich experiences in literature and poetry, such as those suggested and discussed in Chapter 13, are highly important in expanding children's word power. Whether such experiences are used to supplement a

real-life experience (as the second grade teacher in our anecdote used the wind poems) or as a recreational or esthetic experience, children respond to the power of words which, when strung together, create vivid pictures or tell appealing stories. Boys and girls often request their favorite descriptive or "ear-pleasing" passages. "Please read that again," one hears when children encounter the singing words and the powerful imagery of selections such as:

"Swoop, splash, splash, the ringed birds were dashing here and there all about Ping." — *The Story About Ping,* by Marjorie Flack.

". . . the apple trees dancing in the moonlight." — *The Little House,* by Virginia Burton.

". . . the snow lay on the mountains like a chilly white blanket." — *Down, Down the Mountain,* by Ellis Credle.

6. The teacher may occasionally vary the nature of the story time by saying, "I think I'll make up a story today." She may then proceed to weave a fanciful, amusing, or absorbing tale about some character or event as we already have suggested (see Chapter 5, p. 61). Children are especially responsive to a teacher's well-timed and dramatic pauses in a story and "fill in" for her when she asks, "I wonder what should happen next?" Some teachers make good use of a familiar central character in their story sequence, a creature or person who pops up in one adventure after another as the spirit moves the teacher and the class.

You will also find it delightful and educationally profitable to urge children to spin their own yarns, as Bob did with an imaginary lad named Tom:

In the latter part of his first grade year, Bob began relating his stories about Tom. By the end of Bob's year in second grade Tom had enjoyed a wealth of adventures, some of which were both exciting and stirring. The class looked forward to hearing about Tom and the children were always curious to find out what new excitement or misfortune had befallen him.

Bob's friend, Ann, helped him to make sketches for his stories. They were encouraged to assemble them in a booklet. The teacher typed some on the primer typewriter, and Bob copied others. "Tom's Adventures" became a well-worn volume on the second grade library table.

When the teacher musters the forces of her own creativity to sensitize children to the power and beauty of words, and encourages them to express their ideas, she breathes gently upon the spark which kindles creativity in children.

CONSIDERATIONS IN BEGINNING HANDWRITING

As children become involved in the variety of incidents which characterize the dynamic classroom, they discover many reasons to communicate in writing. The teacher in the primary grades should keep the idea of mastery of writing skills in proper perspective—perceiving mastery as a *means* to expression rather than as the *end* result in language development.

Opportunities for Meaningful Writing. Opportunities for *functional* writing during the primary years should be sought so as to provide a framework to support and strengthen the teaching of writing skills. The first grade cookie sale, which was described in Chapter 13, is a useful example of how day-to-day living in school can create a need for writing—say, the messages on posters for announcements or invitations to other classes to "come and buy." Writing is also involved in such activities as making records of progress, preparing notes to parents asking for supplies, recording the money obtained from children who purchased a basket of cookies, and announcing the time and date of the sale.

Here are some events which actually took place in a first grade and which illustrate the functional or applied use of writing for reasons that boys and girls understand and accept.

Mrs. Frank told the first grade they might use the facilities of the kitchen on Friday for baking. It was decided to write the notes requesting parents to permit children to bring supplies on Wednesday. The teacher wisely commented that, "If we forget our materials Thursday morning we can bring them on Friday." On Tuesday the group composed the letter each child would copy and carry home. As the children decided on the phrasing, the teacher wrote their ideas on the chalkboard. The notes read as follows:

Dear Mother,

     We are going to bake cookies.
We will make snickledoodles.
May I bring ____ ____ ____ ____ ?

       Love, (Name)

As the teacher wrote, she called attention to various aspects of the mechanics of writing in an informal fashion; thus:

"What kind of *d* shall I make when I write 'Dear'? What mark comes after mother? Who remembers where we start to write 'We are going to make'? What kind of mark shall I put after cookies? After snickledoodles? Why? At the end of the last sentence? Why? Who knows where we sign our names? Show us, Betty. Will you write 'name' there so we'll all know where to put our names? (Betty was helped with spelling as needed.)

"Let's read our letter again." (The class and teacher read it together.) "Did we remember to say everything we need to say?"

"We didn't tell when to bring the things," cried Karen.

"That's right, we didn't. Where can we add it?"

"We could put 'tomorrow' after sugar or flour or whatever we're bringing," offered David after a little thought. "What would it say then?" asked Mrs. Frank. "Do you agree with David? Then we'll erase the question mark and write *tomorrow*. What mark do we need after tomorrow?

"Yes, we still need the question mark. It is still a question, isn't it? Who will read the question again? Let's read the letter once more to be sure we're all satisfied."

The next morning, when it was time to write the letters, the class reviewed the form and words to be used before starting to copy the message.

"What words begin with capitals?" asked the teacher. The children enumerated them. "Which word is the longest?

"Yes, snickledoodles is a long word, isn't it? Name the tall letters in it. Yes, *k*, *d*—how many *d*'s?—and *l*. Does it have any letters that go below the line?

"No, it doesn't, does it? How tall will you make the other letters in it? Yes, the *s*, *i*, *n*, *o*, and *e* are just half as tall. Do you remember what you are asking to bring? Can you find your name on the chart next to it?

"Are there any questions? Well, then, let's get started."

Since this experience occurred rather late in the year (it was at Easter time), many children had become sufficiently skilled in writing to copy the complete letter. The teacher, however, had previously prepared dittoed copies of the letter complete except for the last sentence, "May I bring _____ _____ _____ tomorrow?" These form letters were on hand for the use of those children who were at an earlier stage on the writing continuum. Even more complete copies were made for two children who still found writing somewhat laborious and were ready for a very limited amount of copying. The entire message was written out for them except for the spaces for the ingredients, *2 cups of flour*, and their signatures.

The recipe for snickledoodles, printed on a chart with a large picture of an inviting display of cookies, was in view on the reading chart rack.

Another chart, posted on a board adjoining the note, contained the recipe broken down into portions or units which each child would bring followed by the names of children who would bring each ingredient:

```
I cup of sugar      {Betty
                     Jack
                     Mary

2 cups of flour     {Bob
                     Ann
                     Sally

I cube of butter    {Eric
                     Glenn
                     Bruce

I egg               {Jean
                     Carol
                     Mike
```

The preceding description of a writing experience is similar in nature to many writing activities which may occur or be devised in the first and second grades. The quantity of copying which is done in any single experience, and how much specific direction and guidance are given before each writing task, is dependent upon the time of year, the complexity of the message, and the stage of physical and linguistic development of the group. The numerous writing opportunities suggested earlier expand with the increasing maturity of the group.

Stages in the Development of Writing Skills. It is desirable to keep in mind the fact that the child progresses through a sequence of steps in his development of writing skill. These steps may roughly be identified with four phases of growing independence and competence:

1. *Dictation—the early oral stage.* The child does no writing. This develops from telling spontaneously about an experience to a more thoughtful, organized, and sequential expression of ideas in letters, group stories, and reports, which are transcribed by the teacher.

2. *Copying—a stage during which the children continue to dictate their ideas to the teacher.* The experience becomes more personal as boys and girls grow in their ability to copy part or all of the material.

3. *Partial independence but with much teacher aid — children write without a sample.* They put their thoughts on paper but need much help from the teacher with respect to letter form, spelling, and spacing.

4. *Increasing independence—characterized by the ability to use self-help materials.* The child has developed so sufficient a mastery of the tools

of writing as to be able to use class word lists and similar self-help and reference materials. At this stage an increasing number of youngsters need a minimum amount of aid from the teacher.

A more detailed presentation of these steps, with additional discussion and comment, may be found in books listed in the bibliography.[1]

Development of fine-muscle co-ordination, a prerequisite to skill in writing, appears at different times in individual boys and girls. Some first grade children's small-muscle co-ordination is so well-developed that they are able to produce a sample of the teacher's writing with an almost photostatic fidelity. Others, whose small-muscle development is progressing more slowly, have the greatest difficulty in reproducing even the simpler straight and curved lines used in manuscript letter forms. Thus, writing assignments made in the primary grades *must not make uniform demands of all children.*

In the *early* part of the first grade the amount of actual writing which children do is, of necessity, very limited. Some children, however, profit by continued opportunities to practice writing their names. Teachers may have cards with the children's names lettered upon them so that they can be used as samples or guides when the children need to sign their names. Notes to parents which the group has composed may be mimeographed or otherwise duplicated and signed by each child so as to personalize the experience.

Later in the year messages may be reproduced with the key word or words omitted: e.g., "We need newspapers ," "We need milk cartons ," or "Come to the party ." As skill in writing increases, many children may be able to fill in the salutation and some important part of the message as well as their signatures. The amount of copying children are able to do increases with the practice gained through experiences of this type as well as with maturity.

Eventually during the first grade children are able to

[1]For example, see Ruth Strickland, *The Language Arts in the Elementary School* (Boston: D. C. Heath, 1957). The four steps listed are adapted from Strickland.

copy whole sentences. Do not be surprised, however, if a few continue to find sufficient challenge in writing their names and copying one word or phrase. Also, expect to find some boys and girls who are carried away by the pleasure they take in their new skill of writing and copy everything in sight: the names of the children on the attendance chart, the names of colors from the color chart, or group compositions from the reading charts about the room. Some continue this practice at home and bring samples of their writing to show the teacher. "These are the names of everyone in my family," a child will say, or "This is a story I wrote:"

My cat is lazy.

She sleeps all day.

Mechanical Aspects of Handwriting. Some teachers who *want* to approach the teaching of writing skills through the use of meaningful material are uncertain *when* and *how* to help children gain successful mastery of the mechanical skills involved.

Especially the beginning teacher is eager to know "When and how do we teach children correct letter forms, packing, and spacing? How much practice do we need to provide on individual letters?" The following suggestions are made as general guides to practice, although the professional judgment of the teacher should dictate the specific timing of the procedures she employs.

1. Beginning writing attempts should be characterized by large and free strokes rather than confined within narrow lined spaces. Blackboards, easels, or large sheets of newsprint may be used. Since the small-muscle control of most fives and young sixes is limited, the use of the large muscles in these initial writing attempts should be encouraged to avoid strain and fatigue.

Although children presumably understand the meaning of the words they copy — *rabbit, party, thank you* — in their initial efforts, most children at first draw the letter symbols with a limited comprehension of the names of *individual* letters or their sounds. Children should not be confused during this stage of their development by having undue stress placed on individual letters or diphthongs rather than on words as a whole.

2. Spaces between which to form letters may be made by folding manila or butcher's paper as children become ready to write within more limited confines.

3. As skill increases, lined paper may be introduced for those children whose co-ordinations suggest that they are *ready* to use lined paper. Beginning spaces are usually made about one inch in height. Some teachers like to use paper, commercially available, which has a dotted line or a

light colored line as a guide for the height of the lower case letters. Such paper, with groups of three lines set one-half inch apart and having one inch spaces between groups, is satisfactory. Also, paper lined according to the teacher's choice may be machine-duplicated for use during this early stage. Caution should be exercised in pacing the children's skill development to their stage of growth.

4. When a child is working at a table, it is suitable to have a sample before him while he works. Since eye-hand co-ordination in these early stages is still developing, too much strain is imposed by looking up and down and back and forth to the blackboard. The teacher may use carbon paper and make two or three sets of samples to accommodate eight or twelve children at a time for a class project. As children become more skillful, they may copy from the board, but should be seated *near* the sample and *facing* it.

5. For their beginning attempts, children may use chalk or crayons to form letters. When they begin to write on lined paper, they may use a large beginner's pencil. Research suggests that standard size pencils are all right to use, too, depending on personal preference.

6. It is important that the teacher's writing be firm, bold, and exact. Teachers who lack certainty and ease in manuscript forms should practice to perfect their skill. The teacher may use a music staff liner for her chalkboard copy so as to indicate for her the heights and relationships existing among the letter forms she writes. Or she may wish to line a portion of the chalkboard with horizontal marks made with a pencil. Pencil marks are almost invisible from a distance of ten feet, but show up clearly when one is at the board. Also, such marks will survive several weeks of repeated washing before they need to be renewed.

a b c d e

abcde

1 2 3 4

7. First and second grade rooms should have a permanent alphabet and a sample of arabic numbers visible for easy reference. These may be written across the top of the chalkboard, printed on tagboard by the teacher, or purchased commercially. (See Chapter 15, p. 275.)

8. As the children gain the understanding that writing is "talk written down," and as they grow in power to

recognize letters, more attention may be focused on the formation of individual letters. For example:

Miss Klein wrote Luke's name on the board, commenting on the way she formed the initial letter. "This is the name of someone in our room. The first letter of the name is very tall! It starts at the top of the line and goes to the bottom of the line. Iᐟ   The arrow shows me where to go. Now, I turn the corner and stop. Lᐟ   Remember this is the beginning letter of the person's name. Now the rest of the name looks like this: Luke .

"Who knows who this is? You're right, Luke, this is *your* name. Can you come and write your name for us? Good. Notice the way he began at the top and went to the bottom of the line.

"Does anyone else's name begin with the same letter? Yes, yours does, Letty. Will you write your name for us? Let's all copy their names in our telephone books."

The teacher walked around the room, giving necessary guidance, as the youngsters wrote the two names in the "telephone books" which each was compiling to take home.

9. The teacher studies the children's written work for clues to their needs and progress. She provides practice situations to help children cope with letters which seem troublesome in their writing activities. In these writing experiences the teacher may choose to emphasize one or two letters (usually one which is repeated in the phrase which is being written) so as to provide concentrated instruction and specific guidance. She often works with small groups on several different writing tasks and gives individual help as children are working.

10. Attention should be given to spacing between letters and between words in each writing experience. Encourage children to study the phrase and to notice that letters within the word are close together with a wider space between words. Manuals listed in the bibliography offer suitable suggestions for specific teaching techniques in packing and spacing.

11. The same general procedures that are followed in teaching manuscript forms may be employed in teaching children how to write *numbers*. As they number pages in their booklets, write telephone numbers and dates, or make calendars, children should be taught where to start and how to form the number symbols.

12. Reversals are often made by children in writing both letters and numbers. *s, N, 3* are among the symbols commonly reversed during the early writing stages. It is desirable to help children establish *from the outset* the left-to-right direction of whole words and phrases as well as to show them *just where* to begin individual numbers and letters.

13. The beginning teacher, or a teacher who is new in a school, has

an initial responsibility in becoming acquainted with the method of handwriting suggested in the curriculum guide used in the school. Often this is a commercial manual, like *Handwriting Aid for Primary Teachers* mentioned in the bibliography, or a mimeographed or printed form that a local committee of teachers has devised.

14. In the course of writing experiences throughout first and second grade, children usually begin to learn various aspects of written language usage—especially punctuation. These include the knowledge that:

   a) A period follows a "telling" sentence.

   b) A question mark follows an "asking" sentence.

   c) A comma follows the greeting in a letter—e.g., *Dear Mother,*—and follows *With love,* in the complimentary close.

   d) Capital letters are used at the beginning of sentences, for names of people, pets, and places (cities, schools, etc.), for days of the week, for the months, and for main words in the titles of stories.

   e) There is a definite prose form for use in writing stories and a letter form for the many letters which they write.

The use of paste, scissors, painting materials, clay, and safe woodworking tools helps develop the eye-hand coordination essential for writing. Work with these art and craft materials is needed to balance any emphasis placed on practice in writing letters of the alphabet in letters, invitations, and so on.

By the end of first grade, a child's writing occasionally indicates that he has a desire and readiness to use cursive letter forms. He may try to connect the letters, adopt a slant, and use some cursive symbols. Usually during the second grade an increasing number of children show this inclination to use cursive writing. They begin to sign their names with connected letters and try to write a few words with the letters linked. These children, more often than not, are "inspired" by older brothers and sisters or by parents who are eager to see them use cursive writing. The teacher may help these youngsters to write their names and some words in cursive form when they request such help, but

Anne
Tom
Alice
Joe

a complete change to cursive writing is usually delayed until some time during the third grade. (See Chapter 4, pp. 49 and 50.)

SPELLING IN THE PRIMARY GRADES: PROCEDURES THAT HELP YOUNGER CHILDREN LEARN TO SPELL

Even though spelling, as such, may not be taught, teachers of kinder-garten-primary children need to understand both the skills involved in spelling and how to use effective techniques in laying foundations which will aid children in developing ability in spelling. Since the teaching of spelling (in the sense of using weekly spelling lists) does not begin in most school systems until some time in the second or early third grade, some uncertainty prevails concerning instruction in functional spelling during the early primary years. An analysis of what skills are involved in spelling is helpful in determining the types of activities which lead to growth in spelling power.

Spelling is a sensory-motor skill. *Seeing, hearing, saying,* and *writing* are involved. Activities in kindergarten-primary years which lead to growth in the ability to listen, observe, and improve muscular co-ordi-nation (including eye-hand co-ordination) are foundations for spelling skills. Exposure to meaningful language experiences is a prime prerequi-site, since the need for spelling occurs only when children are *motivated to spell* by their experiences.

Teachers recognize that any *one* activity or task in which children engage involves many learnings. This is particularly true at the kinder-garten-primary level. In the following suggestions descriptions are given of a few of the many activities which have a high potential for fostering skill in spelling—along with many other language skills.

Learning to Spell Through Speaking. Since oral language power ripens sooner than the ability to use written language, the procedures discussed in Chapter 11 with respect to the development of facility in oral language *are equally applicable to the development of spelling skills.* Accurate pronunciation, enunciation, and articulation are particularly important in spelling since children tend to spell what they hear. The following are some of the daily activities in a kindergarten-primary pro-gram which foster readiness for spelling:

1. *Rhymes, jingles, poems, and stories which foster auditory skills.* Children and teachers may become their own "poets" and make up rhymes after many experiences with verses and books such as Fritz Eichenberg's *Dancing in the Moon:*[2]

---

[2]From *Dancing in the Moon,* copyright 1955 by Fritz Eichenberg. By permission of Harcourt, Brace and Company, Inc.

> 1 raccoon dancing in the moon
> 2 moose scaring a papoose.

Some mature kindergarten children, and nearly all first and second grade children, love the delightful rhyming quality of books such as *Madeline*, by Ludwig Bemelmans:[3]

> In the middle of the night
> Miss Clavel turned on her light
> and said, "Something is not right."

and of course the lovely nonsense verses in Dr. Seuss's rhyming books are perennial favorites. Consider *Horton Hatches the Egg:*[4]

> Then out of the wagon
> And onto a ship!
> Out over the ocean . . .
> And oooh, what a trip!

2. *Make use of pupils' names as a basis for simple spelling—their own names.* Children *know* them so well and *use* them so much! They provide a basis for the simple beginnings in learning to read, to write, and to spell. In kindergarten and first grade, children can be encouraged to try to discriminate likenesses in the beginning sounds of names and names which rhyme:

"Whose name begins like Marilyn's?" (Margaret, Matt, and Milton respond.)

"Listen carefully while I say Mary's name. Can you think of a name that rhymes with Mary? Yes, Larry, your name does."

3. *Make use of music.* Many of the lyrics in songs for young children have a wonderful rhythmic repetition of words or initial sounds as well as rhyming features.

> . . . Jump, Jim along,
> Jim along Josie.

> . . . There was an old woman and she had a little *pig*.
> It didn't cost much and it wasn't very *big* —
> Oink, oink, oink.

Distinguishing between animal sounds, such as the "oink" of the pig and the "quack" of the duck, is a pleasant way to encourage the early beginnings in auditory discrimination.

Visual discrimination is essential in spelling. Ability to discriminate likenesses and differences in sizes and shapes—tall, short, curved, angular,

---

[3]From *Madeline* by Ludwig Bemelmans, copyright 1939. By permission of Viking Press, Inc.

[4]From *Horton Hatches the Egg* by Dr. Seuss, copyright 1940. By permission of Random House, Inc.

thin, and fat—is provided by many kindergarten-primary
activities. The grasping of spatial concepts such as *above*
and *below, over* and *under, in* and *on,* is also a prerequisite
for subsequent success in spelling. Opportunities for increasing the sharpness of children's visual discrimination
include:

1. *Block play* to give children practice in discriminating
shapes and sizes. "I need a long one for this track." "I
need a round one here for the wheel."

2. *Working with puzzles* which involve discrimination of
shapes, sizes, and colors. Children learn how to "fit pieces
together to make a 'whole' configuration."

3. *Observing and discussing abstract shapes and sizes.*
Children become acquainted with the concept of a *circle*
through their circle games, balls, hoops, and many other
materials used. *Triangles* are used for rhythm instruments
and called by this name. Square and rectangular blocks are
used and the teacher refers to these by name. "You need
one of the 'square' blocks." Many other ways of introducing
quantitative, spatial, and relationship concepts occur every
day in every classroom.

Learning to Spell Through Reading. A young child,
in learning to read, is acquiring skills that will be helpful
to him as he becomes a speller. Some of these double-edged
learnings are:

1. The left-to-right direction of our word structure.

2. The configuration of the word to be considered which
shows letter height, shape, and length.

3. The ability to visualize words.

4. The ability to recall words.

After the beginning reader develops a small sight vocabulary, his attention may be focused upon the *elements* in
a word. These skills may also be helpful to the beginning
speller:

1. Recognition of initial consonants—learned in the order

in which they appear in the child's reading vocabulary.

2. Recognition of final consonants—consonants heard at the ends of words.

3. Recognition of common elements in words, such as *an, all, at.*

4. Recognition of consonant digraphs—two letters that spell or make one sound such as *wh* as in *what, ch* as in *children.*

5. Recognition of consonant blends—such as *pl* in *play, fr* in *from.*

6. Learning suffixes such as *ing, s, ed, ly,* and using them in building new words—*helping, boys, talked, slowly.*

7. Building compound words such as *something* and *into.*

Learning to Spell Through Writing. Children in the first and second grades learn to spell through the functional writing activities in which they engage. The child's first spelling task is to make sure that he has copied correctly. This is done by checking to see that his word or words match the sample he is using. In these activities he is progressing through certain of the basic steps in learning to spell: "see it, say it, think it, write it, and check it."

As the teacher keeps an eye on children's problems and progress in functional writing activities, she encourages their careful scrutiny of the words written. In the beginning she calls attention to the general configuration of the word. As children grow in their reading skills and learn letter names, she encourages the use of the word analysis skills which they are learning. For example:

1. The teacher encourages children to pronounce the words accurately and is careful in her own pronunciation so that children hear the final *t* in *kept, d* in *stayed,* the *ru* in *February,* or the *em* in *them.*

2. The teacher asks for comments on the general shape of the word, such as the unusual length of *snickledoodles.* She asks children to notice the capital letters, the "tall letters," or the letters that extend below the line.

3. The teacher helps early first grade children to see likenesses and differences in general word configuration. Later the teacher encourages more specific analysis. In the letter asking for cookie ingredients, which was reproduced in a preceding section, the group's attention was focused on the words *make* and *bake.*

"How are they alike?" asked Mrs. Frank.

"They end the same," said Peter.

"And the last 3 letters are the same," Mike volunteered.

Then Mrs. Frank asked, "How are they different?"

"The first letters are different! *Make* begins with an *m* and *bake* begins with a *b*," offered Nell.

The teacher at this point may ask the children if they can think of any other words that sound like *make* and *bake*. Children may volunteer *take*, *lake*, and *brake* or *break*. At this point the teacher might demonstrate the two spellings of "break" and "brake" and discusses the meanings of each. The teacher may also write all these words on the board so that the children may see as well as hear the words. Often, too, the teacher supplies clues for building words—e.g., "If I put an *r* in front of *ake*, it means something you use to gather leaves. What is it?"

4. The teacher sometimes writes the phrase or sentence and asks for volunteers who will try to spell some of the words. "We have had the word *we* in many of our stories and letters. Who can tell us what letters are in the word *we?*" "With what letter does *mother* start?" "When we write *boys*, what letter must come at the end to show that we are writing about more than one boy?"

5. The teacher takes the opportunity to help children visualize words. In this way they develop the ability to proofread, to sense errors in copying. A misspelled word just "doesn't look right" to the child with growing powers of visual acuity.

6. The teacher aids children as they begin to write "on their own" without a sample. In their initial independent attempts, the teacher quickly supplies the word or phrase, preferably on a slip of paper, or she may write it on the chalkboard.

7. The second grade teacher develops word lists from words most frequently used in children's writing, words like *dear, we, mother, father, the, thank, you, come, like, and,* or *need*. These words may be written on a chart for quick reference. During a particular class interest, word charts may be made of words used in a given project or unit of study —"farm" words, "food" words, or "airplane" words, for instance.

Some children may be helped to make individual dictionaries of words they use. Shoe boxes with alphabetical index cards cut to the desired length have been used successfully by some teachers. Children write the words they have requested and file them for future reference. Beginning dictionary skills are encouraged in this manner. The teacher may also have words in alphabetical order on some of the word lists for class reference.

To sum up, *first grade spelling skills are developed in the context of the children's functional writing experiences.* This approach continues in the second grade. When children are writing to serve real purposes, they will *want* to learn how to spell and assume some responsibility in this learning.

Later in the second grade or in the beginning third grade, *a more systematic approach to spelling may be introduced.* The teacher often uses word lists made up of the words which are of particular interest for the group, words which have given trouble in the children's writing, or may check the needs with a published basic word list.

It must be remembered that all children do not learn to spell in the same manner. Visual approaches meet the needs of most children, but some children are more dependent upon learning by ear or through kinesthetic approaches. As in all teaching, individual differences must be recognized, studied, and acknowledged through constant modification of the program as intelligence dictates.

CHAPTER 15

Reference Helps for the Teacher
Beginning Language Instruction
with Younger Children

The Teacher's Grasp of Current Professional Language Arts
Resources

Selected and Annotated List of Supplementary Readings in the
Language Arts

Books about the Young School-Age Child and How He Grows
General Books and Pamphlets about the Young School-Age Child
and His Development in the Realm of the Language Arts
Supplementary Readings Treating the Young School-Age Child and
His Experiences as a Reader and a Writer
Supplementary Readings about the Young School-Age Child and
His Experiences as a Speaker and a Listener

Favorite Books, Old and New, for the Fives, Sixes, and Sevens

Books that Help to Answer Children's Questions about People, Ani-
mals, Places, and Things
Books that Inspire and Stimulate the Imagination
Books that Have Ideas that Are Funny
Books that Have Ideas that Are Linked to Their Illustrations

Literary Readers

Instructional Materials for Use in Language Instruction

Books Which Are Helpful in Reviewing and Selecting Books for
Young Children
Collections of Materials for Sharing with Children
Publications Which May Be Used in Fostering Observation and
Communication through Science Interests
Audio-Visual and Music Materials Which Are Useful for Developing
Listening and Observing Experiences
Resources for Speech Activities
Supply and Equipment Catalogs and Pamphlets
Tests, Spelling, and Handwriting Aids

Reference Helps for the Teacher
Beginning Language Instruction
with Younger Children

Chapter 1 stressed that when the young child comes to school he is on the threshold of a new world of meanings. Those who work with him must strive to understand and to meet his present communication needs. This means constant renewal of our knowledge and continuing review of the available resources for bettering the language development of the kindergarten-primary child.

THE TEACHER'S GRASP OF CURRENT PROFESSIONAL LANGUAGE ARTS RESOURCES

This section of *Beginning Language Arts Instruction with Children* is built around three categories of professional resources:

1. An annotated list of language arts books for adults.
2. Old and new favorite books of the fives, sixes, and sevens.
3. Instructional materials which are useful for teaching the language arts in the classroom.

None of our selections are exhaustive, but are chosen for the following reasons: they are (1) generally available, (2) explicitly helpful to the teacher in her efforts to broaden the language arts program, and (3) highly readable.

SELECTED AND ANNOTATED LIST OF
SUPPLEMENTARY READINGS IN THE LANGUAGE ARTS

A. Books about the Young School-Age Child and How He Grows
   1. Almy, Millie. *Child Development*. New York: Henry Holt & Co.,
   1955.
   The first eight chapters, in particular, present a lucid and creative
   interpretation of the child's development.
   2. Gesell, Arnold L., and others. *The Child from Five to Ten*. New
   York: Harper & Brothers, 1946.
   Presents developmental profiles of the elementary school child. A
   very helpful resource in understanding general growth patterns.
   3. Jenkins, Gladys Gardner, Helen Schacter, and William W. Bauer.
   These Are Your Children (expanded ed.). Chicago: Scott, Foresman and Co., 1953.
   Developmental patterns and characteristics of children from birth
   to fourteen. Stories of children are supplemented with excellent
   pictures. An easy-to-read volume. Valuable supplementary material
   to share with parents.
   4. Stone, Laurence Joseph and Joseph Church. *Childhood and Adolescence*. New York: Random House, 1957.
   A book of well-presented material on understanding child growth
   and development. Written for both the professional person and the
   layman. The authors are members of the Department of Child Study
   at Vassar College. Chapter 7 will be of most use to the kindergarten-
   primary teacher. Individual differences are adroitly developed.

B. General Books and Pamphlets about the Young School-Age
Child and His Development in the Realm of the Language Arts.
   All of these volumes contain sections on oral language, listening, literature, writing, spelling, handwriting, dramatic interpretation, and
   so forth.
   1. Association for Supervision and Curriculum Development. *Creating a Good Environment for Learning*. Washington, D. C.: National
   Education Association, 1954.
   Contains exceptionally good illustrations and suggestions for teachers. The many forces which contribute to a good learning environment are discussed. Chapter 1, which would be of interest for all
   teachers of grade one, is a diary account of school living.
   2. Dawson, Mildred A. and Marion Zollinger. *Guiding Language
   Learning*. Tarrytown-on-Hudson, N. Y.: World Book Co., 1957.

A comprehensive discussion of many of the language art skills: listening, speaking, writing, reading, literature, etc.

3. Gans, Roma, Celia Stendler and Millie Almy. *Teaching Young Children*. Tarrytown-on-Hudson, N. Y.: World Book Co., 1952. This book presents the child development point of view in teaching. The understanding of children and their world are guideposts in developing the curriculum. Part III, Chapters 7 and 8, will be of particular interest to the classroom teacher in the language arts, for they discuss the child as a reader, a speaker, a writer, and a listener.

4. Herrick, Virgil E., Leland B. Jacobs, *et al. Children and the Language Arts*. Englewood Cliffs, N. J.: Prentice-Hall, Inc., 1955.
Contributions are made by eighteen language arts authorities, including Alvina Treut Burrows, Robert Pooley, Dora V. Smith, and Miriam Wilt. The book has three sections:

a) Section One is related to *The Role of Language Arts in the Elementary School.*

b) Section Two is related to *Modern Teaching Practices in the Language Arts.*

c) Section Three is related to *Modern Practices in the Organization of the Language Arts.*

Section Two will be particularly interesting to the classroom teacher, for it devotes eleven chapters to discussions of the child's experiences in speaking, writing, reading, and listening. Research findings are presented, and a selected bibliography is helpful for suggestions for further reading.

5. Hildreth, Gertrude. *Readiness for School Beginners*. Tarrytown-on-Hudson, N. Y.: World Book Co., 1950.
An excellent book for all first grade teachers. The concept of readiness is carefully developed throughout. Chapters 15 and 16 deal with specific techniques in developing readiness for reading.

6. National Council of Teachers of English, Commission on the English Curriculum. *Language Arts for Today's Children*, Vols. I and II. New York: Appleton-Century-Crofts, Inc., 1954.
Volume I has an excellent bibliography on language arts books in specific subject areas as well as on general references. (441-480) Volume II is specifically focused on the language arts in the elementary school.

7. Shane, Harold G., ed. *Research Helps in Teaching the Language Arts*. Washington, D. C.: Association for Supervision and Cur-

riculum Development, National Education Association, 1955.

A resume of hundreds of research studies which "deal with the language arts questions that teachers probably ask most often." These questions are considered under nine categories: reading, handwriting, creative writing, spelling, language usage, children's literature, listening, foreign language, and oral English.

8. Strickland, Ruth. *Language Arts in the Elementary School.* (Rev. ed.). Boston: D. C. Heath, 1957.

An excellent revision of a good book. The full range of language arts is covered: language development, speaking, reading, handwriting, creative writing, spelling, dramatics, literature, etc. It is a readable, practical, and attractive volume.

C. Supplementary Readings about the Young School-Age Child and His Experiences as a Reader and Writer

1. Applegate, Mauree. *Helping Children Write.* Evanston, Ill.: Row, Peterson & Company, 1954.

The author of this practical volume is not offering patterns for creative writing, but is describing situations in which some teachers have helped children release the creativity within them. She states that for the most part the writings were done by average children. She does record techniques which other teachers might find helpful.

2. Association for Childhood Education. *More About Reading.* Washington, D. C.: The Association, 1960.

Places emphasis on individualized reading and self-selection in reading.

3. Causey, Oscar S. *The Reading Teacher's Reader.* New York: The Ronald Press Co., 1958.

The compilation of the viewpoints of distinguished contributors makes this book a valuable addition to the professional library of a school or an individual. Thirty-five of eighty-one articles deal with effective methods and procedures in the teaching of reading. The remaining articles deal with the nature of the reading process, phonics, vocabulary, emotional factors, and other important considerations in the teaching of reading.

4. Freeman, Frank N. *Teaching Handwriting: What Research Says to the Teacher.* Washington, D. C.: Department of Classroom Teachers, American Educational Research Association, National Education Association, 1954.

This booklet will give the in-service teacher the most important suggestions for the teaching of handwriting that have been discovered through research.

5. Gans, Roma. *Reading is Fun.* New York: Bureau of Publications, Teachers College, Columbia University, 1949.
   This book is helpful to parents and teachers seeking an understanding of some of the problems which confront children in learning to read. The emphasis is on making initial reading experiences of children satisfying.

6. Hildreth, Gertrude. *Teaching Reading.* New York: Henry Holt and Co., 1958.
   This is a comprehensive book on the teaching of reading. Chapters 9, 10, 11, and 12 have particular interest for kindergarten-primary teachers.

7. Hildreth, Gertrude. *Teaching Spelling.* New York: Henry Holt and Co., 1955.
   Trends in spelling instruction and the learning process in spelling are discussed in the first two chapters. Chapters 3 and 4 deal with instructional techniques in the readiness and early primary periods.

8. Hymes, James L., Jr. *Before the Child Reads.* Evanston, Illinois: Row, Peterson & Co., 1958.
   An easy reading volume on "pacing" a child in pre-reading and reading skills capitalizing on the child's ideas, skills, and natural drives. Excellent for parents and teachers of young children.

9. McKim, Margaret G. *Guiding Growth in Reading.* New York: The Macmillan Co., 1955.
   A comprehensive review of the reading program for both the experienced teacher and the beginner. Concrete suggestions are given in relation to such things as skill development, evaluation, and the interrelatedness of reading with all language arts experiences.

10. Miel, Alice, ed. *Individualizing Reading Practices.* No. 14. New York: Bureau of Publications, Teachers College, Columbia University, 1958.
    An inspirational pamphlet giving practical suggestions for the teaching of individualized reading. Leland Jacobs lists and discusses thirteen "insights" essential to the program. Reports of classroom practices enliven the monograph and give information on teacher guidance of skill and interest development. The appendix includes a bibliography of books and periodical articles related to individualized reading.

11. Monroe, Marion. *Growing into Reading.* Chicago: Scott, Foresman and Co., 1951.
    Interprets the nature of reading readiness and its relationship to

the many aspects of child development. The teaching problems are clearly presented with specific procedures which may be employed in promoting readiness to learn to read.

12. Neubauer, Dorothy, ed. "Handwriting," *The National Elementary Principal*. XXXVIII: No. 5, entire issue (February, 1959).
Nine excellent articles on the subject with a Handwriting Bibliography featured on page 30. Perhaps the first three articles, pages 8—15, will be of primary interest to the teacher of beginning writers: *Handwriting in the Primary Program, Handwriting and Child Development and Suggestions for the "Lefties."*

13. Neubauer, Dorothy, ed. "Spelling," *The National Elementary Principal*. XXXVIII: No. 7, entire issue (May, 1959).
The May issue of this publication features material on spelling. The teacher of young children will find some help in understanding the psychology and techniques of teaching spelling. The usual, well related bibliography is found on page 23.

14. Olson, Willard C. *Seeking, Self-Selection and Pacing in the Use of Books by Children*. Boston: D. C. Heath and Co., 1952.
Mentioned in text. Refer to "Individualized Reading," Chapter 13, page 194. Also included in Jeannette Veatch's book (see reference 17 below).

15. Rehage, Kenneth J., ed. "Selected References on Elementary-School Instruction: II. The Subject Fields," *The Elementary School Journal*. LX, No. 2 (November, 1959).
Each year the Elementary School Journal presents a series of three well selected lists on instruction in the elementary school. The second list of the 1959 edition offers references on foreign languages, the language arts, and the library program. The lists are by no means exhaustive, but are well chosen and timely. A usable reference for a teacher.

16. Skinner, Blanche. "Spelling and the Language Arts," *Elementary English*. XXXI: 79-81 (February, 1954).
An account of second grade activities in which spelling was an outgrowth of other language arts activities.

17. Veatch, Jeannette. *Individualizing Your Reading Program*. New York: G. P. Putnam's Sons, 1959.
A champion for individualizing reading describes this approach and collects action research articles to substantiate her cause.

D. Supplementary Readings about the Young School-Age Child and His Experiences as a Speaker and a Listener

1. Adams, Bess Porter. *About Books and Children*. New York: Henry Holt and Co., 1953.

   A readable, helpful volume on children's literature. Mrs. Adams obviously enjoys both children and books, and serves as an excellent guide in the field.

2. Arbuthnot, May Hill. *Children and Books* (Rev. ed.). Chicago: Scott, Foresman & Co., 1957.

   This is a comprehensive volume treating reading interests from toddler to adolescent. It is encyclopedic in its proportions, offering material on the history of children's literature, poetry, books, authors, illustrators, instructional suggestions, book lists, etc.

3. Association for Childhood Education. *Storytelling*. Washington, D. C.: The Association, 1942.

4. Association for Childhood Education International. *Children and TV*. No. 95. Washington, D. C.: The Association, 1954.

   Suggests ways of helping children build up standards and habits in relation to TV listening and selection. Contributors include Paul A. Witty and James L. Hymes, Jr.

5. Association for Childhood Education. *Learning to Speak Effectively*. Washington, D. C.: The Association, 1943.

   A pamphlet on speech education which is focused on helping parents and teachers of young children. Speech specialists are the chief contributors, and offer material on recognition of speech defects and how to understand their causes. A section on activities that give practice in learning to speak effectively is included.

6. Frank, Josette. *Television: How to Use it Wisely With Children*. New York: Child Study Association of America, 1959.

   The picture of TV and its effects, both good and bad, on children. Suggestions are given for obtaining better programing.

7. Lease, Ruth and Geraldine Brain Siks. *Creative Dramatics in Home, School, and Community*. New York: Harper and Brothers, 1952.

   This is a down-to-earth, creative dramatics book focused toward encouraging the child's self-expression. Written with sincerity and enthusiasm, it has many practical suggestions for procedures, materials, objectives, and possible outcomes. This book also serves to increase confidence in the adult developing the activity.

   Chapter 2 is particularly helpful to the primary teacher. The three appendices give many examples of poetry and stories for dramatization, possible pantomimes for simple play, and a good bibliography on creative teaching and child psychology.

8. Meyer, Alberta L. "Television, Radio, Films: Barrier or Challenge?" *Childhood Education.* XXXI:431-34 (May, 1955).
Among other things, the article reported that 163 communities (at the time it was written) had educational radio stations. They featured some in-school programs focused toward language arts, science, social studies interests, etc.
The author discusses the adult's responsibility in helping the child build standards of taste, good judgment, and critical appreciation for each type of communication media.

9. Sawyer, Ruth. *The Way of the Storyteller.* New York: The Viking Press, 1942.
The title is descriptive of the contents of the book. A helpful volume in stimulating the adult's creative imagination for storytelling.

10. Siks, Geraldine Brain. *Creative Dramatics, an Art for Children.* New York: Harper & Brothers, 1958.
This book is a supplement to Mrs. Siks earlier book (see number D-7 above, Lease and Siks). The art of Creative Dramatics is clearly explained, the role of the leader is clarified, pictures of participating children are described, and another good list of suitable material is given.

11. Thompson, Barbara K. "Improving the Young Child's Speech," *N.E.A. Journal.* December, 1959. 13-14.
A very readable article which discusses the main objectives for speech improvement in the kindergarten-primary program. Suggested activities are included which may serve as a guide to the classroom teacher.

12. Thompson, Elizabeth Engle and Arthur E. Hamaloinen. *Foreign Language Teaching in Elementary Schools.* Washington, D. C.: Association for Supervision and Curriculum Development, 1958.
This study reports or discusses:
a) Existing types of foreign language programs in our schools.
b) Problems of when, where, and how instruction begins.
c) Suggestions for evaluating the program.
d) General value of the program.

13. Ward, Winifred. *Playmaking with Children, From Kindergarten Through Junior High School* (Rev. ed.). New York: Appleton-Century-Crofts, Inc., 1957.
Chapter 2 is especially helpful for the kindergarten-primary teacher. This is an inspirational book for the adult, giving excellent sugges-

tions for creative leadership. A very good bibliography, story list, and record list are included.

14. Witty, Paul. *Reading in Modern Education*. Boston: D. C. Heath and Co., 1949.
Points up children's needs and interests as motivation for reading. Discusses prevention of reading difficulties.

15. Witty, Paul A. and Robert A. Sizemore. "Studies in Listening— A Postscript," *Elementary English*. XXXVI: 297-301 (May, 1959).
The title adequately describes the content. An excellent bibliography on listening.

16. Witty, Paul. "You and TV: End of the First Round," *National Parent-Teacher*. LIV, No. 3: 8-10 (November, 1959).
A summing up of a decade of TV's effect on our children and an estimate of the outlook in the succeeding decade. Special emphasis is directed toward need for good programming and for varied, well-balanced scheduling of all daily activities.

FAVORITE BOOKS OLD AND NEW FOR THE FIVES, SIXES, AND SEVENS

This booklist is built around the four categories of books noted in the text as means of stimulating children's ideas through prose. (See Chapter 13, p. 201.) Suggested grade levels are indicated.

A. Books that Help to Answer Children's Questions about People, Animals, Places, and Things.

1. Aulaire, Edgar Parin d' and Ingri d'Aulaire. *Abraham Lincoln*. Doubleday, 1939 (2-3).

2. Baruch, Dorothy. *Pitter Patter*. W. R. Scott, 1943 (k-3).

3. Bate, Norman. *Who Built the Bridge?* Scribner, 1954 (1-3).

4. Behn, Harry. *All Kinds of Time*. Harcourt, 1950 (1-3).

5. Behn, Harry. *The Painted Cave*. Harcourt, 1957 (1-3).

6. Beim, Jerrold. *Twelve O'Clock Whistle*. Morrow, 1946 (1-3).

7. Beim, Lorraine and Jerrold. *Two is a Team*. Harcourt, 1945 (1-3).

8. Bendick, Jeanne. *All Around You*. McGraw (Whittlesey House Publications), 1951 (1-3).

9. Berkowitz, Ethel Strachstein. *The Size of It*, by Ethel S. Berkley (pseud.) W. R. Scott, 1950 (k-2).

10. Berkowitz, Ethel Strachstein. *Ups and Downs*, by Ethel S. Berkley (pseud.) W. R. Scott, 1951 (k-2).

254 GUIDING LANGUAGE LEARNINGS

11. Black, Irma S. *This is the Bread That Betsy Ate.* W. R. Scott, 1942 (2-3).
12. Blough, Glenn. *The Pet Show.* Row, Peterson, 1945 (1-3).
13. Blough, Glenn. *Wait for the Sunshine.* McGraw (Whittlesey House Publications), 1954 (2-4).
14. Branley, Franklyn Mansfield. *Book of Satellites for You.* Crowell, 1958 (1-3).
15. Bronson, Wilfrid S. *Cats.* Harcourt, 1950 (2-5).
16. Bronson, Wilfrid S. *Coyotes.* Harcourt, 1946 (2-5).
17. Brown, Margaret Wise. *The Seashore Noisy Book.* W. R. Scott, 1941 (k-2).
18. Buck, Pearl S. *The Chinese Children Next Door.* Day, 1942 (1-4).
19. Clark, Ann Nolan. *In My Mother's House.* Viking, 1941 (1-5).
20. Clark, Ann Nolan. *Looking-for-Something.* Viking, 1952 (1-3).
21. Coblentz, Catherine. *Martin and Abraham Lincoln.* Children's Press, 1947 (2-4).
22. Cook, Gladys Emerson. *Zoo Animals.* Grosset, 1943 (k-2).
23. Dalgliesh, Alice. *The Thanksgiving Story.* Scribner, 1954 (k-3).
24. DeAngeli, Marguerite L. *Yonie Wondernose.* Doubleday, 1944 (1-4).
25. Dickey, Albert. *About Rivers.* Melmont, 1958 (2-3).
26. Duvoisin, Roger. *A for the Ark.* Lothrop, 1952 (k-1).
27. Elting, Mary. *The Big Book of the Real Circus,* by Benjamin Brewster (pseud.) Grosset, 1951 (k-2).
28. Felt, Sue. *Rosa-Too-Little.* Doubleday, 1950 (1-3).
29. Fine, Aaron. *Peter Plants a Pocketful.* Oxford, 1955 (k-3).
30. Flack, Marjorie. *Boats on the River.* Viking, 1946 (1-3).
31. Fletcher, Sydney E. *Big Book of Cowboys.* Grosset, 1950 (4-7).
32. Fletcher, Sydney E. *Big Book of Indians.* Grosset, 1950 (3-7).
33. Floethe, Louise Lee. *The Cowboy on the Ranch.* Scribner, 1959 (k-2).
34. Gall, Alice Crew. *Flat Tail.* Oxford, 1935 (3-5).
35. Gall, Alice Crew. *Wagtail.* Oxford, 1932 (3-5).
36. Garelick, May. *What's Inside?* W. R. Scott, 1955 (2-5).
37. Gates, Richard. *The True Book of Conservation.* Children's Press 1959 (2-4).
38. Green, Mary M. *Everybody Eats.* W. R. Scott, 1946 (k-1).
39. Green, Mary M. *Everybody Has a House.* W. R. Scott, 1944 (2-3).
40. Green, Mary M. *Is It Hard? Is It Easy?* W. R. Scott, 1948 (k-3).
41. Henrioud, Charles. *A Little Donkey—Un Petit Anê,* by Matias (pseud.) Walck, 1959 (k-2).

42. Hogner, Nils. *Spiders*. Crowell, 1955 (2-5).

43. Huntington, Harriet. *Let's Go Outdoors*. Doubleday, 1939 (1-4).

44. Huntington, Harriet. *Let's Go to the Seashore*. Doubleday, 1941 (2-5).

45. Hurd, Edith T. *Engine, Engine, No. 9*. Lothrop, 1940 (1-3).

46. Hutchinson, William M. *A Child's Book of Sea Shells*. Maxton, 1954 (k-3).

47. Ipcar, Dahlov. *Ten Big Farms*. Knopf, 1957 (k-3).

48. Kramer, Bettina Leonard. *Book of Big Beasts*. Melmont, 1954 (2-4).

49. Lattimore, Eleanor Frances. *The Journey of Ching Lai*. Morrow, 1958 (1-3).

50. Lattimore, Eleanor Frances. *Little Pear and His Friends*. Harcourt, 1935 (3-5).

51. Leaf, Munro. *Wee Gillis*. Viking, 1938 (2-4).

52. Lenski, Lois. *Cowboy Small*. Oxford, 1949 (k-2).

53. Lenski, Lois. *Let's Play House*. Oxford, 1944 (k-2).

54. McClung, Robert M. *Bufo, the Story of a Toad*. Morrow, 1954 (k-3).

55. McClung, Robert M. *Tiger, the Story of a Swallowtail Butterfly*. Morrow, 1953 (1-3).

56. Meyer, Jerome. *Picture Book of Astronomy*. Lothrop, 1945 (3-5).

57. Miner, Opal Irene Sevrey. *The True Book of Our Post Office and Its Helpers*. Children's Press, 1955 (1-2).

58. Miner, Opal Irene Sevrey. *The True Book of Policemen and Firemen*. Children's Press, 1954 (1-3).

59. Mitchell, Lucy S. *Fix It, Please!* Simon and Schuster, 1947 (k-1).

60. Pease, Josephine. *It Seems Like Magic*. Rand McNally, 1946 (2-4).

61. Petersham, Maud and Miska. *The Story Book of Food*. Winston, 1933 (3-5).

62. Peterson, Barbara and Russell F. *Whitefoot Mouse*. Holiday House, 1959 (2-4).

63. Politi, Leo. *Song of the Swallows*. Scribner, 1949 (k-3).

64. Robinson, William Wilcox. *At the Seashore*. Macmillan, 1942 (1-3).

65. Scarry, Richard, illustrator. *The Great Big Car and Truck Book*. Simon and Schuster, 1951 (k-1).

66. Schneider, Herman and Nina. *Follow the Sunset*. Doubleday, 1952 (1-3).

67. Schneider, Herman and Nina. *How Big is Big?* W. R. Scott, 1950 (3-6).

68. Selsam, Millicent. *All About Eggs*. W. R. Scott, 1952 (k-3).

69. Selsam, Millicent, and Betty Morrow. *See Through the Sea.* Harper, 1955 (3-6).
70. Street, Julia Montgomery. *Candle Love Feast.* Coward-McCann, 1959 (k-2).
71. Thayer, Jane. *The Second Story Giraffe.* Morrow, 1959 (k-2).
72. Tousey, Sanford. *Cowbody Tommy.* Doubleday, 1932 (2-4).
73. Traver, Dorothy. *Growing Oranges.* Melmont, 1958 (2-4).
74. Tresselt, Alvin. *Follow the Wind.* Lothrop, 1950 (k-2).
75. Tresselt, Alvin. *Sun Up.* Lothrop, 1949 (1).
76. Tresselt, Alvin. *The Wind and Peter.* Oxford, 1948 (k-1).
77. Vacheron, Edith. *Here is Henri!* Scribner, 1949. *Voici Henri!* par Edith Vacheron et Virginia Kahl. Scribner, 1959. (1-3)—(The grade level assigned above is based on the English text.)
78. Webber, Irma E. *Bits That Grow Big.* W. R. Scott, 1949 (2-5).
79. Webber, Irma E. *Travelers All.* W. R. Scott, 1944 (2-4).
80. Webber, Irma E. *Up Above and Down Below.* W. R. Scott, 1943 (2-4).
81. White, Anne Terry. *All About Great Rivers of the World.* Random House, 1957 (2-7).
82. Zaffo, George J. *The Big Book of Real Airplanes.* Grosset, 1951 (3-5).
83. Zim, Herbert S. *Dinosaurs.* Morrow, 1954 (4-7).
84. Zim, Herbert S. *Elephants.* Morrow, 1946 (2-4).
85. Zim, Herbert S. *What's Inside Me?* Morrow, 1952 (2-5).

B. Books that Inspire and Stimulate the Imagination.

1. Adshead, Gladys. *Brownies—Hush!* Oxford, 1938 (k-2).
2. Adshead, Gladys. *Brownies—It's Christmas!* Oxford, 1955 (k-2).
3. Agle, Nan and Ellen Wilson. *Three Boys and a Light-House.* Scribner, 1951 (2-4).
4. Andersen, Hans Christian. *The Emperor's New Clothes.* Houghton, 1949 (1 and up).
5. Ardizzone, Edward. *Tim All Alone.* Oxford, 1957 (1-4).
6. Asbjørnsen, Peter Christen and J. E. Moe. *The Three Billy Goats Gruff.* Harcourt, 1957 (1-4).
7. Austin, Margot. *Peter Churchmouse.* Dutton, 1941 (k-1).
8. Bannerman, Helen. *The Story of Little Black Sambo.* Lippincott, 1923 (1-3).
9. Bannon, Laura. *Patty Paints a Picture.* A. Whitman, 1946 (2-4).
10. Beatty, Hetty B. *Little Wild Horse.* Houghton, 1949 (k-1).
11. Becker, Charlotte. *Judy Goes Sailing.* Scribner, 1943 (1-3).

12. Beim, Jerrold. *Smallest Boy in the Class.* Morrow, 1949 (1-3).

13. Brown, Marcia. *Felice.* Scribner, 1958 (k-3).

14. Brown, Margaret Wise. *SHHhhh . . . . . Bang!* Harper, 1943 (k-2).

15. Brown, Margaret Wise. *Two Little Trains.* W. R. Scott, 1949 (k-1).

16. Brunhoff, Jean de. *Story of Babar.* Random, 1933 (1-3).

17. Brustlein, Janice. *Minette,* by Janice (pseud.) McGraw (Whittlesey House Publications), 1959 (k-2).

18. Budney, Blossom. *A Kiss is Round.* Lothrop, 1954 (k-2).

19. Buff, Mary. *Dash and Dart.* Viking, 1942 (1-4).

20. Chalmers, Audrey. *Mr. Topple's Wish.* Viking, 1948 (k-3).

21. Chan, Chih-yi and Plato Chan. *Good-Luck Horse.* McGraw (Whittlesey House Publications), 1943 (2-4).

22. Charles, Robert Henry. *Roundabout Turn.* Warne, 1930 (k-3).

23. Credle, Ellis. *Down, Down the Mountain.* Nelson, 1934 (3-5).

24. Dalgliesh, Alice. *Little Wooden Farmer.* Macmillan, 1930 (k-1).

25. Daugherty, James H. *Andy and the Lion.* Viking, 1938 (1-3).

26. Davis, Lavinia R. *The Wild Birthday Cake.* Doubleday, 1949 (1-3).

27. Denney, Diana. *Little Red Engine Gets a Name,* by Diana Ross (pseud.) Transatlantic, 1945 (1-3).

28. Dennis, Wesley. *Flip.* Viking, 1941 (k-3).

29. De Regniers, Beatrice Schenk. *The Child's Book of Dreams.* Harcourt, 1957 (k-3).

30. De Regniers, Beatrice Schenk. *A Little House of Your Own.* Harcourt, 1954 (k-2).

31. Donaldson, Lois. *Karl's Wooden Horse.* A. Whitman, 1931 (k-2).

32. Du Bois, William Pène. *Lion.* Viking, 1956 (k-3).

33. Duvoisin, Roger. *Christmas Whale.* Knopf, 1945 (k-3).

34. Duvoisin, Roger. *Easter Treat.* Knopf, 1954 (k-3).

35. Duvoisin, Roger. *Petunia Beware.* Knopf, 1958 (k-2).

36. Ehrlick, Bettina. *Pantaloni.* Harper, 1957 (k-3).

37. Ets, Marie Hall. *In the Forest.* Viking, 1944 (k-3).

38. Ets, Marie Hall. *Mister Penny's Race Horse.* Viking, 1956 (1-3).

39. Fatio, Louise. *Happy Lion Roars.* McGraw (Whittlesey House Publications), 1957 (k-3).

40. Field, Rachel. *Prayer for a Child.* Macmillan, 1944 (k-3).

41. Fischer, Hans. *The Birthday.* Harcourt, 1954 (k-2).

42. Fischer, Hans. *Puss In Boots:* adapted from Charles Perrault. Harcourt, 1959 (k-2).

43. Flack, Marjorie. *Angus and the Cat.* Doubleday, 1931 (k-2).

44. Flack, Marjorie. *Angus and the Ducks.* Doubleday, 1930 (k-2).

45. Flack, Marjorie. *Ask Mr. Bear.* Macmillan, 1932 (k-2).
46. Flack, Marjorie. *Story About Ping.* Viking, 1933 (1-3).
47. Flack, Marjorie. *Wait for William.* Houghton, 1935 (k-2).
48. Flynn, Helen M. *The Quiet Book.* Wonder Book, 1958 (k).
49. Freeman, Don. *Fly High, Fly Low.* Viking, 1957 (k-1).
50. Fritz, Jean. *How to Read a Rabbit.* Coward-McCann, 1959 (2-4).
51. Gág, Wanda. *ABC Bunny.* Coward-McCann, 1933 (k-2).
52. Gág, Wanda. *Gone is Gone.* Coward-McCann, 1935 (1-3).
53. Gág, Wanda. *Millions of Cats.* Coward-McCann, 1928 (k-3).
54. Gannett, Ruth S. *My Father's Dragon.* Random House, 1948 (2-4).
55. Garbutt, Katharine K. *Michael the Colt.* Houghton, 1943 (k-1).
56. Godden, Rumer. *The Mousewife.* Viking, 1951 (2-4).
57. Gramatky, Hardie. *Homer and the Circus Train.* Putnam, 1957 (k-2).
58. Gramatky, Hardie. *Little Toot.* Putnam, 1939 (k-3).
59. Heyward, Du Bose. *Country Bunny and the Little Gold Shoes.* Houghton, 1939, (k-2).
60. Hurd, Edith. *Benny the Bulldozer.* Lothrop, 1947 (2-4).
61. Jones, Jessie Mae (Orton). *Small Rain.* Viking, 1943 (1-4).
62. Jones, Patricia, adapted by. *Rumpelstiltskin.* Rand McNally, 1955 (1-4).
63. Kahl, Virginia. *The Duchess Bakes a Cake.* Scribner, 1955 (k-3).
64. Kahl, Virginia. *Habits of Rabbits.* Scribner, 1957 (k-2).
65. Krauss, Ruth. *I Can Fly.* Simon and Schuster, 1958, new edition (k-1).
66. Krauss, Ruth. *A Very Special House.* Harper, 1953 (k-2).
67. Kuskin, Karla. *Which Horse Is William?* Harper, 1959 (k-1).
68. Lathrop, Dorothy. *Who Goes There?* Macmillan, 1935 (2-4).
69. Leisk, David Johnson. *Ellen's Lion,* by Crockett Johnson (pseud.) Harper, 1959 (1-3).
70. Lenski, Lois. *The Little Fire Engine.* Oxford, 1946 (k-2).
71. Lent, Henry B. *Tugboat.* Macmillan, 1936 (3-5).
72. Lindman, Maj. *Snipp, Snapp, Snurr and the Red Shoes.* A. Whitman, 1932 (1-3).
73. Littlefield, William. *The Whiskers of Ho Ho.* Lothrop, 1958 (k-2).
74. McCloskey, Robert. *Time of Wonder.* Viking, 1957 (k-2).
75. Moore, Clement. *'Twas the Night Before Christmas.* Houghton, 1912 (1-3).
76. Munari, Bruno. *The Elephant's Wish.* World, 1959 (k-1).
77. Piper, Watty. *The Little Engine That Could.* Retold from the *Pony*

Engine by Mabel C. Bragg. Platt, 1930 (1-3).

78. Reyher, Rebecca. *My Mother is the Most Beautiful Woman in the World.* Howell Soskin, 1945 (3-5).

79. Sauer, Julia Lina. *Mike's House.* Viking, 1954 (k-3).

80. Schlein, Miriam. *The Big Cheese.* W. R. Scott, 1958 (k-2).

81. Schlein, Miriam. *Elephant Herd.* W. R. Scott, 1954 (1-3).

82. Schreiber, Georges. *Bambino Goes Home.* Viking, 1959 (2-4).

83. Seignobosc, Françoise. *Biquette the White Goat,* by Francoise (pseud.) Scribner, 1953 (k-2).

84. Seignobosc, Françoise. *Jeanne-Marie Counts Her Sheep,* by Francoise (pseud.) Scribner, 1951 (k-1).

85. Seignobosc, Françoise. *Jeanne-Marie At the Fair,* by Francoise (pseud.) Scribner, 1959 (k-2).

86. Seignobosc, Françoise. *What Do You Want to Be?* by Francoise (pseud.) Scribner, 1957 (k-2).

87. Slobodkin, Louis. *Trick or Treat.* Macmillan, 1959 (k-2).

88. Smith-Masters, Margaret. *The Cock, the Mouse, and the Little Red Hen,* by Félicité Lèfevre (pseud.) Macrae, 1945 (k-3).

89. Tripp, Edward. *The Tin Fiddle.* Oxford, 1954 (k-3).

90. Villarejo, Mary. *The Tiger Hunt.* Knopf, 1959 (k-2)

91. Weil, Lisl. *The Busiest Boy in Holland.* Houghton, 1959 (k-2).

C. Books that Have Ideas that Are Funny.

1. Bishop, Claire. *The Five Chinese Brothers.* Coward-McCann, 1938 (1-3).

2. Bright, Robert. *Georgie.* Doubleday, 1944 (k-3).

3. Bright, Robert. *Georgie to the Rescue.* Doubleday, 1956 (k-2).

4. Bright, Robert. *Me and the Bears.* Doubleday, 1951 (k-1).

5. Brock, Emma L. *Greedy Goat.* Knopf, 1931 (2-5).

6. Brown, Marcia. *Stone Soup.* Scribner, 1947 (1-3).

7. Chalmers, Audrey. *Hundreds and Hundreds of Pancakes.* Viking, 1942 (1-3).

8. Clark, Mary E. *Poppy Seed Cakes,* by Margery Clark (pseud.) Doubleday, 1943 (2-4).

9. Davis, Alice V. *Timothy Turtle.* Harcourt, 1940 (k-3).

10. De Regniers, Beatrice Schenk. *What Happens Next?* Macmillan, 1959 (k-2).

11. Elkin, Benjamin. *Gillespie and the Guards.* Viking, 1956 (1-3).

12. Fatio, Louise. *The Happy Lion.* McGraw (Whittlesey House Publications), 1954 (k-3).

13. Fatio, Louise. *The Three Happy Lions.* McGraw (Whittlesey House

Publications), 1959 (k-2).

14. Freeman, Don. *Beady Bear*. Viking, 1954 (k-1).

15. Freeman, Don. *Space Witch*. Viking, 1959 (1-3).

16. Garrett, Helen. *Angelo the Naughty One*. Viking, 1944 (1-3).

17. Geisel, Theodor. *And To Think I Saw It on Mulberry Street*, by Dr. Seuss (pseud.) Vanguard, 1957 (k-3).

18. Geisel, Theodor. *The 500 Hats of Bartholomew Cubbins*, by Dr. Seuss (pseud.) Vanguard, 1938 (1-3).

19. Geisel, Theodor. *Horton Hatches the Egg*, by Dr. Seuss (pseud.) Random House, 1940 (k-2).

20. Geisel, Theodor. *McElligot's Pool*, by Dr. Seuss (pseud.) Random House, 1947, (k-3).

21. Gramatky, Hardie. *Hercules*. Putnam, 1940 (1-3).

22. Haywood, Carolyn. *Eddie Makes Music*. Morrow, 1957 (2-4).

23. Haywood, Carolyn. *Little Eddie*. Morrow, 1947 (2-4).

24. Hurd, Clement. *Run, Run, Run*. Harper, 1951 (k-1).

25. Kahl, Virginia. *Duchess Bakes a Cake*. Scribner, 1955 (k-3).

26. Kepes, Juliet. *Five Little Monkeys*. Houghton, 1952 (k-3).

27. Kessler, Ethel and Leonard Kessler. *Crunch, Crunch*. Doubleday, 1955 (k).

28. Krasilovsky, Phyllis. *Cow Who Fell in the Canal*. Doubleday, 1957 (k-3).

29. Kraus, Robert. *Junior the Spoiled Cat*. Oxford, 1955 (k-1).

30. Kraus, Robert. *Ladybug, Ladybug!* Harper, 1957 (k-2).

31. Krum, Charlotte. *The Four Riders*. Wilcox & Follett, 1953 (k-3).

32. Leaf, Munro. *The Story of Ferdinand*. Viking, 1936 (1-4).

33. Lipkind, William. *Circus Ruckus*. Harcourt, 1954 (k-3).

34. Lipkind, William. *Four-Leaf Clover*, by Will (pseud.) Harcourt, 1959 (k-2).

35. MacGregor, Ellen. *Theodore Turtle*. McGraw (Whittlesey House Publications), 1955 (1-3).

36. Merrill, Jean. *The Very Nice Things*. Harper, 1959 (k-2).

37. Newell, Hope. *The Little Old Woman Who Used Her Head*. Nelson, 1935 (k-3).

38. Payne, Emmy. *Katy No-Pocket*. Houghton, 1944 (k-3).

39. Rey, H. A. *Cecily G. and the 9 Monkeys*. Houghton, 1942 (k-3).

40. Rey, H. A. *Curious George*. Houghton, 1941 (k-2).

41. Rey, H. A. *Curious George Takes a Job*. Houghton, 1947 (k-2).

42. Slobodkin, Louis. *The Amiable Giant*. Macmillan, 1955 (k-3).

43. Slobodkin, Louis. *Magic Michael*. Macmillan, 1944 (k-2).

44. Slobodkina, Esphyr. *Caps for Sale*. W. R. Scott, 1947 (k-2).
45. Titus, Eve. *Anatole*. McGraw (Whittlesey House Publications), 1956 (k-2).
46. Weisgard, Leonard. *The Clean Pig*. Scribner, 1952 (k-2).

D. Books that Have Ideas that Are Linked to Their Illustrations. (Unless Indicated, the Author Illustrated the Book.)

1. Anderson, C. W. *Billy and Blaze*. Macmillan, 1936 (1-3).
2. Anderson, C. W. *Blaze and the Mountain Lion*. Macmillan, 1959 (k-1).
3. Ardizzone, Edward. *Nicholas and the Fast Moving Diesel*. Walck, 1959 (k-2).
4. Armer, Laura Adams. *Forest Pool*. Longmans, 1938 (2-4).
5. Aulaire, Edgar Parin d' and Ingri d'Aulaire. *Animals Everywhere*. Doubleday, 1954 (k-3).
6. Aulaire, Edgar Parin d' and Ingri d'Aulaire. *Don't Count Your Chicks*. Doubleday, 1943 (1-4).
7. Bannon, Laura. *Manuela's Birthday in Old Mexico*. A. Whitman, 1939 (1-3).
8. Bemelmans, Ludwig. *Madeline*. Simon and Schuster, 1939 (1-3).
9. Bemelmans, Ludwig. *Madeline and the Gypsies*. Viking, 1959 (k-3).
10. Beskow, Elsa. Trans. by Marion Letcher Woodbyrn. *Pelle's New Suit*. Harper, 1929 (1-3).
11. Bromhall, Winifred. *Belinda's New Shoes*. Knopf, 1945 (2-4).
12. Brooke, L. Leslie. *Golden Goose Book*. Warne, 1906 (2-4).
13. Brooke, L. Leslie. *Johnny Crow's Garden*. Warne, 1904 (k-3).
14. Brown, Marcia. *Little Carousel*. Scribner, 1946 (k-2).
15. Brown, Margaret Wise. *Golden Egg Book*; illustrated by Leonard Weisgard. Simon and Schuster, 1947 (k-1).
16. Brown, Margaret Wise. *Little Island*, by Golden MacDonald (pseud.) illustrated by Leonard Weisgard. Doubleday, 1946 (1-3).
17. Brown, Margaret Wise. *Wheel on the Chimney*; illustrated by Tibor Gergely. Lippincott, 1954 (k-3).
18. Bulla, Clyde Robert. *The Poppy Seeds*; illustrated by Jean Charlot. Crowell, 1955 (1-3).
19. Burton, Virginia Lee. *Katy and the Big Snow*. Houghton, 1943 (1-3).
20. Burton, Virginia Lee. *Little House*. Houghton, 1942 (1-4).
21. Burton, Virginia Lee. *Mike Mulligan and His Steam Shovel*. Houghton, 1939 (1-3).
22. Caldecott, Randolph. *Picture Books* (4 volumes). American Book

Co., 1926 (k-3).

23. Chönz, Selina. *A Bell for Ursli*; illustrated by Alois Carigiet. Oxford, 1950 (k-2).

24. Delafield, Clelia. *Mrs. Mallard's Ducklings*; illustrated by Leonard Weisgard. Lothrop, 1946 (2-4).

25. Eichenberg, Fritz. *Dancing in the Moon*. Harcourt, 1955 (k-2).

26. Flack, Marjorie. *Boats on the River*; illustrated by Jay Hyde Barnum. Viking, 1946 (1-3).

27. Gay, Zhenya. *Look!* Viking, 1952 (k-1).

28. Gergeley, Tibor, illustrator. *The Great Big Fire Engine Book*. Simon and Schuster, 1950 (k-3).

29. Graham, Al. *Timothy Turtle*. Robert Welch, 1946 (1-3).

30. Greenaway, Kate. *Under the Window*; engraved and printed by Edmund Evans. Warne (k-3).

31. Hader, Berta and Elmer. *Cock-a-Doodle-Doo*. Macmillan, 1939 (k-3).

32. Hader, Berta and Elmer. *The Big Snow*. Macmillan, 1948 (k-3).

33. Hader, Berta and Elmer. *Farmer in the Dell*. Macmillan, 1931 (1-4).

34. Hader, Berta and Elmer. *Home on the Range*. Macmillan, 1955 (1-3).

35. Handforth, Thomas. *Mei Li. Doubleday*, 1938 (1-3).

36. Ipcar, Dahlov. *One Horse Farm*. Doubleday, 1950 (k-2).

37. Ipcar, Dahlov. *Ten Big Farms*. Knopf, 1958 (k-2).

38. Iwamatsu, Jun. *Village Tree*, by Taro Yashima (pseud.) Viking, 1953 (k-3).

39. Iwamatsu, Jun. *Umbrella*, by Taro Yashima (pseud.) Viking, 1958 (k-2).

40. Kirn, Ann. *Full of Wonder*, World, 1959 (2-4).

41. Krauss, Ruth. *Growing Story*; illustrated by Phyllis Rowand. Harper, 1947 (k-1).

42. Lathrop, Dorothy. *Animals of the Bible*. Lippincott, 1937 (1-4).

43. Lathrop, Dorothy. *Hide and Go Seek*. Macmillan, 1938 (k-3).

44. Lipkind, William. *Finders Keepers*. Harcourt, 1951 (k-3).

45. Marokvia, Mireille. *Jannot, a French Rabbit*. Lippincott, 1959 (2-4).

46. McCloskey, Robert. *Blueberries for Sal*. Viking, 1948 (k-3).

47. McCloskey, Robert. *Make Way for Ducklings*. Viking, 1941 (k-3).

48. McCloskey, Robert. *One Morning in Maine*. Viking, 1952 (k-2).

49. McGinley, Phyllis. *All Around the Town*; illustrated by Helen Stone. Lippincott, 1948 (k-3).

50. Milhous, Katherine. *Egg Tree.* Scribner, 1950 (1-3).
51. Newberry, Clare T. *Mittens.* Harper, 1936 (k-3).
52. Palazzo, Tony. *Susie the Cat.* Viking, 1949 (k-3).
53. Petersham, Maud and Miska. *Christ Child.* Doubleday, 1931 (1-6).
54. Petersham, Maud and Miska. *The Rooster Crows.* Macmillan, 1945 (k-3).
55. Politi, Leo. *Juanita.* Scribner, 1948 (k-3).
56. Seignobosc, Francoise. *Springtime for Jeanne-Marie,* by Françoise (pseud.), Scribner, 1955 (k-1).
57. Seignobosc, Françoise. *The Things I Like,* by Françoise (pseud.) Scribner, 1960 (k).
58. Sewell, Helen M. *Blue Barns.* Macmillan, 1933 (k-2).
59. Tresselt, Alvin. *Autumn Harvest;* illustrated by Roger Duvoisin. Lothrop, 1951 (k-2).
60. Tresselt, Alvin. *White Snow, Bright Snow;* illustrated by Roger Duvoisin. Lothrop, 1947 (k-3).
61. Udry, Janice May. *A Tree is Nice;* illustrated by Marc Simont. Harper, 1956 (k-1).
62. Ward, Lynd. *The Biggest Bear.* Houghton, 1952 (k-3).
63. Wenning, Elizabeth. *The Christmas Mouse;* drawings by Barbara Remington. Holt, 1959 (k-2).

Some of the books listed above are excellent ones to be used by a beginning reader in a self-selection program. Phyllis Fenner in Chapter 13 of her fascinating book *The Proof of the Pudding: What Children Read,* John Day and Co., 1957, discusses books of this type. Martha Olson Condit, librarian of the Montclair, New Jersey, Public Schools, reports on the Graduate School of Library Service at Rutgers University study which was made "to try to identify those trade books which can be read independently by the first and second grade reader who has normal interests and no special reading problems." The article appears in the *Wilson Library Bulletin* (the H. W. Wilson Co.) : "Trade Books for Beginning Readers," XXXIV, No. 4: 284-301 (December 1959). Fifteen pages of the selection are lists of books graded for the primary reader.

Examples of such books are:

Grade One
1. Carroll, Ruth (Robinson). *Where's the Bunny?* Walck, 1950.
2. Elkin, Benjamin. *Big Jump and Other Stories.* Beginners Books: Random, 1958.
3. Eastman, Philip D. *Sam and the Firefly.* Beginners Books: Random, 1958.

4. Geisel, Theodor. *Cat in the Hat Comes Back*, by Dr. Seuss (pseud.) Beginners Books: Random, 1958.
5. Holland, Marion. *Big Ball of String*. Beginners Books: Random, 1958.
6. Krauss, Ruth and Crockett Johnson. *Is This You?* by Ruth Krauss and David Johnson Leisk (pseud.) Scott, 1955.
7. Miles, Betty. *A House for Everyone*. Knopf, 1958.
8. Rey, Margret. *Curious George Flies a Kite*. Houghton, 1958.
9. Tensen, Ruth M. *Come to the Pet Shop*. Reilly and Lee, 1954.

Grade Two

1. Branley, Franklyn M. and Eleanor K. Vaughan. *Mickey's Magnet*. Crowell, 1956.
2. Bright, Robert. *I Like Red*. Doubleday, 1955.
3. Hoff, Syd. *Danny and the Dinosaur*. Harper, 1958.
4. King, Patricia. *Mabel the Whale*. Follett, 1958.
5. Krauss, Ruth. *Carrot Seed*. Harper, 1945.
6. Minarik, Else Holmelund. *Little Bear*. Harper, 1957.
7. Shaw, Charles G. *It Looked Like Spilt Milk*. Harper, 1947.
8. Slobodkina, Esphyr. *Behind the Dark Window Shade*. Lothrop, 1958.
9. Tresselt, Alvin. *Wake Up, Farm!* Lothrop, 1955.
10. Zolotow, Charlotte. *Not a Little Monkey*. Lothrop, 1958.

LITERARY READERS

Jacobs, Leland B., Johnson, Eleanor M., and Turner, Jo Jasper, *Treasury of Literature* Series. Columbus, Ohio: Charles E. Merrill Books, Inc., 1960.

A six-book series (grades 1-6) containing all types of the best children's literature by 231 outstanding children's writers. Illustrations (over half in full color) by 30 children's book artists. A completely planned literature appreciation program designed for use independently or co-basally.

Shane, Harold G. and Kathleen B. Hester, *Gateways to Reading Treasures*. River Forest, Illinois: Laidlaw Brothers, Inc., 1960 and 1961.

A seven-volume (grades 1-6) series of high-interest tales which includes many original stories as well as established favorites. Designed as a co-basal series and written with a controlled vocabulary. Contains full-color drawings especially selected to provide picture clues and to add meaning to the stories.

INSTRUCTIONAL MATERIALS FOR USE
IN LANGUAGE INSTRUCTION

A. Books Which Are Helpful in Reviewing and Selecting Books for Young Children.

1. *A Teacher's Guide to Children's Books,* by Nancy Larrick (Charles E. Merrill Books, Inc., Columbus, Ohio). A clear and simple introduction to children's literature, organized by grade level, which contains an annotated list of over 400 books for children.

2. Five suggestions for booklists you might wish to own are

   a) *Adventuring With Books* (National Council of Teachers of English, 704 S. 6th Street, Champaign, Illinois). A list of almost 500 outstanding books. Revised every two years.

   b) *A Bibliography of Books for Children* (Association for Childhood Education International, 1200 15th Street, N.W., Washington 5, D.C.). About 1,700 books, well indexed with many cross references. Revised every two years.

   c) *Children's Books for $1.25 or Less* (Association for Childhood Education International, 1200 15th Street, N.W., Washington 5, D.C.). About 1,000 inexpensive books. Revised every two years.

   d) *Children's Books Too Good to Miss.* Second Revised Edition (Western Reserve University Press, 2035 Adelbert Road, Cleveland 6, Ohio). 1959.

   e) *Treasure for the Taking,* by Anne Thaxter Eaton (Viking Press, 625 Madison Ave., New York 22). Revised 1957. 1,580 books in 64 categories ranging from books for the youngest to selections for adolescents.

3. Three suggestions for types of lists you will find in library reference material:

   a) *Basic Book Collection for Elementary Grades* (American Library Association, 50 E. Huron Street, Chicago 11, Illinois; 7th ed., 1960).

   b) *Children's Catalog* (H. W. Wilson Co., 950 University Ave., New York; 1956 ed.). A new catalog is published every five years. Supplements are available for the years that intervene.

   c) Rue, Eloise. *Subject Index to Books for Primary Grades.* (American Library Association, 50 E. Huron Street, Chicago 11, Illinois; 1943. Supplement, 1946.)

4. Six suggested periodicals featuring reviews of children's books:

   a) *Bulletin of the Children's Book Center* (The University of Chicago

Library, Children's Book Center, Chicago, Illinois). Published monthly except August.

b) *Childhood Education* (1200 15th Street, N.W., Washington 5, D.C.). Published September through May.

c) *Elementary English* (704 South 6th Street, Champaign, Illinois). Published monthly from October through May.

d) *The Horn Book Magazine* (585 Boylston Street, Boston 16, Massachusetts). Published six times a year in February, April, June, August, October, and December.

e) *New York Herald Tribune Book Review Weekly* (New York Tribune, Inc., 230 West 41st Street, New York City).

f) *New York Times Book Review*, weekly (Times Publishing Co., Times Square, New York City).

B. Collections of Materials for Sharing with Children.

1. Collections of stories and poems:

a) Arbuthnot, May Hill, compiler. *The Arbuthnot Anthology of Children's Literature.* Chicago: Scott, Foresman, 1953.

b) Child Study Association of America, Inc. *Read Me Another Story;* illustrated by Barbara Cooney. New York: Crowell, 1949.

c) Child Study Association of America, Inc. *Read To Me Story Book;* illustrated by Lois Lenski. New York: Crowell, 1947.

d) Huber, Miriam Blanton, ed. *Story and Verse for Children.* New York: Macmillan, 1955.

e) Johnson, Edna, and Frances Clarke Sayers, and Evelyn R. Sickels, ed. *Anthology of Children's Literature.* Boston: Houghton Mifflin, 1959.

2. Collections of stories:

a) Association for Childhood Education International. *Told Under the Blue Umbrella.* New York: Macmillan, 1933.

b) Association for Childhood Education International. *Told Under the Green Umbrella.* New York: Macmillan, 1930.

c) Association for Childhood Education International. *Told Under the Magic Umbrella.* New York: Macmillan, 1939.

d) Brock, Emma Lillian. *Till Potatoes Grow on Trees.* New York: Knopf, 1947.

e) Gruenberg, Sidonie, compiler. *Favorite Stories Old and New,* revised and enlarged edition. Garden City, N.Y.: Doubleday, 1955.

f) Hollowell, Lillian, ed. *Book of Children's Literature.* New York: Rinehart, 1950.

g) Hutchinson, Veronica S., compiler. *Chimney Corner Stories.* New York: Putnam, 1925.

h) Ward, Winifred, ed. *Stories to Dramatize.* Anchorage, Kentucky: The Children's Theater Press, 1952.

3. Collection of poems:

a) Aldis, Dorothy. *All Together.* New York: Putnam, 1952 (2-4).

b) Association for Childhood Education International. *Sung Under the Silver Umbrella.* New York: Macmillan, 1935 (2-5).

c) Barrows, Marjorie, compiler. *Read-Aloud Poems Every Young Child Should Know.* Chicago: Rand McNally, 1957 (k-2).

d) Brewton, John. *Gaily We Parade.* New York: Macmillan, 1940 (3-7).

e) Brown, Helen Ada and H. J. Heltman, compilers. *Let's-Read-Together Poems.* Evanston, Illinois: Row, Peterson, 1949 (k-3).

f) Doane, Pelagie, compiler. *A Small Child's Book of Verse.* New York: Oxford, 1948 (k-2).

g) Ferris, Helen. *Favorite Poems Old and New.* Garden City, N.Y.: Doubleday, 1957 (all ages).

h) Geismer, Barbara Peck and Antoinette Brown Suter, compilers. *Very Young Verses.* Boston: Houghton Mifflin, 1945 (1-3).

i) Love, Katherine, compiler. *A Little Laughter.* New York: Crowell, 1957 (2 and up).

j) Milne, A.A. *Now We Are Six.* New York: Dutton, 1927 (1-4).

k) Milne, A.A. *When We Were Very Young.* New York: Dutton, 1924 (1-4).

l) Roberts, Elizabeth Madox. *Under the Tree.* New York: Viking 1930 (2-5).

m) Thompson, Jean McKee. *Poems to Grow On.* Boston: Beacon Press, 1957 (k-3).

n) Untermeyer, Louis, compiler. *The Golden Treasury of Poetry.* New York: Golden Press, 1959 (all ages).

o) Werner, Jane, ed. *The Golden Book of Poetry.* New York: Simon and Schuster, 1949 (k-2).

4. Periodicals for children:

a) *Children's Activities.* 1111 South Wabash, Chicago 5, Illinois (3 to 9 years).

b) *Humpty Dumpty.* 52 Vanderbilt Avenue, New York, New York (3 to 7 years).

c) *Jack and Jill.* Curtis Publishing Co., Independence Square, Philadelphia 5, Pennsylvania (5 to 10 years).

d) *My Weekly Reader* (for primary grades), News Reader. American Education Publications, 1250 Fairwood Avenue, Columbus 16, Ohio.

C. Publications Which May Be Used in Fostering Observation and Communication through Science Interests.

1. Teacher references
   a) Blough, Glenn O., Julius Schwartz, and Albert J. Huggett. *Elementary School Science and How to Teach It.* Dryden Press, 1958.
   Comprehensive text by outstanding science educators.
   b) Freeman, Kenneth and others. *Helping Children Understand Science.* Philadelphia: Winston, 1954.
   Suggestions for teachers on *how* to develop science interests with children.
   c) Greenlee, Julian. *Teaching Science to Children.* Dubuque, Iowa: Wm. C. Brown, Co., 1956.
   This reference and the following one offer many practical suggestions for science interests and activities.
   d) Hubler, Clark. *Working with Children in Science.* Boston: Houghton (Riverside Press), 1957.
   e) Sheckles, Mary. *Building Children's Science Concepts.* New York: Bureau of Publications: Teachers College, Columbia. 1958.
   Experiences with rocks, soil, air, and water.
2. Books to use with children
   a) Experiments:
      (1) Freeman, May and Ira. *Fun with Chemistry.* New York: Random House, 1943.
      (2) Freeman, May and Ira. *Fun with Science.* New York: Random House, 1943.
      (3) Larrick, Nancy. *See For Yourself, A First Book of Science Experiments.* New York: Aladdin Books, 1952.
      (4) Podendorf, Illa. *The True Book of Science Experiments.* Chicago: Children's Press, 1954.
      (5) Schneider, Herman and Nina. *Let's Find Out; A Picture Science Book.* New York: W. R. Scott, 1946.
      (6) Schwartz, Julius. *It's Fun to Know Why; Experiments with Things Around Us.* New York: McGraw, 1952.
      (7) Wyler, Rose. *The First Book of Science Experiments.* New York: Watts, 1952.

b) Other simple science concepts:
  (1) Andrews, Roy Chapman. *All About Dinosaurs*. New York: Random House, 1953.
  (2) Clark, Mary Lou. *The True Book of Dinosaurs*. Chicago: Children's Press, 1955.
  (3) Darby, Gene. "The What Is It Series": Chicago: Benefic Press (Division of Beckley-Cardy). *What is a Chicken*, 1957. *What is a Fish*, 1958. *What is a Turtle*, 1959.
  (4) Eggleson, Joyce. *Things That Grow*. Chicago: Melmont, 1958.
  (5) Friskey, Margaret. *The True Book of Air Around Us*. Chicago: Children's Press, 1953.
  (6) Hogner, Dorothy (Childs). *Snails*. New York: Crowell, 1958.
  (7) Lewellen, John. *The True Book of Moon, Sun and Stars*. Chicago: Children's Press, 1954.
  (8) Parker, Bertha. *Air About Us*. Evanston, Ill.: Row, Peterson, 1941.
  (9) Parker, Bertha. *Animals of the Seashore*. Evanston, Ill.: Row, Peterson, 1942.
  (10) Pine, Tillie S. and Joseph Levine. *Magnets and How to Use Them*. New York: McGraw (Whittlesey House Publications), 1959.
  (11) Pine, Tillie S. and Joseph Levine. *Water, All Around*. New York: McGraw, 1959.
  (12) Podendorf, Illa. *The True Book of Space*. Chicago: Children's Press, 1959.
  (13) Schneider, Herman. *Everyday Machines and How They Work*. New York: McGraw, 1950.
  (14) Selsam, Millicent. *Play with Plants*. New York: Morrow, 1949.

Other books containing simple science concepts are included on page 253 in the list of *Books That Answer Questions About People, Animals, and Things*.

D. Audio-Visual and Music Materials Which Are Useful for Developing Listening and Observing Experiences.

1. *Films, film strips, and slides*
   You may wish to consult audio-visual supply agencies such as the public library in your community. Professional educational journals frequently include appraisals of newly released audio-visual material. Other readily available and important printed sources of data may be found in *A-V Instruction, Materials and Methods*, Brown, James

W., Richard B. Lewis and Fred F. Harcleroad. New York: McGraw,
1959. Reference catalogs for selection of 16 mm. films, 35 mm. film
strips, and the slides are listed below:

a) Film guides:

   (1) *Directory of 2002 16 mm. Film Libraries.* Washington, D.C.:
Superintendent of Documents, Government Printing Office,
annual.

   Annotated listings of centers which maintain 16 mm. films
for rental.

   (2) *Educational Film Guide,* compiled by Frederic A. Krahm.
New York: H. W. Wilson.

   Annual list of 16 mm. films with separate title and subject
index, age level, and description. Quarterly supplements.

b) Film strip guides:

   (1) *Filmstrip Guide,* compiled by Frederic A. Krahm. New York:
H. W. Wilson.

   Revised editions issued periodically: semi-annual and annual
supplements available also.

   (2) *Educator's Guide to Free Filmstrips.* Randolph, Wisconsin,
Educators Progress Service, annual.

c) Free or inexpensive catalogs listing films and film strips are available from film companies such as the following:

   (1) Academy Films, 800 N. Seward Street, Hollywood, California.

   (2) Association Films, Inc., 347 Madison Avenue, New York 17,
New York.

   (3) Athena Films, Inc., 165 West 46th Street, New York 36,
New York.

   (4) Bailey Films, Inc., 6509 DeLongpre Avenue, Hollywood 28,
California.

   (5) Coronet Films, 65 E. South Water Street, Chicago 1, Illinois.

   (6) Curriculum Films, Inc., 10 East 40th Street, New York 16,
New York.

   (7) Encyclopedia Britannica Films, Inc., 1150 Wilmette Avenue,
Wilmette, Illinois.

   (8) Frith Films, 1816 North Highland Avenue, Hollywood 28,
California.

   (9) International Film Bureau, Suite 308-316, 57 East Jackson
Boulevard, Chicago 4, Illinois.

   (10) Johnson Hunt Productions, 6509 DeLongpre Avenue, Hollywood 28, California.

(11) McGraw-Hill Book Company, Text-Film Department, 330 West 42 Street, New York 36, New York.

(12) National Film Board of Canada, 1270 Avenue of the Americas, New York 20, New York.

(13) Society for Visual Education, Inc., 1345 West Diversey Parkway, Chicago 14, Illinois.

(14) Teaching Films Custodians, Inc., 25 West 43rd Street, New York 36, New York.

(15) Tompkins Films, 960½ Larrabee Street, Los Angeles 46, California.

(16) United World Films, Inc., Castle Films Department, 1445 Park Avenue, New York 29, New York.

(17) Weston Woods Studios, Inc., Westport, Connecticut.

(18) Young America Films, Inc., 18 East 41 Street, New York 17, New York.

d) Selected examples of some films and film strips from these distributors for kindergarten-primary use in listening and observing are:

(1) Film strips:

(a) "Ann Visits the Zoo." Curriculum Films, Inc.

(b) "The Bakery." Curriculum Films, Inc.

(c) "Elephants." (Referred to in Chapter 12, p. 168). "Animal Friends Series." Encyclopedia Britannica Films.

(d) "The Fireman." Society for Visual Education.

(e) "Shep—The Farm Dog." Encyclopedia Britannica Films.

(2) Films:

(a) "Circus Animals." 11 min./or color. Academy Films.

(b) "Exploring a Harbor." 11 min./or color. Frith Films.

(c) "Here Comes the Milkman." 10 min./or color. Bailey Films, Inc.

(d) "Rumpelstiltskin." 10 min./or color. Coronet.

(e) "Visit with Cowboys." 11 min. Encyclopedia Britannica Films.

e) Distributors of slides:

(1) Society for Visual Education, Inc., 1345 Diversey Parkway, Chicago 14, Illinois.

A leading producer of 2 x 2 slides.

2. *References to music resources for teachers: books, collections of songs, and records*

a) Books:

272

(1) Andrews, Gladys. *Creative Rhythmic Movement for Children.* Prentice-Hall, Inc., 1954.
(2) Association for Childhood Education International. *Music for Children's Living.* Washington, D.C.: The Association, 1955. The section on music for 6-9's discusses rhythmic expression, rhythm instruments, listening, and creative activities.
(3) Driver, Ann and Rosalind Ramirez. *Something Particular,* London: Hodder and Stoughton, Ltd., 1955.
An expensive but inspirational book for dance and rhythm techniques with children.
(4) Ellison, Alfred. *Music with Children.* New York: McGraw, 1959.
Non-technical book for classroom teachers to aid them in releasing the music within children. Many specific suggestions for music activities in the typical classroom situation. Appendices A, B, C, D include readings, recordings, song lists, and collections. See pages 267-281.
(5) Landeck, Beatrice. *Children and Music.* New York: Sloane, 1952.
Music for enrichment of children's lives in family and school. Emphasis on folk music.
(6) Sheehy, Emma Dickson. *Children Discover Music and Dance.* New York: Holt, 1959.
Excellent source for the classroom teacher. Surveys various aspects of music and dance experiences with children. Good bibliographies of source materials.
b) Collections of songs:
(1) Landeck, Beatrice. *Songs to Grow On.* New York: Edward B. Marks Music Corporation and William Sloane Associates, 1950.
Also, *More Songs to Grow On.* 1954.
Suggests dramatizations and instruments.
(2) Lloyd, Norman. *The New Golden Song Book.* New York: Simon and Schuster, 1955.
(3) MacCarteney, Laura Pendelton. *Songs for the Nursery School.* Cincinnati: The Willis Music Co., 1937.
(4) Seeger, Ruth Crawford. *American Folk Songs for Children.* Garden City, N.Y.: Doubleday, 1948.
A fine collection of folk songs for children including an interesting discussion of the songs.

c) Records: Consult your local music supply houses for lists of records suitable for use with children. Beatrice Landeck's and Emma Sheehy's books also contain helpful lists. (See p. 272.) The following examples are representative of the variety of recorded music which may be used effectively in providing musical experiences in the classroom. Although complete albums may be expensive for some school budgets, the same selection can often be obtained on single records.

(1) Listening:

    (a) *R.C.A. Victor Basic Record Library for Elementary Schools*

        Listening Program for Primary Grades, Vol. 1. *Album E-77;* selections from:

            Brahms, "Lullaby" and "Little Sandman"
            Pierne, "March of the Little Lead Soldiers"
            Bizet, "Impromptu" from *Petite Suite*
            Beethoven, "Minuet"
            and others

        Listening Program for Primary Grades, Vol. 2. *Album E-78;* selections from:

            MacDowell, "Of a Tailor and a Bear"
            Schumann, "The Wild Horseman"
            Brahms, "Waltz in A Flat"
            Rubinstein, "Melody in F"
            Debussy, "Golliwog's Cake Walk"
            and others

        Listening Program for Primary Grades, Vol. 3. *Album E-79;* selections from:

            Gounod, "Allegretto" from *Faust*
            Grieg, "March of the Dwarfs"
            Haydn, "Toy Symphony"
            Schubert, "The Bee"
            Chopin, "Waltz in D Flat" (Minuet Waltz)
            and others

    (b) *Introduction to Master Works Series.* For example:

        Selections from *Swan Lake Ballet, Columbia J-215.*
        Selections from Tchaikovsky's *Nutcracker Suite, J-214.*

    (c) R.C.A. Victor Educational Series, *Victor Album No. E-104. Instruments of the Orchestra.*

(2) Examples of story records:
  (a) *Camden (R.C.A.) CAE-296. One String Fiddle*—Paul Wing.
      Story with musical background.
  (b) *YPR 1007. The Emperor's New Clothes*—Told by George Rasely.
(3) Rhythms:
  (a) *Decca DI 8471. Marching Along Together.* (A collection of familiar marching songs including "The Army Air Corps" and "The Marine's Hymn.")
  (b) *Estamae's*, 2829 Seventh Avenue, Pueblo, Colorado (directions for dance with album)
      Album No. 1—*Toy Shop and Other Rhythms for Little Folk*
      Album No. 2—*Let's Have Fun Dancing* (Easy Couple Dances)
  (c) *James, Phoebe. Elementary Rhythms.* Box 134, Pacific Palisades, California.
      AED 2—Free Rhythms
      AED 5—Fundamental Rhythms
      and others
  (d) *R.C.A. Victor Record Library for Elementary Schools,* Volumes 1, 2, and 3 (Basic Rhythms Program for Primary Grades)
  (e) *YPR 9002. Swing Your Partner*—Molarsky.
      Many of the records listed under other categories—listening records and folk music records, for example—may also be used for rhythmic activities.
(4) Singing games:
  (a) *R.C.A. Victor Basic Record Library for Elementary Schools*
      Singing Games for Primary Grades. *Album E-87.*
      Four records containing selections such as:
      "The Big Gray Cat"
      "London Bridge"
      "Way Down in the Paw Paw Patch"
      "Looby Loo"
(5) Singing and action songs:
  A few examples of the *many* song and action records which encourage children's listening are:

   (a) *Children's Record Guild:*
       CRG 1004. Little Red Wagon—B. Landeck.
       CRG 1025. Rhyme Me a Riddle.
   (b) *Columbia J-187. Put Your Finger in the Air*—Tom
       Glazer.
   (c) *Decca 88125 (k-85). I Know an Old Lady*—Burl Ives.
   (d) *R.C.A. Victor—Singing Program for Primary Grades.*
       Album E-83. (Nursery rhymes, evening prayer, The
           Tailor and the Mouse, and many others.)
   (e) Young People's Records:
       YPR 711. Building a City—Tom Glazer.
       YPR 225. Little Bitty Baby; Twelve Days of Christmas
           —Tom Glazer.
       YPR 618. When the Sun Shines.
       YPR 702. What the Lighthouse Sees.
       YPR 706. Trains and Planes.
       YPR 713. Circus Comes to Town and others.

E. Resources for Speech Activities.
These are non-technical books for the use of the classroom teachers
in a speech improvement program. They contain games, poems,
rhymes, and stories which may prove valuable to teachers of primary
grades.
1. Abney, Louise and Grace Rowe. *Choral Speaking Arrangements for
   the Lower Grades* (Rev. ed.). Boston: Expression Co., 1952.
2. Barrows, Sarah T. and Katherine H. Hall. *Games and Jingles for
   Speech Development.* Boston: Expression Co., 1936.
3. Keppie, Elizabeth F., Conrad Wedberg and Mariam Keslar. *Speech
   Improvement Through Choral Speaking.* Boston: Expression Co.,
   1942.
4. Rasmussen, Carrie. *Choral Speaking for Speech Improvement* (Rev.
   ed.) Boston: Expression Co., 1952.
5. Scott, Louise Binder and J. J. Thompson. St. Louis: Webster Publishing, 1951.

F. Supply and Equipment Catalogs and Pamphlets.
1. General
   a. *Catalog of Free Teaching Aids* (revised regularly). By Gordon
      Salisbury and Robert Sheridan, Box 943, Riverside, California.
   b. *Elementary Teachers Guide to Free Curriculum Materials* (re-
      vised yearly). Educators Progress Service, Randolph, Wisconsin.

c. *Free and Inexpensive Learning Materials* (revised yearly). Division of Surveys and Field Services, George Peabody College for Teachers, Nashville 5, Tennessee.

d. *More Sources of Free and Inexpensive Materials.* National Council of Teachers of English. 704 S. Sixth Street, Champaign, Illinois.

e. *Supplies and Equipment Instructional Aids for the Seven- and Eight-Year-Olds of the Good Elementary School.* Monograph 5. San Francisco 2, California: Elementary School Administrators Association, 693 Sutter Street, 1957.

f. *Sources of Free and Inexpensive Educational Materials* (revised regularly). Merchandise Mart Plaza. Chicago 54, Illinois: Field Enterprises, Inc., Educational Division.

2. The following commercial catalogs are representative of supply sources where instructional aids in language such as puzzles, flannel boards, alphabet charts, and many other materials may be purchased:

a) *Bacon and Vincent Co., Inc.,* 1 Ellicott Street, Buffalo, New York.

b) *Childcraft Equipment Co., Inc.,* 155 East 23rd Street, New York 10, New York.

c) *Creative Playthings, Inc.,* P.O. Box 1100, Princeton, New Jersey.

d) *Gel-Sten Supply Company,* 913 South Hill Street, Los Angeles 15, California.

e) *The Judy Company,* 310 North Second Street, Minneapolis, Minnesota.

f) *Play Art—Educational Equipment Company,* 116 S. 20th Street, Philadelphia 3, Pennsylvania.

G. Tests, Spelling and Handwriting Aids.

Reviews on these tests may be found in publications edited by Oscar Krisen Buros, the latest book entitled *The Fifth Mental Measurements Yearbook.* The Gryphon Press, Highland Park, New Jersey, 1959.

Prices may be obtained from the most recent catalogs which publishers will send on request. The test publishers' names have been abbreviated and the key is listed below:

BP Bureau of Publications, Teachers College, Columbia University, 525 W. 120 St., New York 27, New York.

CTB California Test Bureau, 5916 Hollywood Blvd., Los Angeles 28, California.

ETB Educational Test Bureau, 720 Washington Ave., S.E., Minneapolis 14, Minnesota.

HM Houghton Mifflin Co., 2 Park St., Boston 7, Massachusetts.

PSP Public School Publishing Co., 345 Calhoun St., Cincinnati 19, Ohio.

WBC World Book Co., 313 Park Hill Ave., Yonkers, New York.

1. Types of tests available for the purpose of evaluating reading:

a) Reading Readiness:

(1) Gates, Arthur I. *Gates Reading Readiness Tests* (Group tests). BP, 1939. Grade 1. One form. Time: about 50 minutes. Five scores: picture directions, word matching, word-card matching, rhyming, letters, and numbers.

(2) Hildreth, Gertrude and Nellie L. Griffiths. *Metropolitan Readiness Tests* (Group tests). WBC, 1950. End of kindergarten and first grade entrants. Two forms, R and S. Time: about 65-75 minutes. Four scores: measures reading readiness, number readiness, drawing-a-man (optional).

(3) Lee, J. Murray and Willis W. Clark. *Reading Readiness Tests* (Group tests). (Rev. ed.) CTB, 1951. Grades Kgn.-1. One form. Time: about 15 minutes. Four scores: letter and word symbols, concepts.

(4) Monroe, Marion. *Monroe Reading Aptitude Tests* (Group and individual test sections). HM, 1935. Grade 1. One form. Time: about 50 minutes (two or three sittings). Included in the battery of seventeen tests are sections on auditory discrimination, memory for a story, motor control, laterality preferences, articulation, etc.

(5) Van Wagenen, M. J. and M. L. G. Klaeger. *Van Wagenen Reading Readiness Scales* (Part 1—Listening Vocabulary) and M. J. Van Wagenen (Part 2—perception of relations, opposites, memory span for ideas, word discrimination, range of information). ETB, 1954. Grade 1 or end of kindergarten. One form. Part 1 and Part 2 may be obtained separately.

b) Intelligence Tests:

(1) Kuhlmann, F. and Rose G. Anderson. *Kuhlmann-Anderson Intelligence Tests* (6th ed.) (Group test). ETB, 1952. Grades 1, 2, etc. through 12. Booklet K is for kindergarten, Booklet A is for first grade, Booklet B is for second grade. One form. Time: 30-45 minutes.

(2) Lorge, Irving and Robert L. Thorndike. *The Lorge-Thorndike Intelligence Tests* (Group test). HM, 1954-57. Level

1, Nonverbal battery, Grades kng.-1. Level 2, Nonverbal battery, Grades 2-3. Time: 35 minutes.

(3) Pintner, Rudolph and B. V. Cunningham. *Pintner-Cunningham Primary Mental Tests* (Group test). WBC, 1923. Grades kgn.-2. Forms A, B, or C. Time: 25 minutes. Seven subtests measure a variety of aspects of general mental ability.

(4) Sullivan, Elizabeth T. and others. *California Mental Maturity Pre-Primary Battery* (Group test). CTB, 1957. Grades: Pre-primary level—kgn.-entering grade 1, primary level—grades 1-3. Time: two periods of about 45 minutes for each administration. It measures intelligence through a sampling of mental processes in five areas: memory, spatial relationships, logical reasoning, numerical reasoning, and verbal concepts.

(5) Terman, Lewis M. and Maud Merrill. *Revised Standford-Binet Scale* (Individual test). HM, 1960 (3rd ed.). Ages 2-Maturity. One form (Combination of L and M forms). Time: 30-90 minutes.

c) Diagnostic and Reading Achievement Tests:

(1) Durrell, Donald D. *Durrell Analysis of Reading Difficulty: New Edition* (Individual test). WBC, 1955. Grades 1-6. Time: 30-90 minutes. Materials for individual diagnosis of reading difficulties.

(2) Gates, Arthur I. *Gates Primary Reading Test* (Group test). BP, 1958 edition. Grades 1-first half of Grade 2. Three forms. Time: 15 minutes each for Types PWR and PSR, 20 minutes for Type PPR. Type PWR: Word Recognition, forms 1, 2, 3. Type PSR: Sentence Reading, forms 1, 2, 3. Type PPR: Paragraph Reading, forms 1, 2, 3.

(3) Gates, Arthur I. *Gates Advanced Primary Reading Test* (Group test). BP, 1958 edition. Grades for second half of Grades 2 and Grades 3. Three forms of each of two types. Time: 15 minutes for Type AWR (Word Recognition); 25 minutes for Type APR (Paragraph Reading). Word recognition and paragraph reading.

(4) Gilmore, J. V. *Gilmore Oral Reading Test* (Individual test). WBC, 1952. Grades 1-8. Two forms. Time: 15-20 minutes. Comprehension, rate and accuracy of oral reading. Analysis of errors used to diagnose reading difficulties.

(5) Lee, J. M. and W. W. Clark. *Lee-Clark Reading Test-First*

Reader (Group test). CTB, 1958 revision. Grades 1-2. Two forms, A and B. Time: about 25 minutes. Primer-Grade 1: 4 scores, Auditory Stimuli, Visual Stimuli, Following Directions. First Reader-Grades 1-2: 6 scores, Completion and Inference added to Primer scores.

    (6) Tiegs, E. W. and W. W. Clark. *California Reading Test.* CTB, 1957. Lower primary grades 1-2. Two forms, W or X. Time: 23-35 minutes (Group test). It tests reading vocabulary and reading comprehension.

2. Spelling Word Lists and Teaching Aids:

    a) Anderson, Paul S. *Resource Materials for Teachers of Spelling.* Minneapolis: Burgess Publishing Co., 1959.

    b) Board of Education, City of New York. *Teaching Spelling.* (Course of study and manual.) New York City: Board of Education, 1954.

    c) Fitzgerald, James A. *A Basic Life Spelling Vocabulary.* Milwaukee: The Bruce Publishing Co., 1951.

3. Handwriting Aids:

    a) Freeman, Frank N. *Handwriting Aid for Primary Teachers.* Columbus, Ohio: The Zaner-Bloser Co., 1948.

    b) The Handwriting Committee of the Madison Public Schools. *Manuscript Writing in the Primary Grades.* Madison, Wisconsin: The Madison Public Schools, Curriculum Department, 1951.

    c) Putnam, Rufus A. (Superintendent) *A Guide to Handwriting, Kindergarten-Grade Twelve.* Minneapolis, Minnesota: The Minneapolis Public Schools, 1956.

    d) Stone and Smalley. *Manuscript Basic Handwriting* (Teacher's Guide). New York: Scribner, 1953.

INDEX

A

About Books and Children (Adams), 251

Adams, Bess Porter
About Books and Children, 251

Adventuring with Books (N.C.T.E.), 265

Aids for the teacher, *see* teaching aids

Allen, Mary Louise
"Sneezing," 206

Almy, Millie
Child Development, 246
Teaching Young Children, 247

Andrews, Gladys
Creative Rhythmic Movement for Children, 272

Anecdotal records, 215

Applegate, Mauree
Helping Children Write, 248

Arbuthnot Anthology of Children's Literature, The, 210

Arbuthnot, May Hill
Books Too Good to Miss, 211
Children and Books, 251

Association for Childhood Education International
A Bibliography of Books for Children, 265
Children and TV, 251
Children's Books for $1.25 or Less, 265
Learning to Speak Effectively, 251
More about Reading, 248
Music for Children's Living, 272
Storytelling, 251

Association for Supervision and Curriculum Development
Creating a Good Environment for Learning, 246

Audio-visual aids
see visual aids
see also music materials for teachers

B

Barrows, Sarah T., 148

Baruch, Dorothy, 199

Bauer, William W.
These Are Your Children, 246

Before the Child Reads (Hymes), 198, 249

Bemelman, Ludwig
Madeline, 237

Biber, Barbara, 111

Bibliography of Books for Children, A (A.C.E.I.), 265

Book reviews, 265-66

Book selection, 210-14

Booklists, 265-66

Books
on music, 272
on science, 268-69
on speech improvement, 275
see also favorite books

Bowman, Clare, 62-64

Burton, Virginia
The Little House, 227

C

Caffery, John G., 88

Caldwell, Charles J., 70

Carrothers, George C., 51

Causey, Oscar S.
The Reading Teacher's Reader, 248

Child Development (Almy), 246

Child from Five to Ten, The (Gesell), 246

Childhood and Adolescence (Stone and Church), 246

Children
five-year-old, 112-13
seven-year-old, 115-17
six-year-old, 113-15
and story selection, 57-59

Children and Books (Arbuthnot), 251

Children and Music (Landeck), 272

Children and the Language Arts (Herrick, Jacob, *et al.*), 247

Children and TV. (A.C.E.I.), 251

Children Discover Music and Dance (Sheehy), 272

Children's Books for $1.25 or Less (A.C.E.I.), 265

Children's Books Too Good to Miss, 265

Children's Catalog, The (Giles and Cook), 211

Church, Joseph
Childhood and Adolescence, 246